A Passage to the Heart

We hear on all sides that East and West are meeting, but it is an understatement. They are being flung at one another with the force of atoms, the speed of jets, the restlessness of minds impatient to learn of ways different from their own. From the perspective of history this may prove to be the most important fact about the twentieth century. When historians look back upon our years they may remember them…as the time in which all the peoples of the world first had to take one another seriously.

Huston Smith

When drinking water, remember the source.

Chinese proverb

A Passage to the Heart

Writings from Families with Children from China

Edited by Amy Klatzkin

YEONG & YEONG BOOK COMPANY
St. Paul, Minnesota

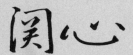

Yeong & Yeong Book Company
1368 Michelle Drive
St. Paul, Minnesota 55123-1459
www.yeongandyeong.com

Designed by Mark Ong

Calligraphy by Pearl Weng Liang Huang

Front jacket and title page photograph © David Sanger

Publisher's Cataloging-in-Publication
(Provided by Quality Books, Inc.)

A passage to the heart : writings from families with children
    from China / edited by Amy Klatzkin. — 1st ed.
        p.   cm.
        ISBN 0-9638472-2-8

        1. Intercountry adoption—China.   2. Intercountry
    adoption—United States.   I. Klatzkin, Amy.

    HV875.5.P37   1999   362.7′34
                                    QBI98-1271

Manufactured in the United States of America

06 05 04 03 02 01 00 99

This book is printed on acid-free paper that meets the uncoated
paper ANSI-NISO specifications for permanence as revised in
1992.

For our children,

and for all those who wait

Contents

The Adoption Journey

Settling In

Health and Development

Adoption after Infancy

Single Parenting

Perspectives

Culture, Language, Identity

Race Matters

Going Back

Adoption, the Lifelong Journey

Introduction

Amy Klatzkin

San Francisco Bay Area FCC

In November 1992 a small group of families with children from China gathered at a Chinese restaurant in New York to celebrate a "first month party." The families—a few of whom had come in from Washington, D.C., and Boston—included some of the first Americans to adopt children from Chinese orphanages under China's new national adoption law as well as some who had adopted even before those regulations were in place.

In January 1993 a slightly larger group gathered to share revolutionary experiences. "We felt," said Susan Caughman, one of the founders of Families with Children from China in New York, "as if we knew an amazing secret that we had the obligation to tell the world about." From then on they began to organize in earnest both to provide a network of support for adoptive families and to encourage others to adopt from China, where orphanages were overflowing with children in need of permanent homes. Most of the children were infants, and most of them were girls. Most of the orphanages were underfunded and understaffed. The need for families was urgent.

In February 1993, just as adoptions from China began to accelerate, China shut the door for an unspecified period while authorities in Beijing reorganized the international adoption program. Months dragged by. Then, on April 11, the *New York Times Magazine* published an article by Bruce Porter that the editors tagged with disastrous headlines: "China's Market in Orphan Girls," "Unwanted and Abandoned Baby Girls Have Become the Newest Chinese Export." Those of us waiting during that period, including my husband and me, feared that in such a climate international adoption from China might never open again.

But it did open again, and despite a few scares, a few slowdowns, and an ever longer queue of waiting parents, adoptions from China have steadily increased nearly every year since the moratorium ended. By the summer of 1998 there were around 13,000 children adopted from China in the United States alone. As thousands more families have adopted Chinese children, more and more adoptive family support groups have sprung up to meet their needs. From Toronto to Tampa, Los Angeles to Seattle, and scores of places in between, most of these groups have followed the lead of the original chapters of China adoptive families in Seattle, New York, and Washington, D.C., and call themselves Families with Children from China (FCC).

A Passage to the Heart brings together for the first time writings from Families with Children from China and similar adoptive family support groups across the United States, Canada, and Britain. Most of the articles were written specifically for parents or prospective parents of children adopted from Chinese orphanages (although a few have had a wider audience), and all were published in one of the many flourishing newsletters sponsored by regional chapters of FCC and like-minded volunteer groups.

One of the oddities of FCC is that it exists all over North America and yet has no central organization. Unlike established nonprofits like the Sierra Club or Resolve, FCC has no national office, no paid staff, no universal by-laws binding chapters together. Indeed, the name Families with Children from China is used by completely independent organizations incorporated in various ways in a growing number of states and provinces. This is the sort of international "organization" that could never have existed without e-mail—a grass-roots movement that rapidly expanded across a continent and beyond largely through the electronic grapevine. Chuck Bouldin founded the FCC web site (www.fwcc.org) as the only truly pan-FCC resource, and that, along with internet discussion groups like "a-parents-China" and "post-adopt-China," is how most of the FCC chapters have found each other and built contacts with similar organizations in North America and Europe. When I was looking for a title for this book, the calligraphic logo on the FCC home page—*guan xin*, "a passage to the heart"—was the obvious choice: it's the only symbol everyone in FCC has in common.

This book began, as many things do across chapters of Families with Children from China, as an e-mail conversation. I had been thinking about the marvelous cooperation among newsletter editors that had quickly developed into a vast network of newsletter exchanges. Like many of my fellow editors, I read every one that comes in—from across the United States, from Canada, from Britain—looking for inspiration and good articles to reprint in our next issue. With so many FCC newsletters circulating, there are always more good articles to reprint than I can possibly fit, and I had been wondering if we could find a way to share these riches with other FCC families, the ones whose lives aren't periodically disrupted by newsletter deadlines.

With the backing of Susan Caughman in New York, I floated the idea to a handful of FCC newsletter editors with whom I'd had contact over the past few years. Wouldn't it be wonderful to have a sampling of great articles from all the FCC (and similar) newsletters gathered together in a single volume? Brian Boyd, the publisher of Yeong & Yeong Book Co. (who brought us the invaluable *When You Were Born in China*), had recklessly agreed to publish it if we could pull it together *fast*. What's more, Yeong & Yeong would donate to the Amity Foundation and the Foundation for Chinese Orphanages the percentage that would ordinarily go to royalties and would also make the book available in bulk to FCC chapters to use as a local fundraiser. Would they be interested in selecting articles to submit to such a collection? Could they do it quickly?

The response was overwhelmingly positive, and from there I searched out all the FCC-like newsletters I could find. Every editor I reached responded positively to the project, and though a few felt that their newsletters were still too new or too local in orientation to have anything to contribute, and a couple of others were unable to meet our short deadline, almost all found the time in their busy schedules to review back issues and choose articles they felt best represented their newsletters and their chapters.

There are many ways—perhaps better ways—a volume like this could have been put together, resulting in a different kind of book. But because community building was an important part of what I wanted the book to do, I asked all the newsletter editors to make their own choices about what to submit. I didn't specify subject matter or even present a predetermined structure for the book. I wanted it to evolve from the editors' choices. What that meant for me as volume editor, however, is that about six weeks later I had a stack of more than 150 "found objects" to organize into a book of around 100 articles.

The articles that made it into this volume (and many that did not) sorted themselves into eleven basic categories—from the emotionally charged period of waiting to adopt, through the adoption journey, settling in as a new or enlarged family, specific issues of health and development in young children adopted from China, the special rewards and challenges of adopting children over the age of one and of single parenting, perspectives on adoptions from China from inside and outside the adoption community, the loaded issues of culture, language, identity, and race, a few accounts of going back to China after adopting, and, finally, a look down the road of adoptive family life at issues that simply don't come up in families formed the "usual" way. Many, many articles touch on more than one of these broad categories. I placed them as best I could, knowing that others, had they been sorting the same collection, would probably have chosen differently. (For example, in a different arrangement there could have been a whole section on blended families—those in which some children were born into the family and others adopted into it. Quite a few of the writers have blended families, it turns out, although that's not mainly what they're writing about.)

While some of the writers are professionals in adoption or health care or childhood development and others are professional writers (or writers of professional quality), most of these articles were not written for a broad audience, let alone an international one, and bringing them together in this volume emphasizes the amicable, collaborative nature of the adoptive family groups they addressed. Although I have edited out most strictly local references, the intimate voice remains, for in many ways our newsletters serve as forums for open conversations among friends and neighbors sharing advice, opinions, and experiences.

This book carries those conversations to a wider audience, where we can listen in on a party line and hear what other parents in other parts of the country or the continent or the world think is important. It is mainly a collection of ideas and personal experiences, not an authoritative guide to raising children adopted from China. And the conversation we're hearing in this book is not complete: when an author praises the "Ferber method" or "holding time," for example, you can bet that plenty of FCC parents disagree. Just as there is no one way to build a family, there is no one way to adopt, to raise adopted children, to handle issues of race and culture. In the end, we all have to decide what makes most sense for our children, our families.

Please don't take anything here as the final word on any subject. Use it, instead, as the starting point for, or as a supplement to, your reading, talking, and research in areas of interest to your family. Above all—and this is a special plea to prospective and waiting parents—don't let the many articles about difficulties discourage you. Yes, difficulties are a part of international adoption—as one article title says, there are no guarantees—but remember also that we newsletter editors receive and publish more articles about the less usual situations simply because they *are* less usual.

Hardly anyone sends us stories about adoption trips where everything goes right. But usually, even if your papers are delayed, your luggage is lost, or your hair dryer blows up, the important things go right.

One striking aspect of this book is its focus on very young children in brand-new adoptive families. There's very little here on children over the age of six—as if the whole world started adopting for the very first time in about 1992. Because adoptions from China have been going on for such a short time, we just don't have a lot of experience with middle childhood yet, let alone adolescence and beyond. A second edition of this book—say, five years from now—would look different: much less on the adoption journey, for example, and a whole lot more about school. In the meantime, it's worth looking beyond the China adoption community for pointers on what to expect in middle childhood—coming up fast for many of our children—and how to prepare for it. Plenty of adoptive families with children from countries other than China have been down that road before us, and there are lots of good books in libraries and adoption catalogs.

Like many other families with children adopted internationally, most families in the United States, Canada, and Britain who have adopted children from Chinese orphanages really stand out in a crowd. In fact, among the first things new adoptive parents have to get used to—along with sleep deprivation and the art of changing diapers—are the constant double-takes in public as passersby look from the parent or parents, usually of European ancestry, to the child, whose beautiful Chinese features don't match a thing in the parents' faces. For many parents, this is the first experience of visibly not fitting in with the majority. And it is powerful.

Soon we develop tactics for coping with unwanted intrusions while navigating supermarket aisles, and we share war stories with other transracial adoptive parents about dealing with unwanted attention and idiotic questions. We may even congratulate ourselves on how much more accepting of diversity we are compared with others of our acquaintance, forgetting how recently we too immediately looked from a child's face to the parent's in expectation of similarities, how much we took (and still take) our majority status for granted.

And yet, much as we think we have weeded out stereotypes, it's remarkable how quickly new ones sprout up. Most of us have a clear notion of what a family with children from China looks like. There is one parent or two, of European descent, and a daughter or two who are Chinese. So why is that *boy* on the jacket and title page of this book? How come the *mom* is the one who stands out? The family whose picture appears on the front of the jacket is not typical of FCC families, just as FCC families are not typical American or British or Canadian families. As a group committed to honoring difference, we need to keep rooting up all the stereotypes we have. It's hard work, because difference, while surely something to celebrate, is also sometimes challenging to live with every minute of every day.

While being visibly outside the mainstream is a new experience for most FCC parents, it's old hat for others. Throughout the FCC community, and especially in areas with large Asian populations, such as San Francisco and Vancouver, many FCC parents have a lifetime of experience as "other"—as Asians in a predominantly white society. Children in transracial adoptive families, however, will not only be minorities in their country, state, province, and, often, neighborhood; they will also be minorities in their own family. While embracing our children as *ours,* we need to acknowledge, respect, and celebrate their differences from us, our differences from "typical" families, and the many different types of families that make up Families with Children from China and similar organizations. I regret that, because of the politics of international adoption, this volume could not acknowledge an important subgroup of FCC families— no photo, no article, represents their special challenges and rewards. That is a shame and a loss for us all. Perhaps one day things will be different, and all the members of our community will feel free to speak their hearts.

As we who have adopted from China think back on our adoption experience and look forward to watching our children grow and prosper, many of us want to make a contribution to improve the lives of the children who remain in orphanages in China waiting for forever families that they may never have. Each purchase of *A Passage to the Heart*—thanks to the generosity of the publisher, the designer, the newsletter editors, and the writers who have brought it to life—will directly benefit two extraordinary foundations doing great work in Chinese orphanages: the Amity Foundation and the Foundation for Chinese Orphanages. The two articles that follow introduce these foundations to the readers of this book. Thank you for supporting their work. Together we can make a difference.

Amy Klatzkin is the newsletter editor for San Francisco Bay Area FCC and the mother of Ying Ying Fry, age five, adopted from Changsha on Jan. 4, 1994.

The Amity Foundation

Aileen Koger
FCC–New York

When we first adopted our precious children from China and experienced the immeasurable joy they brought to our lives, many of us were mindful still of the babies, toddlers, and disabled children we encountered in the orphanages. These "sisters and brothers"—our children's cribmates and friends—remained behind, their futures uncertain. Some would soon be adopted, but others would have to wait a long time for a place to call home and a family to love them. And some of these children would spend their entire childhood in the care of an orphanage.

We asked ourselves what we could do. We knew that many parents, and their relatives and friends, were eager to find ways to support the children remaining in China's orphanages. So we set ourselves the task of discovering how we could help in an effective and meaningful way.

In the fall of 1995, as Families with Children from China in New York was growing in size and establishing itself as a not-for-profit organization, we began our research. We looked into different ways that might enable us to get support to children in need in China's orphanages. We contacted international relief agencies, aid organizations working in China, adoption agencies, private foundations. We learned that while a number of groups were interested in beginning support programs and several projects were getting under way, including some sponsored by adoption agencies, there were few established programs providing assistance to orphanages in China.

Our research led us to an experienced China-based humanitarian aid organization. The Amity Foundation, a well-respected and innovative social service organization based in Nanjing, had been working in orphanages for almost ten years. It met our criteria: Amity was an estab-

XX
The Amity Foundation

lished aid organization with a significant track record of projects that both had the approval of the government and were well received at the local level. It worked in a number of different orphanages, providing a range of direct and vital services to children. And Amity offered a full accounting to its contributors of funds received and how they were used, providing letters of acknowledgment, receipts, reports of medical treatment, and photographs of the children who were being helped.

Amity was founded in 1985 in a period of openness by members of China's Christian community and other reformers, including leading educators, to improve the lives of the poorest in China. In a recent study of nongovernmental organizations (NGOs), the Ford Foundation reported that Amity is "perhaps the most active indigenous development NGO in China." Amity's officers, board of directors, and Nanjing staff are all Chinese. Hundreds of volunteers work in Amity-supported projects across China. In addition to its work in orphanages, Amity conducts rural development projects and directs health, education, and social welfare programs for those in need. Families and communities benefit from work-training programs and projects to enhance agricultural production. Amity is active in relief efforts, providing food, clothing, medicine, and shelter during natural disasters. It brings a measure of independence to the blind and deaf and to victims of polio through programs in education, job training, and rehabilitation services.

Amity's first program for orphaned children involved the sponsorship of a rehabilitation unit for disabled children at the Nanjing Children's Welfare Institute in 1988. Amity launched its "Grandmother's Program" in Nanjing as well, recruiting retired physicians and nurses to work in orphanages, provide special attention to infants and young children with disabilities, train staff, and improve health care. Amity also began to fund corrective surgeries, meet expenses related to basic child care, and pay fees for children to attend community schools.

Impressed with Amity's record of service, FCC–New York launched a fundraising campaign in November 1996 in support of Amity's orphanage assistance projects. The response from our members and their families, friends, and colleagues has been overwhelmingly positive. Now in its second year, our fundraising effort has received close to $150,000 in contributions. As an all-volunteer organization, FCC is able to send 100 percent of the donations it receives to orphanage programs, with the Amity Foundation's projects the primary beneficiary of our support thus far.

We have been rewarded in our work with Amity. The funds we have sent them over the past two years have gone to some of the orphanage projects Amity already had in place, such as the Grandmother's Program in Wuxi and school fees for children in Changzhou. And with our support Amity has begun some exciting new projects. When we first learned of Amity it was working in a dozen orphanages, primarily in Jiangsu province. By mid-1998 Amity had extended its reach to 24 orphanages in five provinces, with FCC directly funding projects in 17 of these facilities. Amity has expanded its Grandmother's Program, seen scores of children through life-saving medical treatment and corrective surgeries, and given dozens of children a more promising future by enabling them to receive an education in community schools. Orphanage conditions have been upgraded with the purchase of new beds, heaters, toys, and rehabilitation equipment. Playgrounds have been constructed for orphanages in Gaoshun and Suzhou, and medical clinics established in Luan and Anqing.

FCC's relationship with the staff of Amity's Social Welfare Division is one of mutual understanding, shared goals, and deep commitment. We have established easy and direct communication and in two site visits have met Amity staff and visited orphanages benefiting from our support. We observed Amity Grandmas at work and saw many of the children whom we have helped. We have received frequent expenditures reports, photographs of the children, and detailed accounts of the services they have received.

A most satisfying aspect of our relationship with Amity is our ability to share in the direction of how the funds we contribute are used and to effect and influence the development of new Amity initiatives. When FCC was asked to direct, if possible, memorial donations to Tongling Children's Welfare Institute, Amity was most receptive to contacting its administrators and developing a project proposal with them. The family of a little girl who died at a much too early age are comforted in knowing that children in the orphanage where she spent her earliest days are benefiting from the joint efforts of FCC and Amity in putting a program in place. In other instances, Amity has responded favorably to FCC's requests to explore beginning projects in certain regions or particular orphanages and to apply a more significant proportion of the funds we contribute to a specific use, such as medical care. As of this writing, Amity has just begun, at FCC's suggestion and with our funding, a pilot project providing intensive nursing care to babies at risk.

The efforts of FCC chapters and their members, through initiatives such as *A Passage to the Heart,* bring hope to those living and working in orphanages in China. We trust that, through the generosity of our many supporters, FCC working together with Amity will continue to make a difference in the lives of some of China's neediest children.

Contributions to Families with Children from China for the Amity Foundation's orphanage projects are welcome. Please make your check payable to Families with Children from China, with the Amity Foundation noted on the memo line or in a cover note. All moneys will be forwarded to Amity, and your contribution is tax-deductible in the United States. Donations may be sent to Families with Children from China, Fundraising Appeal, Box 865 Ansonia Station, New York, NY 10025, USA.

Aileen Koger chairs FCC–New York's Charitable Initiatives Committee.

The Foundation for Chinese Orphanages

Rita Guastella
FCC/New England

Founded in 1996, the Foundation for Chinese Orphanages (FCO) is an American 501(c)3 foundation created by Families with Children from China/New England. This chapter, 500 families strong, developed this outreach from a collective sense of gratitude for the children who have come into—and transformed!—our lives. Each year the Foundation sponsors projects undertaken in cooperation with the Chinese govern-ment to support the children still living in Chinese orphanages. Its aims are to help the children in rural or less-traveled orphanages with direct-care items and to recognize the many people who cared for our children before they became ours—from birth parents to municipal officials to orphanage workers to foster parents.

One hundred percent of the money donated is tax deductible and is sent to China for use in the orphanages. There is no administrative over-head either in the U.S. or in China.

What Happens to the Children Left Behind?

The goals of the FCO are different from other charitable organizations through which FCC chapters work. "While all organizations do vital humanitarian work," states FCC/New England fundraising chairman Liane Welch, "the Foundation allows us to enter into a dialogue with the Chinese authorities at both the central and provincial levels, to involve them in the realization of a shared dream, and to acknowledge that the Chinese people care as deeply about helping the children as we adoptive parents do."

"Most important," says FCC/New England president Shanti Fry, "the Foundation enables us to build a bridge to the Chinese orphanages so that when our children ask, 'What happened to the children left behind?' we will have an answer....We know that the more we can bring to life the spirit of caring that connects us all, the healthier our children's outlook will be."

The Red Envelope Campaign, Your Invitation to Help

In 1997, the Foundation, with the help of many FCC chapters and similar organizations, launched its first annual fundraising appeal, the Red Envelope Campaign. This theme was chosen for the appeal because Chinese New Year is traditionally a time of giving to children. It allows those participating to teach their children about the Chinese tradition of *hongbao* and "to give back" to children still living in Chinese orphanages. Families can put money into the red envelope provided following in this tradition and that of American philanthropy. Each donor gets a tax receipt letter for his or her records and each child, in whose name the donation is made, gets a certificate with a red ribbon and gold starburst in the current Year of the Zodiac.

Building a Bridge to China, One Picture at a Time

Because the Foundation is building a relationship with the Chinese people, we've incorporated a personalized response into our giving. We know from experience that the orphanage workers love to see photographs of our children. That's why each year we ask donors to include a 3" x 5" photo of their child and a short greeting on the cards sent out. We collect the photos and messages from each contributor, have them translated into Chinese, and present them in large-format leather-bound albums with the name "Families with Children from China" in gold leaf. These beautiful albums (all donated materials) are sent to the CCAA in Beijing with copies sent to the American Embassy and other offices involved in adoption. Because the photos and messages are organized by orphanage, we are also able to bind large-format color photocopies of these pages and send them to the individual orphanages, sharing the tangible symbol of our gratitude at both the central and local levels.

The messages of goodwill and caring offer joyous feedback to those who continue to do the hard work in China. A typical message reads:

Anna has been a joy and has enriched our lives with her exuberant, joyful personality. She loves her kitty—who is also coming to love her, although cautiously. Therefore, we feel a strong connection to China and particularly to the orphaned children. We are happy to help in what small way we can with the large task of caring for them.

Adopted from Wuhu orphanage in Anhui province

The response from Chinese officials to the albums has been terrific! Mr. Dou Yu-pei, Director of the Social Affairs Department of the Ministry of Civil Affairs, who oversees policies affecting international adoption, described the album as his "most precious gift from this trip to North America." Having received his copy of the album, Ambassador Qiu Shengyun, Consul-General of the People's Republic of China in New York, wrote the following:

I am so deeply impressed by [FCC/New England's and the Foundation's] devotion to international adoption affairs and by your love and care for the adopted children from China and every effort you have made for all these smooth adoptions. [This] work has certainly contributed to the friendship and understanding between the peoples of China and the U.S.A. I wish you and the adoptive families great happiness and harmony.

The Projects

This year the Red Envelope Campaign will provide foster care for children in the small, rural orphanages of Hubei province. A donation of $100 will cover one child for four months; $300 covers one child for one year; $600 covers two children for one year; $1,000 covers three children for one year. Last year, the Red Envelope Campaign raised more than $41,000, which provided industrial-grade washers and dryers for more than 2,000 children in rural orphanages in Hubei province.

The Foundation allows you to extend your reach—and that of your child—to change the lives of children in small and out-of-the-way orphanages.

We are profoundly grateful to Amy Klatzkin, the editor of this publication, as well as Mark Ong, the designer, Brian Boyd of Yeong & Yeong Book Co., the publisher, and to all the authors and newsletter editors for donating their time and expertise to helping us bring the story of the Foundation to the largest group of FCC parents ever. Foster care is the single most cost-effective way to help the children left behind. We thought it would take years before adoption officials would be willing to expand foster care beyond the limited number of programs now available. Now our hope is that, based on this year's successful campaign in Hubei, other provinces will start foster care programs, perhaps with our support.

We gratefully acknowledge your support too, FCC reader, because a portion of every purchase of this book aids the Foundation in its work with Chinese orphans. Should you care to put your name on our FCO mailing list or make an additional contribution, please send a note or check made out to: FCC/Foundation for Chinese Orphanages, 8 Berkeley Street, Cambridge, MA 02138, USA. Or look for our Foundation page on the FCC/New England website at www.fwcc.org/NewEngland. For those making contributions who are not yet on our mailing list, we will gratefully forward the FCC materials to include your note and photo in the Foundation album. Thank you!

The Foundation for Chinese Orphanages was created by Shanti Fry, president, FCC/New England and mother of Victoria, with support from, among others, Liane Welch, Foundation chairman, as well as special adviser Weihang Chen, a professor from Wuhan University who helped make possible some of the first adoptions to the U.S., and copywriter Rita Guastella, a single mother who adopted from the Wuhan Foundling Institute in 1992.

Ready and Waiting

Of course we need children! Adults need children in their lives to listen to and care for, to keep their imagination fresh and their hearts young and to make the future a reality for which they are willing to work.

Margaret Mead

Surviving Waiting Parenthood

Some Completely Useless Advice from One Who's Been There

Shanti Fry
FCC/New England

"Have you got the baby's room ready?" I must have heard this question a dozen times in the five days between THE call and the airport. Short answer, "No." Medium answer, "Irish Catholics don't believe in baby showers let alone doing the room. It's bad luck." Long answer, "What baby? I'm just going to China on the off chance this is one fertility treatment with more promise than the others. But, jeez, I'm not so dumb as to think it will work the first time."

So how does a person who doesn't really think she's getting a baby get through the twilight zone of waiting parenthood? Answer: You go a little crazy.

Our situation isn't like a biological pregnancy with its clearly delineated stages and sense of progress. It's a free fall through eternity. No one is presenting you with cute sonograms and saying stuff like "You may be late," meaning a one-week adjustment to the due date. You don't even have a due date. And you sure don't have a baby. Or do you?

The best and worst part of waiting adoptive parenthood is that there is nothing that will make the date come any sooner. However out of control you felt before you signed the last document, that feeling is multiplied when your dossier goes to China. While people can simply repress a lot of that feeling, it tends to rebound with a vengeance when the adoption agency doesn't return your calls (usually because the social worker doesn't know any more than you do). So here is a list of the barely rational things I did as a waiting parent besides pick fights with my husband.

Things That Turned Out to Be Useful Even Though They Were Strange at the Time

I wrote a new will. My fertile friends couldn't believe this. "You're writing a will in favor of someone you don't know?"

"I know her name," I replied defensively.

My thinking was even more tortured than they could have guessed. I thought that if I got a child, Jeff and I could be traveling back with her from China and the plane could crash and somehow I would die and Jeff and the baby would survive—in the middle of the Pacific Ocean! You see what I mean by crazy.

Things That Were Fun Even Though They Were Weird at the Time

I planned the trip to China as if I were going as a tourist. When we were assigned our child and given two weeks to prepare, I took off early, hooking up with my best friend from business school. Jeff and the other parents arrived a week later.

In my week as a tourist, my friend and I toured Beijing, Shanghai, and Suzhou. Despite all the Chinese books and movies I had read, China was a wonderful surprise. We found a country bursting with energy and expansion. I felt that in discovering the country I was discovering something about my daughter.

At the time of THE call, I hesitated to do this trip even though I had planned it this way. But in a moment of mixed anger and clarity, I thought that I hadn't come to motherhood the "normal" way and why didn't I take advantage of that liberation by celebrating the differentness of Victoria's arrival?

Things That Were Useless Then and Still Are Three Years Later

The day after THE call, an experienced mother took me baby clothes shopping, since we now had an age to attach to our baby's name (though not a weight, which I quickly discovered would have been more helpful). While Sheryl wisely took me first to a children's clothing outlet, we somehow ended up at Saks Fifth Avenue. There, I purchased a baby garment no child will ever wear. It was an Italian pink wool baby suit with an embroidered lawn collar costing $64. This was such a foolish purchase that I still laugh about it today. I wish I could at least say that this represented my romantic dream of motherhood, but the truth is that I didn't even want the kind of daughter who would happily inhabit such a garment. Who knows what primitive myth took hold of my shaking psyche and credit card?

Things I Should Have Done

I should have read a baby book. I should have read a pediatric medical text. At midnight in our hotel in Wuhan with less than 12 hours to go before we got our baby, I started speed reading the first nine chapters of *What to Expect the First Year* so I could figure out how to handle a nine-month-old baby. I was hysterical. My husband, not unreasonable, asked why I hadn't read this book previously, since we had come to China to get a baby. We had? I had reached the limits of denial. It wasn't a pretty sight.

Instead, I had spent my endless pregnancy reading Chinese history and classical literature. While this material may lack a certain relevance to first-time parenthood, it does offer a singular advantage to waiting parents—it's long. *The Dream of the Red Chamber* is published in five volumes by Penguin. It is the equivalent of Shakespeare for its influence on Chinese literature. By focusing on the desolation of one eighteenth-century aristocratic family, it covers the struggle between romantic love and married love with plenty of higher spirituality and eroticism as well.

Two survey histories are outstanding: John Fairbank's *China* and Jonathan D. Spence's *The Making of Modern China,* which starts with the Ming dynasty. Ross Terrill's biography of Mao is a good read, too. When the son of the Wuhan orphanage's director pointed out the place at the Yangzi River from which Mao swam, I asked, "The first or the second time?" Believe me, this made a big impression. Later I had a fantasy about a Chinese couple coming to America to adopt and telling me that they had read *Tom Sawyer* and Arthur D. Schlesinger. I thought I would be really touched by their desire to be connected to the best of my country.

Every group of parents faces their own problems when adopting from China. For us, it was the 16-month shutdown in 1993–94. I can't say whether it was better or worse than what parents face today. The only real comfort I can offer waiting parents is to tell you that I haven't met one FCC family that is sorry they went to China.

As for the baby's room. Once I had Victoria in my arms, I called our beloved house painter, Gaspar, from Wuhan and asked him to paint the corner room "Shantung." Seemed like our bad luck was over.

Shanti Fry is president of FCC/New England. She lives in Cambridge, Massachusetts.

Choosing an Agency

Jane Brown, M.S.W.
San Francisco Bay Area FCC

As both an adoptive parent and a social worker, I have been involved with international adoption for over twenty years. Here are some of the things I might consider in choosing an agency:

International adoption is so very difficult, stressful, and ever-changing that I would want an agency to have lots of experience and to have more than one or two international country programs in case one program closes or changes and is no longer a realistic possibility for me.

I would look for an agency that has an in-country facilitator/advocate with a *very, very* good reputation for getting referrals quickly, with travel times following within a reasonable time.

I would want an agency that is very financially stable so that my money or a portion of my money could and would be refunded if the adoption fell through or I had to switch programs and/or agencies because the agency could not refer a child through one of their programs.

I would want the agency to escort me to the child's country when I adopt. If they do that, I would know that they probably have the ability and willingness to advocate for me should something go wrong there (i.e., help me to get *quality* medical care, find a different child if the child I received were, for example, thought to be mentally challenged and I had not been prepared to parent a child with severe challenges, or I got into difficulties with the mechanics of the adoption while in-country).

I would not choose an agency because they are "nice." All agencies are nice when they are selling themselves—it's how they run their program, how satisfied families are, and whether they continue their commitment to the children that they place beyond the final adoption that counts with me.

I would not choose an agency because they are cheap. They are often cheap because they cut important corners, and to me, this is not the place to cut corners unless we are talking about airline tickets, accommodations, or other inconsequential things.

I would not choose an agency that makes big promises or speaks of a definite time frame—a reputable agency would hesitate to do so because the only thing predictable about international adoption is that it is ever-changing. I would rather look for an agency that can say that this is what is happening with families currently, but be prepared for delays, changes, even moratoriums in any given program. I would rather have honesty than surprises, I suppose, because then I could trust what they say about other things to be true.

I would insist on working with an agency that is licensed in my state.

I would absolutely, positively insist that they provide education about adoptive parenting *before* and *after* the fact. In experienced agencies, they know that adoptive parenting involves extra work, extra understanding of issues that the general public is not knowledgeable about. These are not the things that you wait to learn after you get a child—you need to start right from the beginning to prepare yourselves, your friends, and your family *before* the child enters the picture. This can make a tremendous difference in children's mental health later on.

I also know—and research backs this up statistically—that children who join their families through adoption have extra issues that they must deal with. I would insist that my agency provide services for post-adoptive families so that when those things come up later, and they most definitely will, families don't have to scramble to find services that are costly and only half-adequate. These issues tend to arise at or about age eight for adoptees, so most families with children from China do not have experience with this unless they have adopted children previously through other programs. China is too new.

Education enables families to identify the issues and pick up on the clues their children give that they need support, help, communication, sensitivity regarding adoption issues. Without the education, most families miss this.

I hope that these suggestions give you something to consider, and I hope that whatever agencies you look at will provide most or all of the things that *you* deem important.

Jane Brown, the mother of eight children (five of them adopted internationally), is a member of FCC-Arizona (she lives in Scottsdale) and a regular contributor to the SF Bay Area FCC newsletter.

How to Decipher and Compare Adoption Agency Fees

Lori Raff

FCC–Capital Area

If you're like me, one of your main concerns about adopting from China is cost. I first decided to adopt domestically because of the expense of international adoption but was frustrated to find that it's nearly impossible to adopt young, healthy children here because of our legal system's reluctance to terminate the rights of biological parents.

So I turned to international adoption and quickly became excited about adopting from China, with its rich, ancient culture, proud history, and the most beautiful children in the world! I became determined to complete this adoption regardless of cost.

I decided to minimize expenses as much as possible. I soon discovered that most expenses, such as U.S. government and Chinese government fees, travel, and accommodations, were beyond my immediate control.

The only expenses I could control were the fees charged by the adoption agency. I began requesting information from some of the agencies I found on China adoption web sites and added more from the APC (adopt-parents-China) e-mail list. Soon I had collected information from 18 agencies, but they all used different ways to calculate total adoption costs, and I was trying to compare apples and oranges. I began by separating expenses into three categories:

1. *Dossier preparation expenses.* These expenses vary considerably, so if an agency included estimates of these costs, I subtracted them from that agency's total fee. They include the home study, INS fees, marriage/divorce decrees, birth certificates, fingerprints, notaries, certification/authentication fees, passports, visas, etc.

2. *Costs that can be "guesstimated."* I estimated round-trip airfare to China, travel between Chinese cities, hotel accommodations, and meals to be U.S.$5,000 for two people and added this cost to each agency's total. (This is a conservative estimate; your travel expenses may be higher.) If the agency included travel expenses in their total fee, I subtracted their estimate and used my $5,000 estimate in order to be consistent. For agencies that charged a separate fee for an interpreter/guide/escort, I added that fee to the $5,000.

3. *Government fees paid in China.* I estimated all U.S. and Chinese government fees in China (including the orphanage donation) to be $5,000 and added this to each agency's total. Again, if these fees were already included, I subtracted them first and used a flat $5,000 for consistency.

After turning all the oranges into apples, I was then able to extract the bottom-line fee that each agency charged for their services. Some agencies provide this information for you, while others make you go through an exercise like the one described above.

And cost is not the only factor you'll want to consider. For example, I'm requesting a toddler-aged "special needs" child. So I want an agency that will pay special attention to my circumstances and help prepare my daughter for the adoption. There are several agencies in the lower price range willing to do this. You'll want to decide if there are any concerns unique to your situation that will narrow your choice of agency.

Remember, though, regardless of the agency you use, assuming it's licensed, experienced, and reputable, the end result is the same—a beautiful child! So save your hard-earned money for the braces and piano lessons.

Lori Raff is an FCC member from Potomac Falls, Virginia.

Adopting on a Budget

Kathy Graves
FCC-Chicago

We had a great desire to adopt a child from China. When we first investigated the possibility with a local agency, the cost estimates were much more than we could afford. We felt disappointed, but we continued to explore other adoption avenues for nine months. After looking into dozens of agencies, we found one that allowed our dreams to come true within our family budget. We were able to bring Emily home at seven months of age in May 1995 with the help of an out-of-state agency that was able to meet our family and financial needs for adoption. We were able to save $8,500 based on the original costs stated by the first agency we approached. Although each family and each adoption will be a unique experience, other families may be able to benefit from some of the lessons we learned along our pathway:

If you are considering adopting more than one child, write in the number 2 or 3 on the INS I-600A form in box 17. We applied for three; we now have 18 months from our INS approval to adopt up to two more times. Also, when talking to an agency, ask if any fees will be reduced for a second adoption at a later date. Often the home study fee is significantly reduced, and the program fee may also be reduced. If you desire to adopt two children, look for an agency that will be cost effective for both adoptions.

Consider using an agency out of your home state. The variety may enable you to find an agency that meets your family's needs. Based on our investigations, agencies in the northwest U.S. seemed less expensive. Adoptive Families of America (800-372-3300 or 651-645-9955) has a booklet titled *Adoption: How to Begin* that lists hundreds of agencies. We called almost 50 agencies to request program descriptions and fee structures. If an agency is out of your area, make sure you check with the agency state licensing authority to see if they are a legitimate agency and to find out if any complaints have been filed against them. We also checked agency references. We asked each agency for the names of families in the waiting stage as well as families that had completed their travel. Waiting families can provide information on the support and attentiveness of an agency; an important issue to us was whether the agency staff returned phone calls promptly.

If using an out-of-state agency, inquire at many different agencies within your state before selecting a local agency to complete your home study. If your state allows independent social workers to complete the home study process, look into this option for cost savings. Check all the fees you will have to pay, and ask about the process for a second adoption. Our search revealed a price range from $750 to $3,500 for the home study.

If you or a family member or good friend is in a frequent-flier program, start saving miles. Ask an agency if they will accommodate individual travel plans. You might find that leaving a day or two earlier, or returning a day or two later, can save money. We decided to use our frequent-flier miles through United Airlines to fly business class on an "open jaw" ticket. We flew into Shanghai and departed from Hong Kong, saving close to $3,000 on airfare.

Much of the expense of adopting from China is in the travel. Ask specific questions on cost, who makes the arrangements, and if they have a tour package. Consider finding an agency that books a total package including in-country travel, food, lodging, translation, and baggage transfers. When you talk with a family that has used an agency, ask if the travel expenses were within the price quoted by the agency. If you travel and pay as you go, you may find that you pay a premium. We met one group while in China and found that they had paid U.S.$40 for a medical exam that cost us only $10.

It may feel uncomfortable to discuss fee structures and anticipated expenses when you are creating or expanding your family through inter-country adoption. But for us it was a necessity, and asking the hard questions helped us realize a dream. One final idea on money: before making your decision, compare the total costs, not just agency fees. We made a comparison sheet with columns for each agency and what fees covered which services to help us make our decision.

Each family needs to find the right route for their journey. We hope our experiences help you pursue the adoption of your dreams.

Kathy Graves lives in St. Charles, Illinois. For details of her anticipated budget for another adoption from China in 1998/99, contact Kathy at ILJOH@aol.com or (630) 587-9560.

Fund-raising to
Adopt Sophie

Sylvia Jefford
Children Adopted from China (UK)

Our decision to adopt a baby from China came at a time when we had exhausted our savings through numerous IVF attempts. As I felt strongly that I wanted to give up work to look after our child, taking out a loan was not an option because we would have had difficulty in meeting the repayments on one salary.

Together with friends from our church we prayed about the situation and asked God for guidance. The decision to fund-raise was the obvious solution, but the prospect of organizing events was daunting given the stress involved in the impending home study and the bureaucracy of the adoption process.

We knew of a couple in a similar situation who had already raised several thousand pounds by a variety of events such as a disco, sponsored walk, raffles, and sponsorship from local firms. We decided on a sponsored walk as our first event. With 23 friends whose ages ranged from 3 to 73 we organized the walk taking into account age and physical abilities. We chose a six-mile circular walk in the Surrey countryside stopping at a pub halfway for a break and were blessed with a beautiful crisp autumn day in November 1995.

We produced our own sponsorship form, giving a brief history of the situation in China relating to the orphaned girls and the costs involved in adoption. We also made appeals at our church through a weekly news sheet and during an evening service. The response was overwhelming both from our church and the company for whom we both work. Sponsorship came from unexpected sources, which included a double-glazing firm in Kent, a number of people in Aberdeen and Holland, and two anonymous donations, one of which arrived in the form of a banker's draft for £1,000 placed inside a Chinese envelope. The walk was intended to be one of several fund-raising events, but we could not have imagined that we would have raised the £7,000 needed with just one event.

Initially we had dismissed the notion of overseas adoption as being something that we could not afford to do; however it proved possible with the help and support of our church and work colleagues. We would encourage others in similar financial circumstances not to abandon the idea of adopting without first considering the possibility of getting together with friends and family to raise the money.

We eventually traveled to Anhui province in China and on the 8th July 1996 we adopted Sophie Li Tian. She is now a happy, healthy 11-month-old who has become quite a celebrity both at our church and our work-place. We feel we have God to thank for giving us such a precious gift.

Sylvia Jefford lives in Ashtead, Surrey, England.

A Second Time Around

Carrie Krueger
FCC-Northwest

Adoption is a very different process the second time around. The anxiety and stress are less when you've already rocked a cradle once. You know enough to know that it *will* work out if you take the right steps. You also know enough to be savvy about the process. But it can still be a confusing and stressful time. Here are some things to consider when you're ready to add to your family…again!

Choosing a Country

For most of us, China holds a very strong pull. Having one child from China, it can feel very natural and logical to try for a second from China. For many people this does make sense. You only have one culture to integrate into your home life. You know the procedure. You may even have contacts at an orphanage in China that can help you the second time through. Plus it makes it a whole lot easier to respond when nosy strangers ask, "Where are they from?" Most significantly, many parents feel their children will share a special bond since they both came from the same country and from similar circumstances.

A few considerations to going with China the second time around are: Most of the children coming from China are girls. If you want a boy, the process could be a bit more complex. However, don't despair. Plenty of people have adopted boys from China, and it can be done. Second, China requires those adopting a second child to accept one with a handicap. Many agencies are saying this could be something very minor, or that they can work around the requirement. You will have to ask yourself how you feel about adopting a child with a handicap, and how you feel about working around a requirement. Traveling to China a second time is an issue for many families. It's one thing to head overseas when you're "child-free." With a second adoption, you've got the first child to think about. Do you leave her home, and return weeks later with a new child? Do you take her along? The travel requirement has led some families to consider other countries that allow escorts for their second adoption. Lastly, some people decide to adopt from a different country the second time as a way of avoiding the constant comparisons that come when two children are somewhat similar. Some fear the "two beautiful little china dolls" syndrome. Others want their second child to have a different identity and origin than the first because they remember what it was like to live in the shadow of a perfect older sibling.

Choosing an Agency

By the time you complete your first adoption, you know your agency pretty well. Are they organized? Do they communicate well? Are they honest, ethical, and fair? You know all their faults, and you know that they get the job done. After all, they helped you adopt one child. The question becomes, "The Devil you know, or the Devil you don't know?" If you feel comfortable with the agency or facilitator you used last time, that tends to be the easier way to jump back into the process. You may be able to do a simple home study update, rather than starting from scratch. And since the agency already knows your family, chances are good they will work extra hard to meet your needs. However, if you are still uncomfortable about something that happened during your first adoption, this is the time to switch!

Finding the Money

International adoption is incredibly expensive. Many of us broke the bank on the first adoption, and have remained broke as new parents. How to get the money for a second try? There is no easy answer to this. Several new agencies believe they can help you adopt for less. At least with the new adoption tax credit, Americans can count on getting a break from Uncle Sam on future adoptions.

Preparing Siblings

Your tummy doesn't grow (unless stress makes you overeat). There's no morning sickness, ultrasound, or hospital visit. But in every way, you are expecting. Soon-to-be siblings will need a special explanation of this blessed event. And be prepared. The new arrival will raise lots of questions about where your other child (or children) came from.

Unlike pregnancy, adoption offers no concrete nine-month time frame. So it can be difficult to decide when to tell children about the adoption. In my own home, I began discussing in vague terms with my daughter the idea of a little brother or sister, around the time that I did my paperwork and home study. As things firmed up, I became more concrete, saying, "Someday you *will* have a brother or sister." When I got a referral and a photo, I couldn't hold back any longer. I shared my excitement and joy with her. I'm not sure she "got" it (she was just shy of three years old at the time), but she took the picture with her to preschool and showed it to friends and visitors. As the arrival date approached (my son was brought by an escort from Vietnam), she discussed him constantly. And it did lead to some questions about how she got here. As always, I tried to be honest and clear in my responses. In fact, I feel in a lot of ways, the arrival of her brother did clarify the whole adoption issue somewhat for my daughter. But, boy, did we do a *lot* of talking!

Meanwhile, those who travel for their second adoption must also consider preparing their first child (or children) for travel, or preparing them for the absence of one or both parents. Again, this will involve a lot of talking. Taking older children along could be the trip of a lifetime or a nightmare, depending on the attitude, abilities, and adaptability of the child. A number of families have done it, and it might make sense to consult them for tips. Leaving a child with grandparents, other relatives, or friends can also be very special, as long as the child has ample preparation and a secure relationship with parents.

Finally, just as with the arrival of a birth sibling, your home and your child's environment must be prepared. I found it helpful to get my first child out of the crib, highchair, and other "baby" equipment well in advance of the new arrival. That way there was less chance of her perceiving herself as being displaced. I actually tried to put as much of this stuff away as I could for a period of several months, and then bring it out again before the baby arrived. The experts recommend against constant use of the "big girl" phrase, as two-, three-, and four-year-olds still need to feel they can be a baby sometimes. We did a lot of talking about the role of "big sister," but I tried to also baby her a lot with extra holding and care. There are a couple of pretty good books on the market geared toward preparing your first child for a birth sibling, but still very useful in families built through adoption.

Preparing for Questions

If you thought you were getting attention from strangers with one child, try it with two. People notice. And perhaps the most irritating thing they say is, "Are they brother and sister?" Of course they are, but you have to be ready for people to ask. What makes this harder is now you have an older child who is listening with sharp ears to everything you say. Those questions about where the new baby is from, how small he or she is, how tragic his or her life might have been, and what a hero adoptive parents are (blah blah blah) take on new meaning when an older child is on hand. As I become more experienced, I am getting better and better at saying nothing, ignoring strangers, or answering in pleasant but vague tones.

A Time to Relax and Enjoy

From my own experience, and that of many others with whom I've talked, a second adoption can be very enjoyable and rewarding. I felt confident because I knew the process and knew how to navigate the paperwork maze. I also had a busy two-year-old to fill my time during the wait. In fact, I think that special time with the child (or children) you already have is one of the most important things to consider when doing a second adoption. Cherish that time and make the most of it. When the new child arrives, life will never be quite the same!

Carrie Krueger traveled to Hangzhou in 1992 to adopt Claire Lilai Krueger. In February 1995 Carrie and Claire welcomed Cameron Krueger from Da Nang, Vietnam. They live in Bellevue, Washington.

The Unbearable Process of Waiting

Mary Jo Leugers

Families of the China Moon (Virginia)

No other journey in your life better warrants the phrase "hurry up and wait" than the adoption process does. By the time you make the decision to adopt, you are way past wanting a child. You've wanted this child for a very, very long time. You've paid your "patience" dues. You've picked an agency, finished your paperwork. Your dossier's been in China for months. You want your child NOW! And you're still waiting…

We asked several families who've already adopted about their experiences waiting and what they did to make it easier. Maybe what they have to say will give you some ideas.

"Two or three days before we were to travel, our trip was canceled. It was awful," Terrie recalls. "We were told all bets were off—the agency didn't know when we'd travel." Terrie and her husband John had gotten caught up in the reorganization in China. To help them through, John's family gave them a "supportive brunch." "We got a lot of nonverbal support with our family gathered around us being very sympathetic." Terrie says she also cleaned the house incessantly. While it is hard to keep the faith, she believes it's important to trust in God or in divine providence, whichever suits your beliefs. Keep that internal dialogue going. "For all my doubts, it finally did happen and it was worth the wait."

"The wait for me was really hard," says Barbara, "I found that being around waiting families was much easier than being with families who had already adopted. It made me realize that I wasn't alone and it just wasn't my agency screwing up." Barbara decided it was best not to buy anything of any size for the baby until she had Gillian's picture. "If it doesn't fit in a large U-haul box that goes in the back of your closet, don't buy it." She did do a lot of window shopping though, and figured out what she wanted to get once she had a picture. Barbara also recommends not planning holidays as if you will have your baby by then. Barbara laughed and added: "What amazes me is how quickly I forgot how painful the wait was. People told me that would happen, but I didn't believe them."

"For us," says Susan, "the hardest part was watching the news about China and worrying whether China would close its program. My adoption agency was able to calm my fears." Susan also said it was hard for her and Jack when they got Audrey's picture and had to wait months to get her. "You realize these kids are growing without you. It's very hard to be a parent long distance." To deal with the wait, Susan started a diary about how she was feeling about waiting, how their lives would change, whether Audrey was born yet and how she would look. "I also started collecting things about China like newspaper articles, and I started planning for the trip by thinking about questions I wanted to ask and pictures I wanted to take to keep for Audrey's life book." Susan had a final point to say to waiting families: "Everyone gets their child—everyone eventually travels to China."

While her wait was shorter than most today, Cary found it helpful to work on getting things done that had been hanging around forever and that she knew she would never get done once she had a child. "Getting organized and keeping busy was the key for me."

Mary Jo Leugers, the newsletter editor of Families of the China Moon, lives in Richmond, Virginia.

The Labor of Waiting

Christine Kukka

Maine Families with Children from Asia

After the initial flurry of gathering documents, attending home study meetings and mailing documents to secretaries of state and embassies, the most grueling part of the adoption process begins: waiting.

For my family, the wait turned into an excruciating test of faith. We had submitted our authenticated package in January of 1993 and were told we would be traveling to China in late March or early April. Then, the *New York Times* Sunday magazine cover story appeared, showing a Chinese baby girl with the headline, "China's Latest Export." China closed its door to adoptions with our authenticated package sitting in some office in Beijing. No one knew when China would reopen its door, if at all.

As in all of life's great challenges, it was unclear to everyone how long this trauma would last or what the true ramifications would be. The international adoption agency we dealt with kept postponing our departure. Maybe next month, they wrote us, month after month.

Finally, we received a letter announcing that the agency didn't know when China would reopen. They asked us to stop calling, because our calls caused their staff too much stress.

Months went by. I entertained all the bleak, self-pitying "why me?" moments. It was hard enough not to be able to conceive children, then to make this bold leap to adopt in a country that had just recently opened to adoptions, and then the shutdown. It was difficult not to feel like a victim.

In adoptions, I find money becomes a symbol for all our hopes and anxieties. I found myself lamenting all the money we had invested, and how now we might lose it all if China never reopened. But it was really my heart I was talking about.

In some respects, we were lucky. I met a woman in Massachusetts who had just received her referral photo when China shut down. She spent eight months in purgatory, looking at that picture and thinking about how her baby was faring in a very distant country and orphanage.

I spent those eight months living day by day, trying not to think about this open wound. After a while, my husband and I stopped talking about it. There was nothing left to say that hadn't been said a dozen times before.

There were two things that pulled me through. I hooked up with a woman in Maine who was in the same travel group as my husband and I. She was waiting and anxious and going crazy, just like me. Neither the local nor the international agency had given us each other's name; it was a mutual friend who linked us up. We tentatively began talking, first guardedly and then openly, about our anguish. Any letter from the agency resulted in a new round of calls and speculation between us. We didn't know what would happen, but we knew we had each other to pour out our hopes and fears onto.

My husband and I visited her and her husband that summer. As we left, we hugged and said, "Maybe next time we meet, we'll be boarding a plane to China together." But our hearts weren't really in it. In our weary way, we were trying to be hopeful, for each other and for ourselves.

There was something else that got me through, and only today do I realize how important it was. A friend at work cut out a photo from a tourist guide that showed a group of Chinese children standing together, giggling at the photographer. I taped it to my computer and speculated daily which child my future daughter might look like. When the going got tough, when I thought China would never reopen, I sometimes stopped looking at the photo. But still it was always there. Three years later, I can still see that photo with my eyes closed.

Finally, that friend and I did board that plane together. Later, she told me that she too had a photo. It was a picture of a friend's adopted daughter. When I visited her last summer, two years after our return from China, it was still taped to her refrigerator door.

During our endless wait, those photos became our talismans, our confirmation that somehow our brave leaps of faith would not be wasted. No longer how painful the wait—and how heartless the international conditions that prolonged it—those pictures promised that if we somehow maintained hope, somewhere out there a child would come to us.

We did not have to speak our hopes and prayers aloud, we had only to glance at these photos to remind ourselves that our children were waiting. If only we were strong enough to stand the wait.

And of course we had to endure that endless year. After all, our children hadn't been born yet.

Christine Kukka and her family live in Scarborough, Maine.

Rebecca's Letter

Rebecca Garland
Mosaic (UK)

Dear Mei Ming,

I am not sure whether you are born yet. I know that you will be one day and that you are waiting for me, or should I say, us. Let me tell you who I am and that might make things a little clearer. My name is Rebecca Catherine Louise Garland. (My parents took six weeks to choose my names.) I started off as Hannah, then Rachel, then Katie, then finally Rebecca, with my Mum's name Catherine next and Louise to round it off. We live in a ragstone house with two bedrooms and that might be a problem. It has a long garden, with a ragstone wall all along one side of it. We have a swing and a sand pit and right at the top is a secret garden where we can have picnics and pretend we are not at home. It is very cold here today, snow has been forecast, and some places have snow already. I am ten years old and I go to school a mile from my house. Our home is in England about 40 miles from the seaside and 40 miles from a big city called London. When you meet us you will think we are funny to look at. Our noses are big, our skin is pale and freckled, and our eyes are round. People have hair of many different colors. Our language is strange too. You will look at us and wonder what we are saying and why we stare at you. When you are ready to be born, you will burst into the world, full of love and hunger. Your mother will take you, perhaps not straight away, but in a little while to a place where you will wait for us. There will be lots like you, waiting. For what? They don't know. Some will always wait, but you, you are waiting for me, Rebecca, to love you and show you all the things I have learnt. To watch you play with toys I used to play

21

with, and help you choose new ones, when you come into our world and stay forever. I know what you look like. You will have beautiful, almond-shaped, deep brown eyes that look jet black. Your hair will be very dark brown or black and your nose will be turned up. Your skin will tan easily. Already I want to learn your language, I want to know where you come from. One day, when you grow up, as old as me, we will travel back together and see the cot that you once slept in and the orphanage and you will want to find your first mother. We won't find her, though, she left no name. I know she would be happy that you were here with us. If only she knew!

With love,

Your sister Rebecca

Rebecca Garland was born on August 13, 1986. Just before her tenth birthday Rebecca traveled to China with her parents to adopt ten-month-old Zhu Fen from the Lanxi Social Welfare Institution in Zhejiang province. She and her family live in Maidstone, Kent.

Open Mind, Open Heart

Karen Braucher
FCC—Oregon and SW Washington

I.

In Changsha, China, in dark orphanage rooms, hundreds
of abandoned baby girls wait. Legend has it that Lao Tsu,
riding off to the desert to die, sick at heart at the ways of men,

was persuaded to write down his teaching for posterity.
*The Tao which can be told is not the eternal Tao. The name
that can be named is not the eternal name.* At the Office of the

Secretary of State of Massachusetts, they affix the proper seals
to our documents. They used to throw them in the river or
bury them alive. *The nameless is the beginning of heaven and earth.*

My husband's birth certificate is lost in the gray cubicles
of New York state. Lao wrote the *Tao te ching,*
The Way of Virtue, in the sixth century B.C.,

essence of Taoism. Now they leave them near the orphanage,
pretend nothing happened, try again for their one chance
at a boy. *The named is the mother of ten thousand things.*

How long it takes to collect the required papers! *It is important
to cast off selfishness and temper desire.* I'm learning
about patience. *He who is attached to things will suffer much.*

II.

Lao Tsu, ancient master of divination and sacred books,
in Hunan province where my future daughter waits,
is said to have met the young Confucius, telling him to

beware of his pride and his ambition. *Being openhearted,*
you will act royally. Being royal, you will attain the divine.
Confucius, hurt, took the message to heart, and found

he was changing. He looked at Lao Tsu and saw
a dragon rising to the sky, riding on the winds and clouds.
Being divine, you will be at one with the Tao.

He vowed to be worthy of the great master, though he
knew his way was the way of the every day.
Though the body dies, the Tao will never pass away.

    III.

Breathe in, breathe out. How many approvals left to go?
In the universe great acts are made up of small deeds.
In Changsha, she waits in a sea of baby girls,

all needing a name. It's not over at six months, or six years,
it's never over. She may have a place in her that is desolate,
a land I can never reach. I dream that

I am standing on top of a cliff looking down on ocean
under a full moon. In front of me there is a staircase
of stone leading down to churning waves of water.

The stairs are narrow and steep, with no railing, and
I am afraid of heights. I want to go down barefoot
on cold stone, a shimmering below where the tide

hits the land, and above a light bathing me in something
both animal and ethereal. I know I will go. But for a moment
I stop and listen. *Darkness within darkness. The gate to all mystery.*

The Adoption Journey

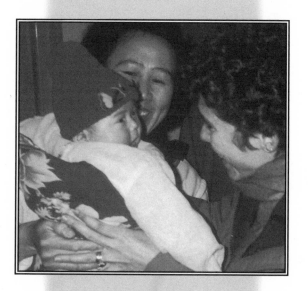

The most important piece of luggage is and remains
a joyful heart.

Hermann Lons

Baby Fear

Vivia Chen
FCC–New York

Just a few months before we adopted our daughter, I confessed to a friend that I had never changed a diaper in my life. My friend, a veteran mother of three boys, looked at me quizzically and said: "If you can make it through law school, I'm sure you can figure out how to change a diaper." Silly me, I thought, of course I would figure it all out. Besides, I remembered that my husband Eric had baby-sat as a teenager, so I assumed he knew the finer points of baby care.

Call it naiveté. Call it arrogance. Call it denial. The simple fact was that neither I nor my husband was prepared for even the most basic aspects of taking care of a baby.

For months, we diligently completed our adoption paperwork, then waited with surreal equanimity for the baby assignment. Once we received our assignment in April of '95, I transformed into a nervous, insecure wreck: I obsessed about the health of our child, issues of bonding, and the possibility of raising a juvenile delinquent. Worrying about the likes of diaper changing was the least of my concerns.

The weekend before we left for China, we summoned up the courage to go to Toys-R-Us for baby supplies (lesson number one: Toys-R-Us is not just for toys). Bombarded with dozens of choices in bottles, nipples, diapers, wipes, lotions, potions, we ran out of the store—dazed, confused, and empty-handed.

Pride had prevented us from taking up offers of baby-shopping assistance from various friends. Finally, shocked by our total lack of preparedness, an old friend literally dragged us to a CVS, where we bought almost $200 worth of baby supplies. We bought things I could never have imagined, much less dreamed of using—like nose aspirators.

Armed with the requisite baby supplies, we set out for our journey to China. Though I took a copy of *What to Expect the First Year* with me onto the plane, I was much too distracted to read it. I figured I would just read the relevant sections of the book on an "as needed" basis.

When we arrived at the Nanjing orphanage, a young nurse brought our three-month-old daughter to the office area to meet us. Though our daughter Sabina was suffering from bronchitis at the time, she was spirited and unquestionably beautiful. When the nurse handed her over to us, we were exhilarated. At the same time, it dawned on me that we were entrusted to take care of a real living human being. In a word, I was petrified.

Back in our room at the Grand Hotel, we were faced with our first challenge: feeding our baby. As she started to cry, we came to the brilliant conclusion that she might be hungry. I read the instruction on the can of ProSobee and clumsily made my first bottle of baby formula. Sabina drank it with relish, and so we thought we had passed the first hurdle.

Next: changing the diaper. This was more challenging as it entailed the removal of the old diaper, cleaning her genitals, and the application of diaper rash ointment and a fresh diaper. Being a quick study, I did figure out that the front of the diaper is where the cartoon is printed. To my surprise, I learned that even babies who consume only formula have bowel movements. What's more, they can poop several times a day. And yes, baby poop does stink. We went into a tizzy when we realized we had to change our daughter's smelly clothes. I remembered someone had said that a "onesie" was what babies wore underneath their street clothes. After several valiant attempts, we slipped the onesie over her head, but we were lost as to how to get her arms into the little sleeves without causing her great pain. As with the diapers, our daughter wailed at each clothing change.

Bathing a baby for the first time also is not for the faint of heart. As our baby screamed and squirmed, I was convinced that she would either go into a convulsion or that she would slip from my arms and drown. After two separate attempts at bathing Sabina, we convinced ourselves of the superiority of good sponging.

The day we left Nanjing for Guangzhou, Sabina started her cycle of incessant, inconsolable crying. To this day the White Swan Hotel in Guangzhou is burnished in my mind as parental hell. For three days and nights, from about two in the afternoon till three in the morning, we struggled to get Sabina to stop crying. We fed her on demand, gave her Infant Tylenol, and rocked her till our arms ached. I got out my copy of *What to Expect* and looked up everything in the index under "crying." Her behavior seemed to fit the description of "colic"—an umbrella term for constant crying with no solid definition or solution.

At times, we thought she was just an incredibly difficult baby. Other times, we became convinced that she was suffering from some horrible ailment and felt guilty that we had attributed her crying to her character. We called our pediatrician in New York four times from China—which must set some sort of record. He assured us that the antibiotic we were giving her for her bronchitis seemed appropriate and to continue with the Tylenol—beyond that, he did not think she needed emergency care.

As it turned out, Sabina was fine. During our stopover in Hawaii, we arranged for Sabina to see a pediatrician—a wise and very reassuring man who pronounced Sabina to be healthy and alert, but told us that we looked terrible and needed a vacation. So, we resumed our original plan and headed for a few days in Maui. Sabina continued her crying spree, but at least we knew she was healthy and normal.

We came back humbled and exhausted by our first venture into parenthood. In retrospect, I wished we had grilled friends about caring for a young baby, read the baby books more carefully, and perhaps rented out a video about basic child care. But the fact is we had no idea of how little we knew. Caring for a baby doesn't come naturally—at least not to us. A little homework certainly doesn't hurt. Better still, bring along a baby nurse.

Of course, there's no replacement for experience. It's been almost a year since Sabina entered our lives, and it seems unbelievable we could have been so inept at basic baby care. Incredibly, I now feel confident about dispensing baby advice—I can tell you the nontraumatic way to put on a onesie (feet first), which nipples don't clog (silicone ones), and how to get your baby to sleep (read Dr. Ferber—it really works!). Believe me, I've come a long way.

Vivia Chen, an interior designer, and her husband Eric Gilioli and daughter Sabina (Nanjing, 1995) reside in Manhattan.

The Journey

Deborah Pope
FCC—New York

I came home from Wuhan with my daughter just three months ago. She is incredibly wonderful, and I feel so lucky to have her with me. I would not want any other baby as my first daughter, and I am overjoyed with my passage to motherhood.

These are some bits of advice I found helpful as I journeyed to China to find my daughter. They are not in any particular order, and they reflect my experience. Your trip will probably be different. Approaching this voyage as a great adventure and greeting it with flexibility are the best things you can do for yourself. Remember that the country to which you are going is the birthplace of your child. It will be nice to have good memories of your trip to share with your daughter as she grows up.

1. Expect enormous obstacles to fall into your path.

2. Expect to feel like everything is disintegrating. Expect to feel out of control.

3. Stay calm.

4. Be confident that everything will work out. Solutions *will* be found to all the enormous obstacles.

5. The Chinese officials *do* want the process to succeed.

6. Treat your hosts with respect and appreciation.

7. Do not exhibit anger or indignation.

8. Do not be afraid of requesting the information and help you need.

9. Understand that the Chinese love their children.

10. Do not expect to meet your child in a calm and quiet environment.

11. Try to ask all the questions you have about your child's history, but do not expect to be able to ask or get answers to all the questions you may have about your child's history.

12. You may bond with your child immediately.

13. You may not bond with your child for days, weeks, or even months.

14. You *will* bond with your child.

15. Do not worry if you wonder if this baby is the right baby.

16. Be calm, follow your instincts, and do not condemn yourself for any doubts you may have.

17. Vent your fears and frustrations to your partner or to a close friend.

18. Make sure that you have carefully researched the least expensive way to make international phone calls from China to the U.S. with your telephone company. Do not make international calls on hotel lines unless calling collect or through AT&T's USA Direct.

19. Understand that you represent the parents who are yet to travel to China for their children.

20. Don't drink the tap water. You *can* take showers without getting water into your mouth.

21. The boiled water in the hotel thermos really is boiled and safe. Bring two Rubbermaid graduated quart bottles to cool it in and to mix formula.

22. Bring mostly lactose-based formula for your baby.

23. Snuglies, or any of the carry slings, are great for transporting your baby.

24. The Chinese tend to swarm around you when you go out with your baby. Don't be afraid of letting them see the baby, and don't be afraid of withdrawing her from view when you feel you must.

25. If you have never been to China, expect it to be completely different from any place you have ever been.

26. Keep your paperwork in one organized packet. Put all new documents and photos in this packet. Take the packet with you when-

ever you must accomplish any official function. Keep this packet with you as much as possible.

27. Always keep your and your child's passports on your person.

28. Don't lose your sense of humor. Your hosts have a sense of humor too.

29. Do not introduce politics into discussions.

30. When leaving China, check your luggage through to the U.S. if you are changing planes in Hong Kong or Shanghai.

31. Ask other parents of children from China about their experiences. Be sure to speak to families who traveled to the same city as you or who have traveled during the same season.

32. Expect this experience to be one of the most exciting of your life.

33. If you are single, seriously consider having someone accompany you. Anyone traveling with you, however, should understand that this is not a sightseeing trip. You and your baby will be the central focus and concern at all times.

34. Expect to be exhausted even before you receive your child. The emotional and psychological strain of this trip is enormous.

35. Expect to be even more exhausted once your receive your child.

36. Expect to play with your child and begin to establish your own routines with her from the very first minute you are together.

37. Through trial and error make sure that the holes in your bottle nipples are large enough for a baby who is used to getting her formula rather quickly.

38. Don't be afraid of using the pacifier.

39. The home recipe for Pedialyte (used to counteract dehydration) is one level teaspoon of sugar and one pinch of salt in eight ounces of water. Pack a few ounces of sugar and salt, carry a teaspoon and cup measure. This is very important. If any of the babies become dehydrated, this mixture will save the day.

40. Bring antibiotics for your baby, but do not administer them until you have consulted with a physician.

41. Before departing for China, consult your pediatrician regarding what medications to bring for the baby.

42. Consult your doctor regarding medications to bring for yourself.

43. Ask your doctor about the immunizations you will need: hepatitis B, hepatitis A, gamma globulin, polio, tetanus...

44. Bring some foodstuffs for yourself. Eating some meals in your hotel room makes life easier.

45. Shop in local stores in China. Find foods from China that you enjoy snacking on.

46. Do not expect your American adoption agency or facilitator to meet all your needs or to tell you everything you need to know.

47. If something goes wrong try to concentrate on how to move forward and solve the problem. Let go of trying to figure out who is to blame and who will pay for the mistake.

48. The only real mistake is wasting energy on anything unnecessary to getting and then keeping your baby happy and healthy.

49. By the time you return home you will feel as if you have been away for a lifetime.

50. You have.

Deborah Pope lives in Brooklyn, New York. Her daughter, Abigail Tao Yu, was born November 13, 1993.

Feeding Suggestions While in China

Deborah Borchers, M.D.
FCC–Greater Cincinnati

Before leaving for China, talk to your child's doctor or nurse practitioner about what formula he/she recommends. Many pediatricians recommend taking a milk-based formula, such as Similac with Iron or Enfamil with Iron. Others recommend Lactofree (a milk with no lactose sugar, but also with no soy protein), as many people of Asian descent have a lactose intolerance. This often does not manifest until the children are older, however. In my experience, Lactofree seemed to be the closest in taste to the Chinese formulas used in most orphanages. The powder packs well, and for a two-week trip five cans will be more than enough. If you have room, take at least one can of a different formula also in case your child refuses the one you brought. You can safely use the water provided in the thermos supplied in your hotel room. Take your own thermos (preferably stainless steel so as to avoid accidental breakage) with a narrow spout or lid from which it will be easy to pour while in dining rooms, on buses, and on planes. A funnel is also helpful for transferring hot water into your thermos without burning yourself.

It does not matter if you take disposable or washable bottles, but take ones that have interchangeable nipples. Different babies prefer different types (standard versus Nuk) and different openings (regular holes versus cross-cut), as well as different textures (latex versus silicon). Although it sounds crazy, the babies are that picky. My younger daughter stopped eating after two days because she preferred a different nipple, so it is worth the trouble to bring the variety. If you need to enlarge the holes in the nipples for your daughter once you are in China, do not enlarge all of the nipple holes. Sometimes children will prefer the formula fast flowing at first, then want to slow down.

Some children from Chinese orphanages are used to the formula being given at temperatures that are outrageously hot by our thinking. Try to use water temperatures that are comfortable to your touch. If your daughter refuses to eat, use water that is a little warmer or cooler. The children adjust easily to a gradual decrease in the water temperature once you are comfortable with their eating habits.

To ease the transition to U.S. baby formulas, many people mix the formula in a lesser strength for a few days. This avoids some problems with constipation and stomach aches. Usually powdered formula in the U.S. is mixed at a ratio of one scoop to two ounces of water. You may wish to mix it for a day at a ratio of one scoop to four ounces of water, then one scoop to three ounces of water for a day. If your child refuses the change in formula, Chinese baby formula (actually made by American companies) is easily available from Friendship Stores. We figured that one scoop of Chinese formula to one ounce of water was the correct ratio, but double check this ratio if you need to use Chinese formula (one ounce is about 30 cc of fluid). After one or two days of feeding the Chinese formula, start mixing in gradually the American formula.

While at the orphanage, ask what other foods your child is being fed. It may be helpful to ask your physician before you go for his/her recommendations regarding other solid foods to be fed while in China. Older children who are on solids can usually easily be fed from the table. Foods that are also eagerly eaten by children on solids include Nutri-Grain bars, Cheerios, Kix, rice cereal, and graham crackers. Be sure to pack such goodies in double bags to avoid crumbs throughout your luggage.

In feeding your daughter, flexibility and patience will be the key to getting through the transition days together. I strongly recommend that all families adopting from China make an appointment with their physician or nurse practitioner prior to travel to obtain their input and preferences regarding these suggestions.

Deborah Borchers, M.D., is a general pediatrician in Cincinnati, Ohio, and the mother of two daughters adopted from China. The information given here is based on experience gathered through her years of pediatric practice, as well as during the adoption of both daughters. This article was revised May 8, 1998, to include the current recommendations of the International Adoption Clinic at the University of Minnesota. If you have questions or need further information, please call Dr. Borchers at Eastgate Pediatric Center, (513) 753-2820, or at home, (606) 331-7026.

Packing Differently the Second Time Around

Kathy Graves
FCC-Chicago

Prior to going to China in 1995 we read every packing list we could find. By following several lists, we used three suitcases and brought way too much stuff. We will pack much differently for our second trip. We had been told that so many things were not available in China; but in Changzhou, Jiangsu province, we did not find that to be the case at all. The key to packing well is to investigate as much as possible before you go to China. The more you know about the provinces and cities/towns in which you will be staying, the better prepared you will be for your stay in China. By talking to others who have been to your child's orphanage, town, or province, you will be able to pack more wisely.

There were many things I packed for our first trip that we did not need:

Too many clothes. In Changzhou the laundry was fast and inexpensive. For our second trip we will bring three or four changes of clothes and plan on doing laundry at least twice in the orphanage town. Laundry charges tend to be higher in major cities like Beijing or Guangzhou or in upscale hotels. Look for nearby local laundries rather than hotel laundries, or get your laundry done before you leave your child's provincial city.

Too many diapers. We were in China only ten days and had Emily for only five of those days. Needless to say, we did not need 88 diapers. Diapers were available in her town and in Guangzhou; they did not seem that expensive.

Too much formula. We chose to give Emily what she had been given at the orphanage to help her adjust to us. We did add sugar and gradually switched her to American formula. For our second trip we will only bring two cans of soy formula. We also found soy formula in Guangzhou.

Too much of everything. We expected China to be more third world than it was. We saw it as both a developed nation and a developing nation.

While we were in China the first time, there were many things I wished we had packed:

Slippers. The hotels we stayed in were carpeted but not very clean; some hotels do provide slippers, but ours did not.

Small audio tape recorder. Our guide explained so much about Emily's town, the culture, why children are abandoned, etc. I took notes, but not enough. I would have liked to tape record our guides' comments for a permanent record of the information that was shared.

Journal. Use the *International Adoption Travel Journal,* by Mary E. Petertyl (888-436-5461), or your own free-form journal to record the emotions and experiences of the trip. Or consider making a video journal each day instead, using a separate tape just for the journal.

Warmer clothes for the plane and hotels. Bring comfortable clothes for layering for yourself and your child; the air conditioning on the plane and in the hotels is cool.

All possible medicines. Bring any type of prescription or over-the-counter medicine that you take; be prepared for the unexpected.

Finally, I want to share what we learned about baby bottles and food on our first trip. Based on our experiences with Emily, I would encourage bringing regular baby bottles. It seemed that infants about seven months and older were used to drinking from regular bottles. To be on the safe side, you could bring disposable and regular baby bottles. We had heard that some babies did not want to drink from a bottle, so we also brought a couple of learner cups. We also learned that children were fed with propped bottles at the orphanage. When we tried to feed Emily cuddling and looking into her eyes, she would not eat. She ate well in the Snugli with the weight of the bottle on her lips.

At our daughter's orphanage we were given formula, calcium tablets, fish oil, sugar cubes to sweeten the formula, an eating schedule, and gifts from Emily's province. We chose to use the Chinese formula to help Emily get adjusted to us. Everything that Emily was used to—sights, sounds, smells, tastes—changed when we adopted her. We chose to give her the same thing to eat because we felt it was important to help her through the adjustment period. Emily was the only child in our group that ate well for the first 24 hours. We found Emily's Chinese formula at the local department store; the vitamin and nutrition information between the Chinese formula and the American formula was almost identical. Over time we did change to American formula, little by little, by blending the two formulas. By the time we arrived home Emily was drinking American soy formula. We brought both soy- and milk-based formula. For our second adoption, I think we will just bring soy, which I only saw available in Guangzhou. If we need milk-based formula we can always buy it in China. We will also consider using the baby supplies that are available in the town. In Changzhou, the state-run department store had an entire aisle of milk-type formulas for infants, children, adults, and older adults.

After we had been home for four months, we found out that Emily is allergic to milk protein and not milk lactose or sugar. Now she is on Toddler Next Step Soy. After having what we thought was a continuous cold, we realized she was having an allergic reaction to milk. For those adopting toddlers one to two years old, you may want to bring some Toddler Next Step Formula in soy or milk.

In our group of seven babies, ages 7–12 months, no one ate anything but formula. We brought baby cereal, but it was also available in China. Parents that have adopted older infants/toddlers have said that their children are usually eating easy table food like rice, noodles, soups, and soft vegetables, which are available with every meal. I did not bring baby food, but I have heard that bringing some prunes or prune juice can help babies that are constipated. We did order baby food for our plane trip home just in case we needed it when Chinese noodles or rice would not be available.

The key to preparing for your trip and packing well is knowing as much as possible about the towns and provinces in which you will be traveling. I hope that some of what we learned from our first trip will be helpful for those who are preparing to travel. It won't be the end of the world if you don't pack everything, but packing wisely can make your adventure more enjoyable and give you more time to spend getting to know your child in China.

Kathy Graves lives with her husband Kevin, twin sons Brian and Kyle, and daughters Emily and Shasha in St. Charles, Illinois. She recently joined the staff of Journeys of the Heart as international program director in their Chicago office. For a detailed packing list, contact Kathy at ILJOH@aol.com or (630) 587-9560.

Emily's Life Did Not Begin When She Joined Our Family

Katharine Cobb

FCC–New York

When my husband, Eric Balber, and I adopted Emily in July of 1995 at the age of four and a half months, we knew there would be limits to what we could learn about our daughter's early life, but we wanted to try to find out as much as we could. We viewed the requirement that we travel to Emily's birthplace as a wonderful opportunity to learn about the country where she was born. We were eager to speak with the orphanage director and acquire as much personal information about her as we could. We knew how much our older daughter, now eight, loves to hear stories about her own birth and early infancy, and we wanted to be able to have stories to share with Emily about her life before we adopted her.

We adopted Emily from the Hangzhou Children's Welfare Institute. We traveled with a group of five other families adopting children from this and other orphanages in Zhejiang province. At first we were told that we would have an opportunity to visit the orphanages during our stay in Hangzhou and be able to ask the orphanage staff questions about our child. However, as a result of an unflattering documentary on Chinese orphanages made secretly by British film makers pretending to be tourists, the government closed all orphanages to anyone traveling on a tourist visa. We were, of course, quite disappointed.

Since we could not go to the orphanages, one official from each of the three orphanages where our children had been came to our hotel to answer questions and receive our orphanage donations. We and two other families met with the deputy orphanage director, who brought with her any notes that had been left with the children and the children's immunization records.

Fortunately, my husband and I prepared for this visit by writing down a list of questions. The interview was an emotional experience, and we would not have been able to remember everything we wanted to ask without the list. (I have included below a list of the questions that we asked; if Emily had been older, we would have asked many more questions about her life in the orphanage.) My husband took extensive notes. This was very important. Later we discovered we had to refer to his notes often, as our memories of what was said were not always trustworthy!

The deputy director was unable to answer all of our questions, but she made a conscientious effort to respond, adding details of her own. We found it was very important to listen closely to the answers and follow up with other questions. Sometimes we did not understand the answer; sometimes the answer suggested other questions.

We learned, among other things, that Emily was found in a parklike area along a river by a passerby at around noon on March 12. She was in a lady's handbag and was wearing cotton baby clothes. We asked the deputy director to mark the location on our map of Hangzhou and to describe a landmark near where she was found. She told us she was left by a statue of children holding hands. This piece of information proved critical in our subsequent efforts to find the location.

Emily was turned over to the police, and three days after she was found she came into the custody of the orphanage. The deputy director did not know the name of the individual who found Emily. One of my regrets is not trying more vigorously to find out who that person was, although it might very well not have been possible. I have heard of a family who was able to identify and actually meet the people who found their child.

A note was left with Emily with her birth date in the Chinese lunar calendar written on a small piece of Buddhist prayer paper. Although we were not permitted to keep the original note, we were allowed to photograph and photocopy it. Seeing the note was overwhelmingly emotional.

Emily was eight days old and tiny when she was found. Her small size led them to conclude that she may have been an "eight-month" baby. In response to our questions about what Emily was like and what made her happy, the deputy director told us that she loved to be held, that she enjoyed "talking" to her nurse in the morning when waking up, and that she especially enjoyed her bath. When asked who named her Sihui, her Chinese name, and why, she smiled and said that she had because she wanted her to be bright and intelligent. (*Hui* means "wisdom," and *si* means something like "emerging" or "thinking"). She told us she was called Wei-Wei as a pet name.

We knew there was an orphanage practice of having newborns share cribs, and we asked who Emily's cribmate had been. The deputy director laughed and pointed to one of the other babies in our group who had entered the orphanage at about the same time as Emily.

We also asked our translator to write down all Chinese names mentioned during our discussion. In addition, we got everyone's business cards.

Although our experience was positive, the experience of other members of our group who had adopted from a different orphanage was disappointing. The representative sent by their orphanage was a business person who knew little about their children, had not come prepared with any information, and seemed not to care.

Later the same day after our meeting with the deputy director, we set out to find the spot where Emily had been found. We had our guide write down the location on a piece of paper that we showed to the taxi driver. Our guide used the location name that was on the certificate of abandonment, a document that is part of the Chinese adoption paperwork. A very puzzled taxi driver took us to that location, a small park and children's playground across the street from a river. However, within minutes of our arrival, it began to rain very hard and we had to leave.

As it turned out, this was a stroke of good fortune. When we returned the next day, we approached the spot from a different direction and saw, along the river, a statue matching the description given to us by the deputy director. First, we searched the little playground where we had been the day before, and finding no statues at all, we crossed the street to the riverbank. We then walked a short distance to the statues we had seen during our taxi ride. There were no other statues along the river, and we were convinced that we had discovered the place where little eight-day-old Emily had been found.

The statue was of a family—two children, a mother, and a father—all holding hands. Although there was not heavy pedestrian traffic in the area, there were a number of people passing by, all of whom looked at the three of us curiously, no doubt wondering what on earth we were doing there. It was apparent to us that Emily was left in a location where she would have been discovered after a short while. I also strongly felt that placing her by this particular statue was a message of hope and love. We took photographs and some video footage. I picked a few flowers from a flowering bush next to the statue to press and save. Something about the location and the moment made me recall the story of another child abandoned out of necessity—Moses left in the bulrushes by his mother. I kept wondering if Emily's birth parents were somehow nearby, watching us.

We did not stay long. It was an incredibly hot day, and we were happy to escape the heat. Returning to the shelter of our air-conditioned hotel room, we felt triumphant and exhilarated, knowing that we would have a story to tell Emily.

Questions to Ask Orphanage Representatives

1. What is her feeding/ sleeping schedule?

2. What immunizations has she had and when?

3. What was her physical condition when she entered the orphanage?

4. What illnesses has she had since she has been in the orphanage?

5. Where and when was she found and what were the circumstances? Are there significant landmarks at the location?

6. Who found her and when and how did she come to the orphanage?

7. Was there a note, what did it say, can we examine it? Was there any other property with her when she was found?

8. How was she dressed when found?

9. How was her birth date known and/or selected?

10. How old was she when she was found?

11. Do you know any background information about her (medical, socioeconomic, etc.)?

12. Can you make any guesses about her background based on how she was dressed, where she was left, the note, or other circumstances?

13. Do you think she was born around here and why?

14. Who named her and how was her name selected? Any "pet names"?

15. Can you tell us something about her personality?

16. What does she like? What makes her happy? Is there something you do to comfort her?

17. Did she sleep with another baby? Who?

18. What was the name of her nurse? the deputy orphanage director? the director?

19. Was she ever in foster care?

20. Is there anything else you can tell us about her?

Katharine Cobb wishes she had thought to visit the police station (recorded on the abandonment certificate) where her daughter's arrival was recorded to learn more about the three days between Emily's abandonment date and her arrival at the Hangzhou orphanage.

A Sister from China

Rebecca Garland
Mosaic (UK)

I'm going to tell you about the trip my family took last summer to get my sister Hannah whom we adopted from China.

We flew on a jumbo jet from Heathrow on 27th July. We traveled to Beijing in China and the journey was 11 hours. When we climbed down the steps from the airplane the heat was like being too near a fire or near an open oven door. People walked slowly and ladies held up colorful umbrellas to shelter from the sun.

We slept that first afternoon having decided to look around Beijing in the evening when it would be cooler. We had a ride on a rickshaw, which is a tricycle with seats and a canopy at the back. We were charged 40 yuan for a short ride in the direction of Tiananmen Square. (The next day we discovered it should only have cost 4 yuan!) We looked at the outside of the Forbidden City where there was an enormous picture of Chairman Mao. People came up to us all the time to take my photograph, because in China there are no blond heads or blue eyes. It was a bit like being a famous film star.

The next day we flew to Hangzhou. On the airplane we were given fans to keep ourselves cool while we were waiting for the plane to take off. We were only expecting to be in Hangzhou for four days but our papers for the adoption hadn't arrived. We were told we would have to wait there for possibly another four days which meant that all the sightseeing that had been organized in Beijing for our return would not take place. We regretted sleeping that first afternoon now.

Monday

Our first day in Hangzhou. We were taken by our guide to the Cave of the Yellow Dragon. This was a good choice because there were lots of trees for shade and water flowing from a natural spring. In the thirteenth century a monk had lived in a wooden hut in the mouth of the cave. The cave was so cool it was a delight to stand in it out of the intense heat. We saw a nightingale in a wooden cage singing to the birds that were free. There was a modern monument there like a large medallion or gong with chains coming from it. On the links of the chains were hundreds of padlocks, all engraved by people who are engaged or married. They each keep a key. It is a favorite place to have wedding photos taken.

In the evening our guide, Li Bing, came back bringing her daughter Yuo Yuo. We walked along the lake called West Lake looking at the views of the beautiful mountains. We bought some sweet bread from a stall—it was delicious.

Tuesday

We went to Li Bing's office to see if our papers had arrived. Then we went by a rickshaw to a tea room. We had a green tea made in a traditional way called a tea ceremony. We ate quails' eggs, dried plums coated with salt, nuts, and dried fruits. Later colorful steamed cakes were brought in in the shape of a cube. We then went upstairs where we had to take off our shoes. We sat at low tables on cushions and I played a form of chess. In the afternoon we asked whether we could go to a street market to buy some bargains. Our guide didn't seem to understand and took us to a Friendship Store, which is like a department store (Harrods or Army & Navy stores). I bought a panda T-shirt and a set of sandalwood bookmarks, also with pandas on. My parents bought a painting in Chinese style.

Our next stop was a tea museum. It was so cool inside but otherwise not very exciting. Outside masses of beautiful colorful butterflies were settling on the trees and bushes. There was an almost deafening noise of crickets. We were approached by a gang of ladies all dressed identically and with the same haircuts trying to sell us some green Chinese tea. They started off asking for 200 yuan. We eventually bought a tin for 40 after haggling. They were very persistent and all spoke at once like the crickets.

Wednesday

In the morning we tried steamed buns for breakfast. They are a bit like dumplings but with meat inside. They are sold in kiosks where they are cooked.

After breakfast we went on a boat with Li Bing and Yuo Yuo which had a canopy for a roof and was rowed by a man to an island in the middle of West Lake. We walked on a series of raised wooden platforms over the water. There were lotus blossoms and water lilies all around. When it was time to return we bought a special sweet rice pudding to eat on the return journey.

In the afternoon we were expecting very important visitors. We rested, bought some cakes, sterilized bottles, and waited. Yuo Yuo and I waited in the foyer of the hotel. Soon we were bursting into the hotel room. "Mum, there's a man and a woman coming with a very thin baby." The orphanage director and a lady from the orphanage entered soon afterwards carrying Zhu Fen dressed in a blue babygro. The baby smiled, blinking her eyes at the same time and sticking her tongue out. She wasn't wearing a nappy. Our store of clothes and nappies were all too big for her. Nevertheless, a nappy was put on. Everyone wanted to hold her but Mum had been promised the first turn. It was love at first sight for us all.

Zhu Fen, though alert, was clearly not well. She was hot, her chest rattled, and she had large boils on her head and body (there were two enormous ones, one on her back and one on her chest). Her legs hung strangely when we picked her up. She could sit up but her back wasn't straight and she slouched forward. Her weight was 4 kilos and she was ten months old. Many babies are born at that weight.

That evening I was invited to go home with our guide Li Bing and Yuo Yuo to stay the night. We traveled to their apartment on a crowded bus.

Yuo Yuo's house was rather dark with five rooms and a balcony. There was a kitchen, dining room, two bedrooms, and a bathroom. Each room was tiny. There were not many objects in the five rooms. The bathroom was the smallest. It had a shower and a long sort of sink where you went to the toilet, and where you flushed the loo you would twist round a thing at the side of the toilet and it would send a stream of water to flush down.

Yuo Yuo and I danced together to Chinese pop music. For supper we had rice, egg, and some meaty things. It was delicious. I used chopsticks and Yuo Yuo used a knife and fork. After that we had some watermelon. Yuo Yuo and Li Bing sucked it in and spat the pips out, so I did the same.

Thursday

Now that Zhu Fen had arrived we could begin the adoption process. Our guide took us to the offices of the registrar. When we had finished there we took Zhu Fen to hospital. The doctors who examined her were insistent that she must be put on a drip for seven hours each day for four days. In the evening we were to bring her back to our hotel room. Mummy and Daddy took it in turns to stay with Zhu Fen in the hospital and sometimes I stayed with Mummy and sometimes with Daddy. The hospital did not have air conditioning and it was very hot The doctors were all very kind and helpful, but it was very different from hospitals in England.

Friday

Another day at the hospital. Zhu Fen was getting better and her boils were starting to clear up. She was also starting to put on weight as we began feeding her on baby milk.

In the evening we ate in the hotel. I had my favorite soup, chicken and sweet corn. For dessert we ordered sweet glutinous dumplings. When they arrived there were about 15 of them sunk at the bottom of a large mixing bowl. They were white and inside there was what looked and tasted like crushed coffee beans and cigarette ash.

Saturday

In between hospital visits we went to a market where there were various different animals, including dogs and eels. In the evening we went to another island on West Lake where there was a theater. We saw what seemed rather like a pantomime with comedy actors and singing and dancing. Even though I couldn't understand what was being said, I enjoyed it very much and loved the music and the bright colors of the costumes.

Monday

Our last hospital visit and our last day in Hangzhou. Zhu Fen was now much better, the boils had almost gone, and she was putting on more weight and doing a lot of smiling. We signed out of the hospital and the doctors said how lucky Zhu Fen was to have us to look after her. We thought how lucky we were to have her in our family.

After leaving the hospital we had to go to another office to complete the adoption and sign some more papers. We had decided that Zhu Fen's English name should be Hannah and this was put on the adoption papers. To celebrate we decided to have an afternoon tea and asked our guide to take us to somewhere by the lake. She took us to a very grand hotel and ordered food for us. Some of it was very tasty but then one dish arrived that smelt so horrid it put Mummy, Daddy, and me off eating anything else, although Mummy did try it and we found out later that it was heart (a Chinese delicacy). In the evening we ate in the hotel and then packed ready to fly back to Beijing.

Tuesday

Flew back to Beijing. We were met at the airport by Cathy, our guide in Beijing, who thought Hannah was lovely but very small. We went to our hotel to get settled in and then went for a walk around Beijing.

Wednesday

In the morning we went to the British Embassy to get Hannah's visa and then went on a trip to the Summer Palace, which is China's largest park and was originally a private garden for the Chinese emperors. It was a very hot day, sunny and humid. I bought a hat which had a propeller at the front powered by a solar panel. It cooled me down a bit. We walked round the buildings and the beautiful gardens and we hired a paddle boat to go out on the lake. As we left in the late afternoon we were surrounded by Chinese men and women trying to sell us souvenirs. They all talked at once and got very excited. We did buy some stamps.

On our last evening in China we went to Tiananmen Square, a large open space in the center of Beijing, in front of the Forbidden City. Up to a million people could fit into this square. The Chinese fly kites there in the evening and we thought we would do the same. We bought four kites to take home as presents and tried to fly one but didn't have much success. We walked back to the hotel and after supper packed ready to fly home to England.

We had arrived in China not knowing quite what to expect or what was going to happen and now we were returning home taking Hannah, my sister, with us.

Rebecca Garland wrote this article in June 1997, when she was ten years old. She is now a pupil at Maidstone Grammar School for Girls in Kent.

Inside Jiande Orphanage

Katharine Hayner
FCC-Northwest

We turned the corner after having traveled by car from Hangzhou on an incredibly bumpy road that was under construction for many miles, and caught our first glimpse of the town where our daughter spent the first four months of her life. Visqueen-covered greenhouses filled with fresh strawberries lined the outskirts of Jiande, a nice, simple town situated along a river, surrounded by lush green fields and rice paddies. Lovely rolling hills and mountains formed the backdrop for this rural burg, which comprised only a few main streets, three of which intersected at a Y in the middle of town. The buildings were relatively new and many of concrete construction.

Jiande was built up as a city (I believe in the 1950s) when the dam that forms 1,000 Island Lake was closed. Many of the initial residents were farmers who were forced off their land as the waters rose behind the dam. The town provided a setting for a variety of shops, department stores, open-air stalls along the street, and, in the center, a lovely river-front park. After turning down a short dirt road where we saw workers busy with construction, we stopped at a new six-story building, the Jiande Social Welfare Institute. The building houses the orphanage, a guesthouse, a kitchen, and a restaurant. We later heard that a home for the elderly or a nursing home was scheduled to go into at least some of the yet-to-be-completed sections of the building. The majority of the interior was unfinished.

The excitement was mounting as we were shown to what became our room for the next five days. We were told it was very modest and that we could move to a hotel if the accommodations were not satisfactory. The room was indeed modest; but it was clean and very adequate for our needs. We certainly would have accepted less just to have the opportunity to stay nearby our daughter. The room had twin beds (very typical of what we have encountered in China) plus a spare cot that was available for our three-and-a-half-year-old son, Eric. We were set.

After settling in a bit, we went downstairs for dinner. There was a fairly large dining room off to the side of the lobby, several of the tables filled with men who were smoking. Opposite and up a short flight of stairs was a smaller, private dining room which held but three tables. We were happy to be segregated from the room full of smokers. We sat down and a lovely feast of very fresh foods was placed before us. I especially enjoyed the dish with the fresh bamboo shoots—a far cry from the canned ones we use at home.

After completing our meal, we were taken upstairs to the orphanage. There we first met four-month-old Wang Dan, soon to be Emily Danmei Syrjala, our beautiful daughter. We had waited many months and come many miles for this moment; we were absolutely thrilled! After spending some time with all of the little girls and their caregivers, we were told that we were welcome to take little Wang Dan down the hall to our room. We (Mom and Dad) shall have forever the vivid memory of our son, Eric, dancing down the hallway singing, "I have my baby sister. I have my baby sister." We could not have been more proud of him or more thrilled with his reaction to meeting his little sister. (And we cannot imagine having come to China without him.)

The orphanage consisted of three small rooms containing a total of 28 children at the time. The configuration of each room was the same as that of the guest room in which we stayed, except that the concrete floor was not carpeted and the walls were unpainted. The area that would have been the bathroom was without fixtures. On the floor in the bathroom area, the caregivers sterilized and filled the babies' bottles. The fires with the large kettles for boiling water for sterilizing were on the landing of the stairway, away from where the children might get access to the fires. Opposite the "bathroom" was a closet that contained clean clothes organized by type.

Our daughter's room contained five green-painted cribs, a cot, and a wooden bench of potty chairs with enameled chamber pots under each hole. The latter we came to call "potty row." There was a clothesline along the wall that had various colorful rags hanging on it, mostly used to wipe babies' faces. Miscellaneous socks of many varieties and colors were kept in a box under the first crib. A few would-be toddlers were in walkers that were tethered to the cribs with a one- to two-foot-long cord. A back door led to an enclosed porch area where the older children played in their walkers on sunny days. The Jiande air was very fresh. Two babies shared each bed, feet to feet. All were lying on their backs with arms sticking straight up, hands covered by long sleeves, and heavily clad in knit clothing. It reminded me of how a toddler looks in a snowsuit. A thick heavy cotton quilt was on top, fastened with a thin bungee-type cord. This, I imagine, was to keep the babies from kicking their blankets off. Names written on tape (in Chinese characters, of course) were placed on the end of each crib.

Clean clothes were put on every few days. The caregivers were very careful to change undergarments without uncovering any body parts or taking off any layers of sweaters. Each baby had an elastic band around her waist. A cotton sheet-like rag was used as a diaper, held in place in the front and the back with this elastic band. There were no diaper pants. Legs were covered with three layers of slitted leggings. The first one was cotton—very soft and quite thin. The next one was a medium-weight knit, and the outer one was a heavy knit. The upper body was covered by similar layers. On top of a very heavy sweater most wore a thick quilted vest. In China, everyone is concerned about keeping babies very warm. Dressing our baby as we were accustomed brought signs of disapproval. When we dressed our daughter, Emily, in clothes we had brought from home, the caregivers and others were very concerned we were not dressing her warmly enough. Only when we added a snowsuit-like bunting over her clothes was approval forthcoming.

Caregivers at the orphanage seemed to give all the babies attention and were genuinely concerned with their health and well being. Babies were fed four times per day on a schedule: 6:30 A.M., 10:30 A.M., 3:30 P.M., and 8:30 P.M. A cow's milk–based formula was mixed with a rice cereal, making a rather thick fluid. This was poured into glass bottles, to each of which a baby's name was taped. This very hot formula was fed to them through a standard nipple with a rather large hole in it. Bottle-propping was standard practice. It took most babies less than five minutes to gulp their fill of 8 ounces. After feeding, they were put in a free spot on "potty row." The chamber pots were checked periodically, and once a baby "produced," she (there were no boys) was put back in bed—lying on her back. Noses were wiped with one of the rags on the line. Frequently, a caregiver carried one of the babies about as she performed her duties, occasionally taking time to cuddle and feed her.

We were happy to spend the next several days with our daughter, getting to know her and exploring the area around where she had spent the first few months of her life, before we embarked on our journey back to Seattle and the next phase of our lives.

Katharine Hayner and family traveled to China in April 1995.

If Only We'd Known

Cathy and John Smith
Children Adopted from China (UK)

Our adoption process took two years from the start of our home study, and just when we were beginning to lose hope and were dreading facing another childless Christmas, a large brown envelope arrived on our doorstep on Christmas Eve.

As we're both self-employed and get lots of boring big brown envelopes in our mail, especially during the Christmas rush, it was almost pushed to one side. Thank goodness it wasn't! It was our invitation to China to adopt our daughter, which the Department of Health (DOH) had held onto for a week.

We received details from the DOH of a particular travel service specializing in China, and we decided to contact them as well as China Women's Travel Service, whom we had heard were good. We wanted to ensure we could get the earliest dates possible to travel as we couldn't wait to meet our longed-for daughter.

We stayed up through the early hours of Christmas night and Boxing Day night faxing and phoning China. We received quotes from both agencies and decided to go with China Women's Travel Service, as they were better on dates, costs, and itinerary. We faxed the other travel service to inform them we would not use them and thanked them for their quote.

With only a week to go, it was a mad, happy panic to sort out visas, flights, and baby gear. We had not dared to buy even one pair of booties in advance! So with Christmas and New Year holidays, a new home in chaos which we had only been in a few weeks, and both running our businesses, not much sleep was had. Our family and friends appeared magically with all sorts of baby goods for us. At last our turn had come.

Then the bombshell dropped. Only a few days before we were due to travel we received a fax from the other travel service. Our heart sank. It read, "It is surprising to know that you have decided to travel to China without our assistance. Thus we have informed the Chinese Embassy in London to cancel your invitation." They also requested a $50 payment.

We could not believe it. Our elation turned to despair. Surely it could not all go wrong now.

Fortunately, it didn't—after a saga of phone calls, faxes, and many very anxious moments, we did eventually get our visa in the nick of time and set off to China on 4th January 1997 loaded up with ski gear and long johns to protect us from the Chinese winter.

Another experience we could have done without happened on our first night with our new daughter and concerned "Mongolian blue spots," something which we knew nothing about. For those who might share our ignorance, they are dark bluish patches on the skin, usually on the buttocks and back, which look like bruises. You might imagine our shock when we put our daughter's first nappy on and discovered very dark blue finger-like marks and what we thought were bruises all over her bottom and up her back.

I shall never forget my feeling of horror that she should have had such an accident or abuse, then the dreadful thought that someone might think we did it. We searched our hotel corridors for someone to act as a witness. We found an American lady who informed us that they were skin pigments, to our tremendous relief.

If you are still waiting to travel to China, find out as much as you can before you go. Our happiness at being a family at last is overwhelmingly wonderful, and our daughter is the joy of our life!

Cathy and John Smith live in Bramley, Surrey, England.

Making It Home

Eliza Thomas

FCC–New York

To set the record absolutely straight as an arrow, my daughter PanPan Amelia, who is graciously napping at the moment, is truly, truly great: jubilant, watchful, defiant, funny, and sweet. Like any parent, I feel blessed to have such a wonderful child, and I cannot imagine life without her. For my daughter and me, however, the beginnings were not very easy; while things did find their own way of working out, there were plenty of confusing and scary moments. In retrospect, I can see that the difficulties I encountered on my trip were maybe worse than some I have heard about, while not nearly as bad as some others—but to me, of course, at the time, they were fairly overwhelming. It's not that I want to dwell on all the doubts and fears and difficulties for their own sake, but I think it is helpful to acknowledge them; for us, anyway, the aspect of Struggle was certainly an important part of the amazing process of becoming a family.

To start off, I know some people who were unswerving in their decision to adopt a child. I, however, was scared and ambivalent, and partly because of that, and partly because of the unpredictable nature of the adoption process, there were false starts and long waits. By the time I got my referral from China—a five-month-old baby girl—I had lived in limbo far too long and asked myself far too many questions. Her photograph showed a child with a thatch of dark hair, wise and kind eyes, and the beginnings of a smile. She seemed oddly, reassuringly familiar, and simply beautiful. It was definitely now or never, and so I made up my mind once and for all, almost as if on the spur of the moment, and off I went.

My first difficulty was an intense last-minute panic attack, which I probably should have foreseen, but which particularly disturbed me since

I had determined to leave my fears behind. In any case, alone on an over-crowded jumbo jet, hurtling through space to halfway around the globe, bound to meet a total stranger who would absolutely dominate the rest of my life, I thought I could see with ghastly clarity what a bizarre notion, what an irresponsible whim this adoption was, after all. I couldn't do it, I shouldn't have done it. I should have just moved my furniture around if I'd wanted to shake up my life. Etcetera, etcetera. I'd like to say I got over it completely before we landed, but in fact whiffs of that attack hung around for quite a long time.

By the time we arrived in the city where our children were—there were four of us "singles" sent as a group—we were all completely exhausted from the two days of travel, and I, for one, so recently panicked, couldn't believe that any of this was actually happening. But the Chinese authori-ties wanted us to meet the babies before we started any paperwork, so we were immediately escorted to a rather disconcertingly plush hotel where the welfare center director met us. We changed, for whatever reason, into whatever we thought to be our best clothes, the director bundled us all into tiny taxicabs, and we drove helter-skelter to the very outskirts of the city, through extreme and ever-increasing poverty, on roads that seemed less and less like roads at all and at speeds that would have truly alarmed me, if I hadn't been so preoccupied. The welfare center lay at the foot of some looming hills—when we arrived, it was too dark to see where we were, but it felt like the middle of nowhere.

And so there, in the middle of nowhere, in the middle of the night, with few preliminaries, we met our children. On some level, the whole event seemed unreal. The staff ushered us into a rather stark room which was the nursery, woke up the babies one by one, and simply handed them out. They gave me an unbelievably small, distressingly thin, and very pale baby: This one is yours, they said. And that was that, there we were, mother and daughter. I didn't know what to feel, or what to do next. I had hoped for a moment of recognition, a feeling of confirmation, but there was none. I was just shocked at how strange and unfamiliar my daughter was to me. She was nothing like her sweet old photograph: her head was shaven, her eyes were unhappy, she was distant and unsmiling, strained and worn out, and much too thin.

I asked why she was so tiny and pale; they said she had been sick, could not eat well, but otherwise was healthy. I was still worried—she certainly was not thriving. Maybe I realized only then what an enormous responsi-bility I was taking on, and what a huge decision I'd made, for her life, as well as for my own. I had no experience as a parent, this looked to be hard, and I honestly didn't know if I could do it. Our first meeting left me both terrified and enormously sad; when I said goodbye to her that night she had begun to cry, and so had I, and that is how our life together began.

About a week later, when we returned for a second visit, things were worse. It was daytime, I was calmer, we could see where we were, the welfare center was awake and full of life, and I had high hopes for a happier encounter. But my baby was frantic. The welfare center staff hovered about us while she screamed and screamed, trying to tell me above the din how much better she was, how she had just developed a bad habit of crying, how maybe she was even a little spoiled, how there was nothing to worry about. Then, after a while and without warning, they brought out another baby. Take this one instead, she's fatter, healthier, doesn't cry so much, they seemed to suggest. We want you to be happy, not to worry so much, they said. They were concerned for us and meant well, but the thought of choosing between two children absolutely horrified me. I didn't want a different baby, I just wanted mine to be okay. I couldn't even look at the second child, and after an awful and confusing moment they took her away again. Finally, finally, my daughter stopped crying. By the end of the visit she lay passed out across my lap, drenched in tears, her desperate energy spent.

As it turned out, she was indeed still sick: she had been chronically ill with gastroenteritis and was having another bad attack. She was taken to the hospital later that same day after we had left, and stayed there for much of the remaining time I was in China. It was very frustrating that no one volunteered any information about her condition—it was several days before I even found out she was in the hospital—and it was hard to ask all the questions I had. The hospital staff spoke very little English, and the adoption agency had no one in place in case of medical problems or other emergencies. The hospital itself was poor and overcrowded. However, her doctor and nurse took wonderful care of her, and in many ways it was helpful to know there might be a treatable cause to her great distress.

Still, it was an anxious time. I had never taken care of a sick baby before, and I didn't know what to expect. My worst nightmare was that something irrevocable had happened to her very spirit, and she would be frantic forever. She would never calm down, she would never smile, I would never sleep again, things would never be all right. Meanwhile, to my great shame and dismay, all my terrible old doubts resurfaced. First and foremost, I was afraid I wouldn't love her, or love her enough. I knew nothing about bonding—I thought it was an event that I hadn't yet experienced, rather than a process just begun. I was afraid I would ruin both our lives. I missed my old life. I missed my dog, who never screamed at me like this baby did. I missed being alone. There were many times when I wondered if I was doing the "right" thing. I stuck with it, took the necessary steps to become her parent, but much of the time I was just going through the motions.

One thing that kept me going through those motions was, frankly, the lack of any respectable alternative. But there were more positive supports as well: the other people adopting children were incredibly helpful, and so were calls home to family and friends. There was, too, a kind of uncontrollable gaiety in our group (most likely the hysteria of extreme exhaustion) when daily challenges—figuring out what was inside those little rolls at breakfast, for instance, without seeming too suspicious, or trying to deal with the scraps of tiny, tattered paper money, or simply trying to get across the street in one piece—sometimes seemed so ridiculously hard. And then finally, there was this: whatever the balance to fear is, it was there, and to me it looked like Hope. Which, coincidentally or not, is what my daughter's Chinese name means. My hope centered around her old photograph: a normal, healthy, happy little girl.

So I did what I was supposed to do: as soon as she was released from the hospital, I held her in my arms all the time, fed her all the soy formula I'd brought along, and gave her all the love I wasn't sure of yet. It was very hot outside, so we would march endlessly, day in and day out, up and down the halls of whatever tourism hotel we were in, me humming along helplessly to the awful canned classical Muzak with whatever was left of my mind. A first-time parent, I was more tired than I'd ever thought possible. But it all really helped both of us get through those first hard times. In retrospect—thank God for retrospects—I see the trip as a final test of faith, appropriate and necessary for my situation, a path for us to find each other and begin to share our lives.

And, fortunately, she started to get better quite quickly, her desperation revealing itself as sheer determination. Maybe I had simply overreacted to the difficulties of her being sick in my fear and anxiety and inexperience. But I also think I needed the struggle. I learned a lot about trust from her in those early days, as she recovered and turned to greet the strange new world around her, as she reached out with her long thin fingers, waved her skinny little feet, began to smile her brand new gummy smile. There would certainly be ups and downs in the months ahead, but I was lucky to feel certain early on that things would eventually be fine.

As I write this, it is just about a year since we have been back. The adjustments have been enormous, of course, but we are doing really well. Sometimes still, I find myself surprised at how totally familiar she has become to me. People tell me how much she has changed, and I do know she has, but to me she seems just like herself, how she has always been.

And sometimes still, I can't believe that this is all really true. Anyway, here she is now, presently up from her nap, my dear and very beloved daughter, looking positively pudgy, sitting on the floor, mashing a banana I gave her with an old, very dusty toothbrush she found somewhere. From time to time, when the fancy strikes, she blows kisses. How? She raises her eyebrows ever so slightly, smacks her lips together ever so softly, and looks over at me with an air of complete authority, undisputed triumph, and great satisfaction. And I know that she knows too: we've made it home.

Eliza Thomas wrote this article in 1995; a revised version appears in her book of essays, *The Road Home* (Algonquin, 1997). She and Amelia live in Randolph Center, Vermont.

Shauna's Story

An Adoption Announcement

Sherry Agard
FCC-Colorado

Hello everyone!

My name is Shauna Joy Shuangdi Agard, at least that's my new American name. I was born in Nanjing, China, at 11:10 P.M. on August 5, 1994, and my twin sister, Shuangling, was born ten minutes later. Actually we were born in the town of Xiaoshi, which is on the northern edge of Nanjing, near the Yangzi River. The city of Nanjing has about 4.5 million people, but outside the city, the area is mostly agricultural. It is very hot and humid in the summer but very cold and damp in the winter (it even snows sometimes).

I guess life is pretty hard here sometimes, and it can be tough to take care of one baby, much less two. Our parents must have loved us, but after a month, I guess they decided that they couldn't take care of us any more. So they put a little note written on bright pink tissue paper on each of us and left us in a safe place where we could be found. The notes said they hoped some kind person would adopt us and that they were very grateful.

A nice policeman found us the next day, on September 10, and took us to the police station in Xiaoshi. Then we were taken to the Nanjing Children's Home. Wow, what a confusing day, and very sad. We cried for our parents and were very scared and hungry. But then some nice ladies at the orphanage fed us and held us and made us feel a little better. They put us in the same crib, so we were able to snuggle up to each other.

The orphanage people didn't know our real names, so we were given the surname of Han, like all the other babies who came to the orphanage in 1994. And since we were twins, they decided our given names should be Shuangdi and Shuangling (both mean twin sister). The room we were in had a couple dozen green metal cribs lined up in double rows, each with a baby like us, under 12 months old. We were like one great big family.

Everyone was very nice to us, but there were so many other babies who needed attention that we didn't get held or fed or changed as much as we did at home. By October, it was starting to get colder, especially at night, so we were bundled in several layers of clothes and a bright blue and green quilt. The coal stove in the middle of the room was the only heat.

My sister was smaller and weaker than I was, and she caught a cold in October. I guess everyone thought it was just a little cold and that she'd get better soon. But she got sicker and sicker until she had pneumonia. Before anyone could help her, she died on October 14. I didn't understand what had happened and felt lonely and sad. But I could also still feel Shuangling's presence, encouraging me to be strong and live on for both of us.

In November, I found out that I was going to be adopted by an American lady named Sherry. The director of the orphanage and the China liaison for the American adoption agency took pictures of me and some of the other babies. Then they filled out bunches of paperwork, added it to all the paperwork my mom and the agency had done in America, and sent it all off to the Central Adoption Agency in Beijing for approval.

In early December, a group of Americans from Colorado came to the orphanage, but my new mom wasn't with them. Some people from the adoption agency took new pictures of me and told me my mom would be there soon, in early January, so I only had a month to wait. It seemed like a long time. And it was getting cold in Nanjing. Even though we were bundled up, a lot of us babies got sick with colds and bronchitis, including me.

Then, on a cold, wet, January 2, 1995, another group of Americans came to visit us. Could my new mom be in this group? All of a sudden my caregiver picked me up and put me in my mom's arms. Sherry looked down at me and smiled at me with a great big smile. There were tears in her eyes but they were happy tears. I just looked up into her eyes and wondered what things would be like for me now. She talked to me in a strange-sounding language, but the words were gentle. I felt very comfortable and fell asleep in her arms.

I didn't see my new mom again for two days. Sherry and all the other adoptive parents had to fill out more paperwork before the eight of us who were being adopted could be with them. Finally, on the afternoon of Wednesday, January 4, the orphanage director, some of the caregivers, and a few of the new parents came to get us. They wrapped us in another pink quilt, loaded us into a van, and drove us to the Central Hotel. The orphanage director carried me down the hall, put me in my mom's arms, and gave us both a big hug.

Actually, I was asleep then, but I soon woke up as my mom changed me and put me in a new pink sleeper. Then she held me and fed me, and I fell asleep again. Later that evening, a doctor from the Nanjing Children's Hospital visited and checked me over. I was all stuffed up and coughing and didn't feel very well, so the doctor told my mom to give me some funny pink medicine to help my bronchitis. He said I was very weak and needed to eat more and sleep a lot to get stronger.

Over the next few days, my mom held me close and talked to me and played with me and fed me whenever I got hungry—what a treat! We spent a lot of time getting to know each other but also visited some of the other babies and their new parents. All the rooms were next to each other, so this part of the hotel was like a dormitory for all of us. I was feeling more and more comfortable with each day, so after a couple of days I gave my mom my first big smile. She smiled back and started crying with happiness (she sure can get emotional sometimes!). I liked it too, so I started smiling back more and more.

I was feeling a little better after a few days, but then my coughing got worse on Saturday night and Sunday. When the doctor visited me again on Sunday night, he said I was very sick with pneumonia and that my heart sounded very weak. He gave me a different antibiotic and some medicine to slow down my heart, but I still felt awful. I was so congested that I couldn't suck on the bottle very well either.

I slept for awhile in the doctor's arms and then slept a few more hours while my mom held me (it made me feel better just to be held and loved like that). While I slept, the doctor and my mom talked about whether I should go to the hospital in Nanjing, but he thought that sleeping undisturbed would be the best thing for me now. He stayed in my room all night just to make sure I would be okay.

I was still very sick on Monday morning, but the doctor thought the worst crisis was over. We were all supposed to leave for Guangzhou (Canton) in southern China that night, but he thought it wouldn't be good for me to travel just yet. So my mom decided we would stay in Nanjing for an extra day or two while the others traveled on to Guangzhou. I know it was a tough decision for my mom, but then we found out that a single father from our group and his new son would also be staying to finish some paperwork that had gotten delayed in Beijing.

So we all just hung out in the hotel for the next two days. I mostly slept, but when I was awake, I felt good enough to smile at my mom and play with my toys in my crib. The doctor visited us several times and said I was probably strong enough to travel on Wednesday. The agency's China liaison also visited us every day and helped make new flight arrangements. It was snowing lightly when we finally left Nanjing on Wednesday night. I guess it was a little sad, too, to leave my birth place, but I hope I can visit again some day.

I slept through most of the two-hour flight to Guangzhou and then all through the night at the White Swan Hotel. It was a good thing I rested a lot that night, because on Thursday morning, we walked all over the place to complete the U.S. immigration paper-work. I bounced around in my Snugli as we walked to the medical offices for a check-up, then to the U.S. Embassy for the immigration interview, then to the photo shop to get visa photos, and then back to the hotel. Whew! But everything was now done and we were ready to go home to America the next day.

After a nice celebration dinner on Thursday night, we headed out early Friday morning, lucky Friday the thirteenth. After a 40-minute flight to Hong Kong, we boarded the big Cathay Pacific jetliner that would fly us for 11 hours across the ocean to America. I know my mom was worried that I might still be too sick for that long flight, but I was excited by all the new sights. I had a nice bassinet on the airplane that was right under the big movie screen, so I watched the bright colors for hours, much to the dismay of my mom, who thought I should be sleeping instead.

I finally slept for the last four hours until we got ready to land. Then my mom held me in her arms as we landed in Los Angeles. I don't know why, but she started crying when we touched down, held me close, kissed me, and said, "We made it, we made it; we're home in America!"

After more than an hour at the immigration line, we finally left the terminal and were met by my grandpa, grandma, and aunt. Everybody was crying and hugging us and was so glad to see us. I, for one, was glad to get out of the Snugli and go to sleep in the car seat.

We drove to my grandparents' house and then to the doctor's office. My mom wanted to make sure I was okay before going home to Colorado. After being weighed (8 lb., 3 oz.) and x-rayed and poked with needles, I'd had about enough. But the doctor said I still had pneumonia and, because I was so small, he thought I should stay in the hospital for a few days. After being poked and prodded some more, I finally got to get some sleep in my hospital crib. My mom had been awake for almost 36 hours, so she fell asleep in my room too.

My stay in the hospital wasn't too bad, except for being awakened every four hours for a breathing treatment or to be weighed or changed or fed. Everyone thought I was cute, even in the oxygen tent, and they were all fascinated to hear my story. After a couple of days, I could breathe much easier and was less congested, so I was able to eat more. I gained almost half a pound by the time I got to leave the hospital on Tuesday night, January 17.

It was nice to spend a couple of relaxing days at my grandparents' house. I even got to visit with my aunt, uncle, and cousins one night when we all went out to a Chinese restaurant (my cousins are pretty neat!).

But finally on Thursday, January 19, we flew home to Colorado. A dozen of my mom's friends met us at the airport with bright balloons and flashing cameras and good wishes. What an adventure it has been and what an adventure it will be! It's so good to be home!

Love to all my new extended family and friends,

Shauna

Shauna is now a happy, thriving, very independent four-year-old. Her first three months in Colorado were spent gaining weight (which doubled in three months) and getting healthy. Although she had some significant developmental delays, particularly in gross motor skills, she's now overcome most of them. She lives with her mom and three cats in Louisville, Colorado.

Kylie's Feet

Steve Huettel
FCC—Tampa Bay

At the end of an exhausting first day of their adoption trip, Andrea Tumi-atti and Patricia Liebau closed the hotel room door just before midnight and undressed their new daughter for bed. What they saw came as a complete shock.

Kylie's tiny feet were blue and so swollen they couldn't see her toes. A red blotch on her lower back framed a hole as big as a dime. The infection was the size of a grapefruit by morning.

How did this happen? The orphanage assured them their daughter was healthy. The only hint of a problem was the gauze pad covering a knot on her head: a mosquito bite that the infant had scratched, they were told.

Andrea and Patricia were living the nightmare of all adoptive parents waiting to travel: What if something is wrong with our baby and we have to decide whether to keep her?

They barely hesitated. Andrea had already bonded with his infant daughter. The only question was how quickly they could get Kylie home and in the care of American doctors. Thanks to a lot of insistence and one hysterical outburst at the U.S. Consulate, the family was on a plane out of Hong Kong by 4:00 the next afternoon.

It was touch and go for months, but the infection finally went away and the hole healed. Her frostbitten feet are moving again. Doctors at the Shriners Hospital in Tampa performed the first skin grafts and will do any further surgery for free.

"We took on something more than we could comfortably handle," says Patricia, now back home in West Melbourne on Florida's east coast. But the real tragedy, she says, would have been getting so scared that they turned away a precocious little fighter they now can't imagine living without. Her message: You find strength when you need it and help where you'd never expect it.

Just getting to China was enough of a struggle. Because Andrea is an Italian citizen who works aboard cruise ships for months at a stretch, few agencies would agree to work with them. The bureaucratic hurdles were exponentially more difficult than American couples face. Ditto for the logistics of traveling on short notice.

Sure enough, Andrea was on a ship in Cuba when the call came from their agency in April 1996. But his passport was in West Melbourne with Patricia, who needed it for travel approvals. They were able to get together in the Caribbean in time to fly over to China. Andrea expected to stay only a few days to sign adoption papers, so he could get back to the ship. Patricia figured she was in for the full two weeks most parents spend to fill out documents.

Immediately on arriving in Guangzhou, Patricia and Andrea stopped at the passport and notary offices. That morning, they were driven two hours to the orphanage in Gaoming. Their paperwork there was already completed.

For five and a half months Kylie seemed incredibly small—9 pounds, including her four layers of clothes. (American doctors later guessed she was two months younger than the adoption papers stated.) She had flea bites, a rash, and that gauze pad on her head but otherwise appeared healthy.

Patricia watched the orphanage workers change her. But she didn't really notice they kept her feet covered and one had a hand over her back at all times. It wasn't until they returned to the Ramada in Guangzhou that Patricia and Andrea got clues how sick Kylie really was. When they put her feet in warm water, some of the color returned, but they still didn't move. Andrea and Patricia didn't know she'd suffered from frostbite or that the angry red blotch was a potentially fatal staph infection. They did know they had to get her home as fast as possible.

The next morning, Chinese doctors examining her recoiled when they saw the hole in her back. But to Patricia's surprise, they gave Kylie a clean bill of health to leave the country. When they went to their appointment at the consulate for her visa, everyone had gone to lunch. Patricia pleaded, then broke down in tears when they told her to come back the next day.

It worked, and by 4 P.M. that day their plane was leaving Hong Kong for Los Angeles. Their total time from picking up Kylie to leaving: 31 hours.

After landing in Los Angeles, they went straight to see a doctor, the husband of a friend of Patricia's. He told them the staph infection probably would have killed Kylie in a few days.

Back in Florida, doctors saw Kylie at the hospital every day for a month and a half to treat the stubborn infection. She wasn't out of the woods until weeks after that. The hole in her back healed itself.

Patricia worked hours on end getting Kylie to exercise her feet so the toes would come down. Layers of dead skin peeled off the tops of her feet where the frostbite had taken hold.

Then help came literally out of the sky. A friend of Patricia's who had also adopted from China called to tell her about someone she'd met on her job as a Delta Air Lines flight attendant: a potentate for Shiners who was looking for kids needing medical help. When the application came in the mail, Patricia noticed someone had already signed the approval block at the bottom.

In March, doctors removed two strips of skin—each the size of an index finger—from Kylie's stomach and grafted them to the tops of her feet. They still don't know if the frostbite damaged any bones. If so, Kylie could receive bone grafts to make sure her feet grow properly. The Shiners will cover any medical expenses to help her walk through age 18.

Looking back, Patricia thinks orphanage officials hid Kylie's medical condition and sped up the paperwork because they knew it was her only chance to survive. She guesses Kylie must have been abandoned on a cold day and got the frostbite before anyone found her. She has no idea about the rest of the problems. The orphanage director later sent word that the hole in her back was caused by "cold weather."

Their agency warned before they left not to let their hearts overrule their heads if they weren't comfortable about accepting their baby. And officials with Civil Affairs said on the day of the adoption that they could cancel if the baby wasn't "as presented."

But Andrea and Patricia can't imagine making any other choice than the one they made that night in the Guangzhou hotel room. And they kept Kylie's Chinese name, Lan, as a middle name. It means orchid, the delicate flower that easily dies in the cold—or blossoms given warmth and loving care.

Steve Huettel lives with his wife, Jennifer Scott, and their three-year-old son, Matthew Si Scott Huettel, in Tampa, Florida. He is a reporter at the *Tampa Tribune* and edits the *Thread*, the newsletter of FCC–Tampa Bay.

Two Babies

The One I Brought Home,
The One I Left Behind

D. Kenyon

FCC–Connecticut, Rhode Island, Central Massachusetts

After many years of tossing around the biggest decision of my life, and nearly tossing it out because of the "what ifs," I became a mom. This spring I traveled halfway around the world and adopted a beautiful baby daughter. It was a wonderful time and a terrible time, and I share my story with you.

For many years I wanted a baby, a chance to be a mother. Permanent relationships eluded me, and I began to consider alternative means to fulfill my dream. One by one, the alternatives looked less attractive (would I get HIV from sperm which I purchased? would the husband of a friend suddenly want to be more than a donor if the baby were a son?) and they fell away. Adoption, a way to help children that I likely would have pursued if I had married, suddenly took on a new question: Could I do this as a single person? I prayed to God for direction.

At some point I realized that God would not answer with a big "yes" or "no" from the sky. So I changed my prayerful question, "Should I?" to a statement: "I'll keep going until I get a feeling from You that I should stop." I never got that feeling, but I did get another message. One Saturday morning, as I was writing checks to pay bills, I suddenly looked up and said, "Gabrielle, Gabriela." I had been thinking of other baby names, but these came to me out of thin air. A name book revealed that the names meant "God is my strength." I took this experience as a message of the name I should give my baby. But why two names? I didn't know for the longest time.

Finally I had a referral picture with which I, like most adoptive parents, bonded immediately. For seven weeks until I traveled to bring her home, she was my baby. I talked about her, proudly showed my picture of my daughter, visualized her around my home and some of the things we would be doing together. I couldn't wait.

I was traveling alone, but with two other adoptive families. Their babies were coming from a different orphanage than my baby, but we would meet them all at the same hotel. We would have our translator there who would help with the forms and so on.

On the plane trip into the country, I was suddenly filled with dread. I couldn't explain it, but I felt that somehow I was making a big mistake. I was angry with myself, thinking, "Fine time for you to feel this."

When we got to the hotel, we immediately spotted the two babies for the other families. They were with their orphanage workers, who were readily interacting with the babies and then with the new parents. The babies were upright in their arms, vocal, bright, and alert. I did not see a third upright vocal baby and assumed that my little girl had not arrived yet. I snapped first family pictures of my friends and their babies.

After about five minutes, one of my friends came to me and said, "Your baby is here." I looked around, still not seeing an upright baby. "Where is she?" I asked.

"She's over there on a couch."

I rushed over for my first glimpse of my bundle of joy. When I looked at her, my heart sank as I thought, "Oh God." She was very thin, lying limply in the arms of an orphanage worker who was not interacting with her. I walked away, thought that it maybe wasn't as bad as it seemed, walked back to her for another look. This time I started to cry as I felt my dreams and expectations take a nose-dive. I was looking at a very unhealthy baby.

I told my translator of my concerns that something was not right with her, confirmed with another friend that something looked wrong, and ran to a bathroom to sob in privacy.

I had anticipated that I would likely have a baby who was underweight by American standards, that she would have some developmental delays from being in an orphanage, and that I might encounter some medical problems such as ear infection or intestinal parasites. I was not prepared for the extreme condition that I saw. Indeed, I decided to adopt from this country because the babies were healthy and often taken from their cribs regularly and socialized with the other babies and workers. I expected less of the emotional problems that are seen with babies from other countries who are often neglected and stay in their cribs.

I took the baby with me overnight in my room. There I called a friend in the United States to talk about my situation. I am halfway around the world, traveling alone and in a tough spot. We tried to determine a developmental age and came up with a strategy for me to use with the officials the next day. At 17 months, she could roll over but had no arm or leg muscle tone. It took me six hours to feed the poor thing six ounces of formula. I kept her with me for 16½ hours and never felt that I could get her to respond to my voice or touch. I was surely looking at a sick little baby.

The next day I stated my concerns and fears to the officials. I took her to a local hospital to have a pediatrician evaluate her. He pronounced her "severely malnourished," but we never talked about a reason. At 17 months she weighed 13 pounds while at 7 months, the age of the referral picture, she weighed 12½ pounds. She had grown in height but looked very thin. I advocated for her to the officials, saying that she looked better at 7 months than 17, that the other babies who were younger also looked better. I felt that I was looking at a severely neglected, not nurtured, and undernourished baby. I also felt that I was looking at a baby with potential long-term neurological problems. Looking ahead, as parents tend to do, when I retired, I wanted her to be graduating from college looking for an apartment, but when I looked at her on this day, I envisioned instead finding placement in a facility for handicapped adults. Mind you, I was prepared, and still am, to handle any crisis that comes to my family. But to start out in a crisis was not something I could readily do.

But it hurt to leave her. In another place, I would have loved to interact with such a challenged baby over time, would love to see what gains she made, how she changed with intensive tender loving care. But I didn't have the luxury of time. During one very long night and part of the next day, I saw no response from any of my caring for her. I wasn't sure that she was able to hear. But I was sure that I would not be able to provide for her for the long term. Did I underestimate myself? Did I underestimate her? Questions I'll never have answered.

I prepared myself for relinquishing her on that second day. I was also prepared to go home with no baby. I had heard that occasionally that happens, and I expected to be one of those rare occasions. As they had since I first saw her, the tears flowed as her orphanage officials took her back at 1:30 in the afternoon. I gave them some clothes and formula for her. A friend and I met the officials at 2:00 to write a letter about why I could not take her. After it was translated, my translator said casually, quietly, "They do have another baby for you. She'll be here in two hours." A baby! I moved from immeasurable sadness to extreme joy in a split second! I was thrilled!

I was lying on my bed waiting for the message that she was here. "Rest," my translator had said, knowing how sleep-deprived and emotionally drained I was. Rest? When I'm about to become a mom? Couldn't do it. At a quarter to four, he knocked on my door and told me to come quickly to another room. I crossed the hall, praying the whole time that I would not be looking at another sick baby. "Lord, I just can't go through it again." I saw a beautiful, upright, round-cheeked baby in the arms of the official. Oh my God! My heart soared. She was healthy!

I signed more papers that I would keep her. I spoke softly to her and let her become comfortable with looking at me, someone different from the faces she was used to. Then I gently took her in my arms and became a Mom, a long-time dream fulfilled. My beautiful daughter! We connected right away.

More paperwork over the next few days, and some touring of my daughter's native country. I took pictures to use when I tell her of the story of how we became a family.

In my heart of hearts, I believe that I was meant to have two babies, and that I brought home the baby who was meant all along to be with me. My refusal to take the first baby let the officials know that they have an orphanage that is not taking good care of the babies. I pray that my behavior will help the first baby and the other babies of that orphanage. My ability to refuse the baby was an act guided by God; God was my strength. I am filled with thanks and praise for the government and adoption officials who worked with me and delivered my healthy daughter to me.

I had two names; the first baby had the first one, my second baby has the second.

D. Kenyon is the pseudonym of a member of FCC–Connecticut, Rhode Island, Central Massachusetts.

Brand

Karen Braucher
FCC—Oregon and SW Washington

I'm in Changsha Children's Center Number 1 holding only
the baby assigned to me. Although it's bright outside, in here
it's dim, heavy with heat and infants flat on their backs on bamboo.
For some reason, all the helpful Chinese women caretakers
are gone. There are at least forty babies sprawled in the half-light,
and most of them are crying. Perhaps one is hungry, another
thirsty, one burning in a soaked diaper, and I am here
holding only one of them. I look across the room and see another
ashen-faced American, a man, holding only his baby.
Our eyes lock like two refugees, two prisoners, and we shake
our heads slowly and do not speak. The miniature bodies around us
continue to cry, roll and writhe, crane their necks trying to get someone's
attention. No one picks them up. No one is going to pick them up
for minutes, hours, and we know you can forget all that crap
about helping others and all that fluff about loving one another,
because we are looking at the unwanted, the castoffs, no matter how
you try to paint it in some other light. The moment passes. We look at
each other again, veterans, and he says, "We've got to get
our babies out of here." And I think, yes, that's the way it is, you can't
save them all. Courage and ruthlessness rise like the south China heat.

In the Baby Hotel

Stephen Phillip Policoff
FCC–New York

It was like being in a dormitory, only with babies, like fasting and adopting at the same time. It was like being trapped on a bad cruise, where they serve terrible food, and your cabin is tiny, and there is no drinkable water, and you have a baby with you, a baby you really don't know. It was like learning to be a parent while on an acid trip. It was awful and exhilarating, surreal and profoundly real.

In September, my wife Kate and I flew to Hangzhou, China, to adopt a baby girl. We had spent the previous seven months enmeshed in documentation hell: fingerprinted twice; every aspect of our lives notarized, certified, exemplified, and sealed by the Chinese consulate.

I even had to obtain the disposition of a long-forgotten court case, in which I and three friends had been arrested for trying to move a table from outside a dormitory at Wesleyan University to the theater for an anti-war poetry reading (it was 1971—the case was thrown out of court, but mysteriously our fingerprints wound up in an FBI file).

Then it was The Long Wait. All summer we fretted, waiting for the official OK from Beijing at a time of troubled relations between China and the United States—Taiwan tension, Harry Wu, sniping over trade.

I was in a state of anxiety the whole time: Would China suddenly shut down the adoption process, as they had done for mysterious reasons two years before? Would the United States cut off ties with China over human rights?

My friend Don kept saying, "As long as Coca-Cola wants to sell Classic Coke to millions of thirsty Chinese, we're not going to cut off ties."

He was right.

In early September I came home to find a message on our answering machine from the woman we had been pestering for weeks at the adoption agency. "I don't like to leave news like this on a machine," she said, "but I can tell you your daughter is adorable!"

In three seconds, I had called her back and she faxed me a picture of our daughter. I laughed—how could I not?—as the somewhat blurry yet discernibly adorable photo emerged slowly from our fax machine.

This is a hell of a way to meet your child, I thought.

In Hangzhou, we joined eight other couples who were all using the same adoption agency. We were met at the airport by a brigade of adoption facilitators and guides. It was a Sunday. We had spent days getting there; we were tired and hungry. We assumed we would go to the hotel, unpack, have some lunch, see a little of the city, and on Monday begin the Chinese paperwork that would allow us, perhaps by week's end, to finally get our babies.

We were wrong.

Instead, the guide, a young man who insisted we call him Roy (because we couldn't pronounce his Chinese name), said, "Please all get on the bus; we are going to the notary office. To the notary office. To begin paperwork. Immediately."

As we got on the bus, he added, "By the way, the babies will be there."

The babies will be there? In an office in downtown Hangzhou?

Well…yes.

Inside the shabby office it was about 97 degrees, and they served hot tea. Two old men sat scribbling away at documents while two women did the translating. All nine of the couples had to answer the same questions (questions we had answered in triplicate earlier—but in international adoption you learn quickly that redundancy is mandatory). It took four hours.

Every few minutes, a young woman from one of the orphanages would appear, carrying a baby, looking for the parents to whom the baby had been assigned. They would circle the long table, and everyone would stop what they were doing to watch the baby being presented to her parents. Our baby was one of the first to appear. Although it was grotesquely humid, she came wrapped in a fleecy blue winter bunting; she looked exactly like the faxed photo, only not so blurry this time. Kate practically leaped across the table to get her, and suddenly it became rather difficult to answer the remaining questions. When they asked us about our family income, we had to look it up in our dossier—at that moment we couldn't even recall what our jobs were.

And then, en masse, we were questioned by the authorities:

"Do you love your babies?"

"Yes!" the whole group shouted, like a responsive reading at a religious ceremony.

"Do you wish to keep your babies?" they asked. I thought: Why would we have come all this way if we didn't wish to keep our babies?

"Yes!" the whole room responded.

"That's all for now," Roy said, and we got back on the bus, nine couples with new babies, all of us, adults and infants alike, in a state of shock. The hotel the adoption agency had booked us into, a "three-star" hotel called the Zongshan, was a pit. The rooms were tiny, the bathrooms were for munchkins, no one spoke any English, and the hallways were so dark we might as well have been in a submarine.

The entire floor was given over to our group, and we acted as if we were back in college, sitting out in the middle of the gray hall to eat the dismal food. We wandered in and out of each other's rooms to offer tips on how to mix baby formula (we were all new at this) or how to obtain distilled water (the tap water in China is seriously contaminated). We formed a circle and tried to decipher the incomprehensible room service menu (which featured such dishes as hedgehog and duck's feet); we laughed that edge-of-hysteria laugh that is almost indistinguishable from crying.

In the baby hotel, time passed in a sort of Isomil-scented mist. Even at 3 A.M. someone would be sitting in the hallway eating cold noodles, rocking a baby. There were several more days' worth of paperwork to be done before we could go on to Guangzhou, to the U.S. Consulate, where we would get the precious visas for our babies. We had hoped to see a little of Hangzhou during that time, and we did manage to stroll the renowned, if murky, West Lake, where we ourselves became a tourist attraction, followed by a curious crowd of onlookers.

But that night our daughter, who had arrived with what seemed like a little cold, began to cough loudly, horribly, sounding like a wounded seal pup; and then she began to cry; and then she turned bright red; and then she began to sweat profusely; and then she had a fever.

We were terrified. We didn't really know this baby yet, much less did we know how to take care of a sick baby, and the only thing that stopped her from crying was carrying her around. I spent most of that night reeling up and down the dank hallway, almost falling asleep several times when I stopped to lean against a wall (but as soon as I stopped she cried, so I woke up fast).

At 4 A.M., when she had a 103.5-degree fever, we panicked. But at 4 A.M. in China it is 4 P.M. in New York. So we did what new parents always do— called our pediatrician.

It took a jittery half-hour to make an international call, since no one at the front desk spoke English.

When we finally reached him, he said, faintly, from across the world, "You don't worry about a baby until the fever is 105. Give her the antibiotics you brought; don't let her get dehydrated; call me back if she is not better in five days. Good luck."

Fortunately one of the husbands on the trip was an emergency room doctor. He had not yet arrived (it's too long a story to tell here; it involves botched paperwork and the plane running out of fuel in Alaska), but his wife kept saying, "As soon as he gets here I'll send him in to look at your daughter."

Meanwhile, we had not eaten much or slept at all, and we were feeling like prisoners of war in some weird international incident, stuck in the baby hotel with a small unwell stranger. The others in the group sensed this and stopped by with bags of semi-edible croissants from Hangzhou's faux-French bakery, refills of baby Tylenol, encouraging words, even offers to baby-sit.

Mostly we paced the cell-like room and tried to comfort our daughter. When the doctor arrived looking lost after a 30-hour journey, he barely had time to take off his jacket before his wife said, "You go right in there and look at that baby!"

And he did. In the baby hotel, when somebody asked you to do something, you did it, because we all felt a little lost, a little helpless.

He listened to her chest, checked her pulse, looked for rashes, shrugged. "A bad tracheo-bronchitis; you see it all the time with kids who have been in orphanages. She'll be fine. Steam her."

So we steamed her. We turned on the lethally hot shower in the tiny bathroom, wrapped our daughter in a towel, and sat there, as if in a sauna, for an hour. She didn't like it much, but it loosened her cough, and she did get better. And on the day our group finally stumbled into the American Consulate in Guangzhou, 52 Chinese infants were processed for adoption by American couples, a new record.

Of course, both my wife and I came down with the world's worst colds, our first gift from our daughter; and the first week home was a near disaster, since she was still on China time and thought that midnight to 6 P.M. was a fine time to play.

But we made it through even that, and as I type this she is rolling around on the floor nearby making strange growling noises (she looks and sounds at times like a small panda cub), demanding my attention. Already she has gained weight and learned new things—she smiled and waived at us last week! Astonishing!

"You have to wait a minute, Cookie," I say, as I try to finish this. But I know that she won't wait, that everything else will, and that, though I may not have known it, her smiling and growling and furious demands are what I've been waiting for myself, for a long time.

Stephen Phillip Policoff's article was originally published in the Feb./March 1996 issue of *New Age Journal.*

Settling In

Our lives are connected by a thousand invisible threads, and along these sympathetic fibers, our actions run as causes and return to us as results.

Herman Melville

Preparing for
Your Child

Marget Wincent
FCC-Chicago

For parents of children from China, it is important to know that children raised in group settings may have special developmental needs. Each child is going to have unique and individual needs depending on their experiences with touch, movement, and play, their general temperament and coping style, and their nutritional status. This article provides you with some ideas, suggestions, and activities to try with your child as you begin to learn about each other and grow together as a family.

There are two general statements that seem to apply to most children:

Follow your child's lead, and

You are your child's most engaging toy.

Following your child's lead means taking the time to really observe how your child responds and reacts to the environment. If you try to gaze deeply and lovingly into your child's eyes, and your child averts her gaze, cries, or closes her eyes, don't worry; you are not a "bad parent." Just follow your child's lead and back off a little. Find other ways of getting close—hugging, carrying your child in a sling, massage, rocking. If you try to gaze deeply and lovingly into your child's eyes and your child smiles, coos, reaches for your face, vocalizes, and looks into your eyes, follow your child's lead and maintain the interaction. Turn the gaze into a game of peek-a-boo or raspberry kisses or tickles or pat-a-cake. The first weeks and months following the adoption can be full of many emotional highs and lows; you and your child will adjust to each other a bit more easily when you remember to follow your child's lead.

Remembering that you are your child's most engaging toy not only makes packing your suitcases easier, it is also more fun for you and your child. The transition from orphanage or foster home to adoptive family (sleeping in hotels, eating in restaurants, traveling, hearing a new language, smelling new aromas, etc.) is a huge shift in the lives of young children. There are many adults who would have difficulty coping with such an event in their lives. To help your child's transition, and your own transition to parenthood, know that you are your child's most engaging toy. Talk, sing or hum to your child; touch your child through lotion rubs or massage; engage your child in simple interactive games like peek-a-boo, pat-a-cake, or (one family's favorite) "who is hiding the Cheerio?" Regardless of the age of your child, it is essential that a feeling of security be established; do not overwhelm your child in a rush to introduce her to all of the toys and material goods that Western parents seem to think are so important.

Following your child's lead and becoming your child's most engaging toy are two ideas that can help smooth the transition to a new family for parents and child. The suggestions that follow are geared toward specific age groups; even older children will benefit from some of the ideas provided for infants and toddlers.

Infant to Six Months

Spend time face to face with your child, talking softly. Your infant will enjoy the sound of your voice and the changing expressions on your face. While you are reclining in a chair, place your baby on your chest to help her learn to enjoy being on her tummy. Most babies in China sleep on their backs and have limited experience being placed on their tummies when awake. Your infant may become upset when placed in this new and challenging position. "Tummy time" is crucial to future movement because several motor milestones develop from the prone position. Start out by placing your baby on her tummy for one minute when she appears playful. Talk or sing, and rhythmically stroke her back while she is prone. Practice this activity for one minute throughout the day; don't be discouraged if your infant seems distressed by this position. Remember to follow her lead—don't overwhelm her, and watch her responses and reactions.

When deciding what to pack for your child, here are a few ideas. A soft cotton blanket is a must. Wash it a few times to soften it and store it with your clothing prior to your trip. The blanket will pick up your scent and will provide your baby with an olfactory connection to you. The blanket can be used for swaddling your baby during feeding times or times of distress. Select one good, high-contrast rattle; black and white patterns are much more interesting and stimulating to your child than light pastel colors. Pack lotion that can be used for daily massages—before and after bath time are great times to add a massage to the routine.

Age 7–14 Months

Don't panic if your child is not rolling or crawling at this age, regardless of what the baby development books tell you. Sitting, rolling, and crawling are all skills that depend on lots of practice and experiences with movement, touch, and exploration. Children who are swaddled or who spend lots of time lying in a crib may be slow to reach the gross motor milestones. You can help by providing "tummy time" throughout the day; make tummy time a playful time by adding exciting things to look at. Play peek-a-boo, look into small mirrors, explore noise-making toys. Help your child roll across your bed or soft blankets by carefully guiding her shoulders and hips as she moves from back to stomach to back. Rolling after a toy that is just barely out of reach can make rolling more interesting. Sitting in front of a mirror can make rolling, tummy time, massage, and just plain cuddling a fascinating experience for you and your child.

When deciding what to pack, the blanket, rattle, and lotion will still be appropriate. You could add a cardboard or texture book and other small noise-making toys that would be easy to manipulate and safe to mouth.

Age 15–24 Months

Even if your child experiences a mild developmental lag, this is still an age for lots of movement and exploration. Follow your child's lead; your child will show you if she is interested in or ready for crawling, pulling to stand, walking with one hand held, or walking independently. Make sure you ask your child's care workers what they think your child does the best and likes the most in terms of movement and play. One family reported that the nurse at the orphanage was very proud that their 18-month-old girl was just learning to stand.

In addition to motor exploration, this is also a time for language/sound exploration and more advanced play with toys. Many games can be created with items in your suitcase. Your child's small bowl, cup, and spoon can be used for pretend play and taking turns "feeding" each other. Stacking cups make great towers to knock over as well as hiding places for Cheerios, other finger foods, and small toys or rattles. Books and music boxes are also popular choices for games. If you pack dolls or stuffed animals, introduce only one and watch your child's responses; for some children, the doll or stuffed animal may overwhelm them while for other children, holding onto one doll or animal helps in the transition from one home setting to another.

Age 24–36 Months

For all children this is a time of observing, imitating, and problem solving. Follow your child's lead in your first weeks together. Your child will need some time to adjust to you and the new environments. It would not be unusual for your child to temporarily "forget" many of the skills she had while in foster care or the orphanage. The emotional needs for security and trust must be met before your child can turn her attention to play and exploration and learning.

Your child may show other signs of distress, grief, or depression. Some signs to watch for include diminished eye contact, lack of affect (a blank stare or gaze into space), crying, tantrums, hitting self or others, refusing to eat. Your child may favor one parent over the other parent during the first weeks, or possibly months. Each family will work through that phase of attachment in their own way and in their own time. Being consistent with your child, speaking in a calming voice, and following your child's lead will help smooth out the transition and the emotional ups and downs everyone is experiencing.

Coming Home

The time you spend with your child in China is important in building your forever family. Once you arrive home, your child may experience another type of transition into her new home and new routines. It is important that your child feels secure in her new surroundings and has time to explore her new world. For many children, having an established routine as soon as possible will help them feel emotional trust and security. Talk with your pediatrician about delaying any immunizations until you have been home for one month. That first month gives your child time to adjust and relieve the stresses of travel and transition. The first month also gives you time to get to know your child's likes, dislikes, strengths, and preferences. All of that will be very helpful to your child's pediatrician in setting up a schedule of immunizations and care.

For some children, developmental delays may persist and you may start wondering what is "normal" for your child. Choosing the right pediatrician for your child could be an important step in understanding your child's pattern of development; the right pediatrician is one who takes the time to talk with you about your own observations and concerns, who knows about children from China or other parts of Asia, who demonstrates an understanding of international families and families created through adoption. In addition to your pediatrician, there are early intervention teachers and therapists that can provide useful information and helpful strategies regarding your child's development.

Marget Wincent is a pediatric occupational therapist and the mother of two children, one through birth, one through adoption from China. Pat Kluzik Stauch, who has worked in early childhood development and special education for more than 14 years, also contributed to this article.

What to Expect When You Adopt Internationally

Patty Cogen, Ed.D., M.A.
New Mexico FCC

There are four types of initial responses (in the first weeks or months) of infants, toddlers, and young children after leaving an orphanage or foster care setting.

Child's Behavior (External)

1. Quiet, withdrawn, observing. Child may repeat a word or sound which may be the name of the former caregiver.

2. Active, constant movement, always happy, nondiscriminatory social behavior (sits on anyone's lap).

3. Rejecting parents, crying, actively searching for lost caregivers.

4. Spacey, in a daze or trance, falls asleep at unexpected times.

Child's Emotional State

1. Anxious, depressed, grieving, waiting or searching for lost caregivers.

2. Living in a perpetual present, denial of major life change.

3. Grieving, scared.

4. Overwhelmed, scared, overstimulated, reacting to being "handed around"; may be reacting to experiences associated with previous separations.

A child may remain in any one state for long periods of time or may shift from one to another. It's helpful for future situations and for other caregivers to know what specific situations can trigger these emotions. These triggers can often be avoided or acknowledged (see below) if they are known ahead of time.

What Parents Can Do

Validate the event that is disturbing.

Validate the child's feelings.

Model appropriate feelings, and describe how feelings "look" or can be expressed.

Be consistent and reliable.

Keep clear boundaries.

The following are suggestions for responding to specific behaviors.

1. *Withdrawal, observing:* Follow your child's lead and attune your responses to her level. Stay with her, holding her if possible or putting her in a carrier. Verbalize what you observe, i.e., "It's hard to join a family. I see you are feeling quiet and just want to watch what's going on. When I feel puzzled I like to be quiet too. We are going to be your parents forever. That means we will take care of you." If you suspect grieving or searching is occurring and have pictures of the foster parents, share those with your child. Engage in "womb"-like activities: warm baths together, swinging, rocking, carrying, slow dancing, etc.

2. *Active, always happy:* Set limits. Try to slow your child down. Don't allow her to engage everyone around her. Provide daily quiet activity time. Help her to focus on the life change she has experienced. Use words, photos, or even a stick figure drawing to tell your child's life history. This is not an ordinary situation; don't underestimate its impact. Use words such as "a really big change" or "hard to understand," "scary," "exciting," "not real yet." Model appropriate feelings such as scared, happy, sad, or confused. Offer opportunities for play that give physical expression to emotion: playdough, water, play/baths, puppets.

3. *Rejecting, crying:* This is the hardest experience for new parents, but it indicates the least numb emotional condition and demonstrates your child's capacity to be in touch with the magnitude of what is

happening. Stay as near as your child will allow; use a carrier (back or front) as a means to be close for long periods and get acquainted. Verbalize what your child is experiencing: "I can see how sad you are. You must miss someone (foster mother, caretaker) a lot. She took good care of you, and she wanted you to have a family. I know it will take time for you to feel comfortable with me, but I am here for you when you need me. I will take good care of you too."

4. *Spacey:* Sometimes children will become spacey from internal feelings and thoughts, and other times there may be a specific external reason why they "space out." Typical triggers are overstimulation, being handed around, being picked up by "strangers," hearing Chinese once you're back in the U.S., riding in cars or planes. If you are not holding your child when you observe this state occur, pick her up immediately. If you can identify the trigger for spaciness, do so and try to protect the child from the trigger if possible. You can ask people in restaurants not to touch your child or speak to her in Chinese. Act as a buffer for your child. You may want to take her to a quiet place. Verbalize what you think caused the spaciness, or just acknowledge that she is in a dazed, overwhelmed state: "This change (being picked up by so many people, having a family) is too much for you. I can understand that; you need a break."

Behaviors Typical of Children from Institutions

1. *Boundary difficulties or social nondiscrimination:* The child will go with anyone, climb onto anyone's lap, take anyone's hand who happens to be near. This behavior happens particularly when your attention is not focused on your child, even if you are physically close. In the orphanage this behavior is a good survival skill. In families it is not appropriate and may even leave the child vulnerable to abuse. It is considered a sign of nonattachment. Intervene immediately when your child behaves this way and verbally educate her and your family about why this happens and how to handle it.

2. *Overeating/hoarding, stealing or hiding food:* Most children have had adequate but limited diets. The hotel fare is overstimulating and overly generous. Limit your child's intake to avoid diarrhea and vomiting; typical responses to overeating. Children may also hoard food both because it was once in short supply and because it is the most basic way to overcome the feelings of loss, grief, and lack of nurturing.

3. *Overstimulation:* Everything that happens to your child is going to be overstimulating, because the situation is overwhelming to begin with. The new environment, many people, and changes of scene will all add to the initial impact of leaving one life and starting another. Try to minimize stimulation. Most children will need to go through a long (months to a year, depending on their age) period of merely exploring the world through their senses. This is part of the deprivation of institutional life. Toys may be meaningless if they haven't had any. Water in the sink may be a great experience while a bath may be scary.

4. *Regression or loss of skills:* Children regress (become less mature) under stress. This can result in the loss of already established skills, including but not limited to dressing, toileting, feeding, walking, crawling, and language. Moving from one culture to another automatically infantalizes children, because their previous knowledge and skills become virtually useless. It is appropriate to accept these skill losses as normal for the situation. Children over one year old will have some sense that they are at a disadvantage, although they will not be able to show or verbally express this. Be sensitive to this unintended but humiliating aspect of moving from one culture to another.

5. *Pseudo-maturity:* This is a behavior or set of behaviors which are beyond what is expected at the child's chronological age, i.e., a five-month-old holds her own bottle, a one-year-old never asks for help, a two-year-old never shows frustration, a three-year-old shares without possessiveness. Pseudo-maturity is easy to miss because it makes the child appear so "good," so "easy." This is a situation in which what looks good is really not. Children who are pseudo-mature do not trust or expect adults to take care of them. They lack attachment and normal dependency. These behaviors can be learned if parents actively teach their children to expect care. This is done by intervening when pseudo-mature behaviors occur and helping the child to learn normal levels of interdependence with an adult.

Patty Cogen, her husband Larry, their son Robin, and their daughter Sun-Jia live in Seattle. Patty is a child development specialist who works with children ages birth to five years and runs the First Year Home Group, a support group for internationally adopted young children and their parents.

The Joys of
Motherhood
after Forty

Marianne Adams
FCC-Arizona

The telephone message from Debbie couldn't have come at a worse time—at the end of a frazzled, exhausting Monday. Debbie, a reporter for a local publication, wanted to do a story on "The Joys of Motherhood after 40," and I—the 49-year-old adoptive mother of two lovely little Asian girls—was to be the subject of that story.

Monday, always hectic at our house, was even more difficult that day. My girls, Johnna, age five and a half, and Leah, three, were exhausted from a too-busy weekend. The telephone in my home office rang endlessly with calls from potential adoptive parents, who always seem to save their questions for Monday morning. But no time to rest—I had lunch duty at Johnna's kindergarten that morning, followed by a meeting, after which I had promised the girls I would take them swimming.

I picked up the phone message from Debbie at the end of that frenzied day and listened with a mixture of puzzlement and annoyance. Puzzled because the message was worded in such a way as to suggest that I was newly married and barely 40 years old. As I relayed the message to Peter and collapsed into bed, I wasn't feeling very joyful. "Worn out" would have been an accurate description—the joys of motherhood—right?

As I waited for sleep, I thought back over the years during which our two little girls had come to us.

Johnna Young Shin had been an infant, only four months old, when she came to us from Kang-won province in South Korea. Sunny dispositioned, chatty, totally comfortable with herself, she has grown, at the age of five and a half years, into a bright and social youngster who enjoys kindergarten, music, and many friends. Johnna's wish for a "baby sister" took us to Fujian province in China in June of 1996, where tiny Leah Chen

Liu, then two and a half years old, became part of our family. Sweet, gentle-hearted, and shy, bright little Leah quickly adapted to her new surroundings, though with a few strange "twists." The Reeboks we brought with us to China were the first real shoes she'd ever had, and for the first several nights she had refused to take them off when she went to bed. Bed was another stranger to her. When, each night after being tucked in, she crept out of bed and crawled under it, it finally became obvious to us that she had probably slept on the floor. Still, I thought as I drifted off to sleep, was "joy" the proper word to describe these experiences?

At midnight, Leah woke up screaming "Mama!" Peter and I rushed to her bedroom just as she vomited all over the bed, herself, and the tile in the hall as we carried her to the bathroom. We spent the next hour cleaning up Leah and the bed, again chuckling over the "joys of motherhood after 40."

In the meantime, sweet Leah, totally confused over what had happened, kept whispering, "I torry [sorry] Mama for making mess." It was the first time in the ten months since she had come to us that she had been sick. When I saw the confusion in her eyes, I asked her if she would like to have me sleep in her room in case she was sick again. I'll never forget how her little face lighted up. If she could have put her feelings into words, I'm sure that she would have said, "You would do this for me?"

I dragged a mattress into her room—where Johnna still slept soundly, unaware of the drama going on around her. As I lay down on the mattress, I replayed the previous day, probably feeling sorry for myself, and then reviewed my to-do list for the next day. All at once, Leah jumped out of bed, planted a kiss on my forehead, and said, "Thank you, Mama, thank you for staying with me." She did this not just once, but five times. What a precious little girl, so thankful for such a simple deed that so many children take for granted. As I lay there, tears running down my face, I prayed, "Thank you, God, thank you for reminding me of what motherhood is all about."

When I awoke the next morning, I found Leah fast asleep on the floor next to my mattress, with her small hand holding mine.

Oh, the joys of motherhood at any age!

Marianne and Peter Adams live in Scottsdale with their two adopted daughters and their 25-year-old biological son, Chad. Marianne is the branch facilitator for China's Children in Arizona.

Coping with the Post-adoption Baby Blues

Barb Ohland

Maine Families with Children from Asia

You are finally home with your new child! You endured the infertility treatments, navigated the uncertain waters of international adoption, finessed the paperwork, survived the scrutiny of strangers during the home study, learned to wait, wait, and wait some more, and finally you returned triumphant with your new little one.

So why do you feel so blue when your dreams have finally come true?

Once the anticipation and excitement of your child's arrival wears off, the blues are not uncommon. Don't be shocked or too surprised. Adoptive parents often feel let down and occasionally mildly depressed after a child arrives. Most new parents suffer from the "baby blues." Unlike postpartum depression, the blues are not influenced by hormonal fluctuations. When parents add a child to their family, whether adopted or not, they can easily get bogged down when faced with the daily effort involved in parenting a new child.

Children are demanding. Their need for food, dry diapers, warmth, and comfort are expressed in the only way they know—by crying. The arrival of a new baby or toddler is nearly always accompanied by weeks or months of sleep deprivation. The inability to follow one's usual routine with any predictability adds to the physical and emotional stress. Meals, housework, and adequate rest frequently get skipped when the parents try to meet the new child's demands. Often, they use what little quiet time they have to catch up on mounting laundry, cleaning, and baby announcements instead of taking a nap.

Adoptive parents are often too embarrassed to admit that they have the blues at this time. They think they should be happy and excited because they consciously chose this route to parenthood. They rationalize that because there was no pregnancy, there should be no depression.

There are numerous factors that contribute to the blues. Becoming a parent is a major life change. It is not uncommon to feel inadequate when faced with the huge responsibility of the new child in your home. Here is how some parents, who asked that their names not be used, described their feelings:

> When our daughter came home, the adjustment was horrendous. We had worked so hard to get her home and then it felt like—now what?

Adopting a five-year-old was also a tremendous adjustment for an experienced parent of two bio children:

> I was not as prepared as I should have been. I had to learn to relax my expectations and adjust my routine to meet my child's needs and mine. I made a basic schedule for our day and let the housework slide as much as possible....I had to teach my new child how to speak English, how to live in a family, and we had to adjust to one another.
>
> I did have times when I felt trapped and overwhelmed, especially when he threw tantrums, whined, cried, and just basically regressed. Things got better when he went to kindergarten for a few hours a day. It gave me time to unwind or sleep. I did not use the time to do chores. I did whatever I needed to do for myself so I could be a relaxed, happy mom when I picked him up.

When the new child has adoptive siblings already in the house who are also adjusting to the new arrival, parenting can quickly become a 24-hour-a-day job.

> I suffered from extreme moodiness during the first six months after our daughter came home. Sometimes I felt mean and unnurturing [to both my kids]. [Looking back,] a lot of the tension, I think, came from all the changes that accompanied adding to the family. Our first child had gotten to an independent age and suddenly I was chasing around a two-year-old who was so clueless about safety. I had to follow her from room to room and couldn't get anything done. I didn't entirely trust [the older sibling] to be nice to her all of the time, either. Suddenly I felt like I was in a straightjacket. [I had] no life of my own.

A new baby or toddler in the home causes upheaval. Schedules and routines usually fall by the wayside. Life can quickly start to feel out of control. A child who cries a lot, is fussy or anxious, or has some unexpected medical problem may create an early parenting experience that is quite different from the idyllic one that was dreamed of for so long. It is also not uncommon for a new baby or young child to bond tightly with one parent and vehemently exclude the other. When this happens, the rejected parent may understand that this is a relatively short-term problem, but it still adds to the stress.

Sometimes when adoptive parents are honest about difficulties they encounter, friends and relatives are not always supportive. One father shared this story:

> Our new child came home right before the holidays. In addition to the adjustment of the new mouth to feed, our child brought home a surprise—hepatitis B. My in-laws have always been compulsive about diseases and illnesses and so we were "outed" from *all* family gatherings over the holiday season.
>
> My spouse felt we were being treated like lepers by those whom she loved and grew up with. It was very hard to adjust at first. We had minimal support from the agency but had strong support from the specialists we were seeing and our clergyman. Plus, we had another young child to keep us busy.

The post-arrival period can be a very trying time for everyone in the family, and it is normal to have emotional highs and lows. Although the blues are common, it doesn't mean that depression might not become severe enough to warrant treatment. Seeking help from his doctor completely turned things around for this dad.

> We had an uncertain waiting period that was longer than most. I volunteered to stay home with the other children and was physically and emotionally drained [after the three weeks my wife was gone]. The baby came home just before the holidays, and it was a difficult time. [My wife] was more tired than I expected, and the baby wasn't ready to deal with me. Our in-laws came and stayed for two weeks A month later, I was exhausted, frustrated at the baby's continued focus on Mom, and stymied at work. I began to have this increasing focus on morbid thoughts that I couldn't shake.
>
> I finally went to a doctor. He did a physical exam and prescribed depression medication for the "pain." I stopped the medication after a week...[but] it helped me to pull out of the trough and focus on the good things. Shortly thereafter [the baby] began to show significant signs of better adjustment, and our lives began to settle into a more agreeable routine. Overall, when I look back, it wasn't a terribly long period of time—but it *was* terrible!

Many parents reported they were not adequately prepared for the child they brought home. When adopting internationally, it is not uncommon to be referred a child that is older or younger than you had anticipated. A long period of time between the referral and travel date can also cause problems in adjusting once the baby gets home.

That happened in my case. We were referred a baby who was under 4 months old, but because of various delays, we didn't bring her home until she was 11 months. Intellectually, I knew she was getting older and developing, but realistically I had not prepared myself. Within days of coming home, our baby was reveling in her new freedom and was crawling everywhere.

She was attempting to scale the stairs, she was putting everything in her mouth, opening drawers and cabinets, dumping the cat's water dish, unraveling the toilet paper, and rarely *ever* napping. I had piles of announcements to send out, photos of our trip to organize, not to mention laundry, housework, and the everyday demands of a six-year-old brother.

On top of that friends kept stopping by to visit. I was exhausted and incredibly frustrated. I felt like my life was out of control. When I had my first child, I had no problem juggling all these tasks after he came home. Why was it so very hard now?

It took me a while to put in perspective the obvious differences: Our son was an infant and slept 16 hours a day. I had a year to get used to my role and adapt to him. Our daughter was almost a year old and had spent the first 11 months of her life in a crib. When she joined the family she was ready to explore her environment like any normal baby that age. It took me several months to adjust my expectations to the reality of the current situation.

When parents bring home a new child, they need time to claim each other and form attachments. When a woman gives birth, most people respect the mother's need to cocoon with her new baby. However, when a child comes to a family through adoption, especially an older baby or child, some well-meaning friends and family ignore this important need.

Some parents report that employers, friends, or family members continued to make all the usual demands on their time, energy, and emotions despite their new arrival. A few recalled that they had received so much attention that they felt they had no privacy. One mom shared the following:

> I did my share of crying. When my family came to meet the baby, she had scabies and was miserable. We were trying to juggle Thanksgiving, entertaining, mailing out adoption announcements, thank-you notes, and decorating for Christmas. My mom wanted to have a big party to introduce the baby to all her friends and kept pushing me to take the baby out and about for show and tell. I just was not prepared for so much going on at once.

For many adoptive parents who traditionally come to the role at a later stage of life, adjusting to the job of a full-time parent and the loss of an independent lifestyle can be very tough. For some, personal self-image is so closely tied to their career that they find parenting a true culture shock. The following account from a mother who adopted a three-year-old was typical:

> My difficulty was getting used to being at home full time…and having someone with me constantly. I found it difficult [when I couldn't get] any personal time to recharge.

One parent surmised that the blues she encountered were partially related to the losses experienced when people change their lives to accommodate a new child.

Some new adopters found that old infertility issues resurfaced briefly after their child arrived:

> Surprisingly, I got very depressed when my sister announced she was pregnant. I really thought I was over all those fertility issues—[but] I was not able or ready to deal with it. All the long waiting and work we went through to adopt...and here she gets pregnant so easily.

Adjusting to a new baby or child, adopted or not, is a major endeavor. If parents expect this period will be a roller-coaster ride emotionally, and they try to take care of themselves during this vulnerable time, the depression, exhaustion, and anxieties may not be as severe or overwhelming.

Adoption professionals recommend parents connect with other adoptive parents to share anxieties, disappointments, and survival tips. Adoptive parents are renowned for their can-do, triumph-over-adversity features. They often ignore, deny, and hide the sadder and more trying adjustments that accompany adoption and new parenthood. But parents must also reach out to each other for support when they need it. Be they mild or severe, post-adoption blues are not an indication that the adoption was a mistake. They simply signal the transition and stresses that all parents experience.

In her book *Launching a Baby's Adoption,* Patricia Irwin Johnston gives these general tips to help parents minimize post-arrival blues:

Realize you are human.

You don't need to be a super-parent. Advocate for yourselves.

Try to limit the number of visitors when you first come home. Between jet lag, a child who is experiencing numerous changes in her life, lack of sleep, and the everyday physical demands of taking care of a new child, parents need help and rest. Do not try to entertain a constant string of well-wishers.

Eat a healthy, balanced diet. If well-wishers ask what they can do, let them know that a prepared meal would be by far the most appreciated thing they could do. While you are waiting to travel, stock your freezer with ready-made dinners.

Exercise to relieve stress. Take the baby for a brisk walk in the stroller, get an exercise video to do while the baby is napping, sit on the floor and do yoga stretches, sign up for a new parents' swim or aerobics class that offers baby-sitting.

Get out with the baby so you don't fell trapped. Meet up with another adoptive parent, go out for lunch or to the children's room at the library.

Feed your soul. Arrange for your spouse, friend, or a sitter to allow you a little time to yourself every day. Read a book, check your e-mail, take a leisurely bath, get a massage, meditate, etc.

Feed your marriage. It is easy for new parents to forget that marriage came first.

Seek help—from other members of your adoptive families support group, your child's pediatrician, or your social worker. If the blues don't start to dissipate in a few weeks, seek help from a therapist.

Whichever parent is staying home should make sure they shower and dress before the other parent leaves in the morning. It will be hard to find the time later to do that when you're looking after young children. A refreshing start can help set the tone for the rest of the day.

Barb Ohland lives in Camden, Maine, with her husband Geof, son Harry, and daughter Lila, who was adopted from Vietnam.

Perspectives on the First Year

Laura Cowan

FCC-Toronto

In September 1994 we met our Emma. After years of medical treatment and years of looking for a child to adopt, we finally found our daughter. It's been quite a year! We had been notified of our proposal of an eight-and-a-half-month-old daughter by telephone, and armed with her name and birth date we left Canada for China eight days later. It was a leap of faith: faith in our adoption agency, faith in the Chinese government, faith in ourselves. It was the best decision we have ever made.

Our trip was full of difficulties—travel arrangements which didn't work out, planes delayed (in Canada!), an unreachable Canadian embassy, missing paperwork, lots of problems. In other words, situation normal for any international adoption. But finally we arrived in Yiyang and met our daughter. I will never forget that moment. We'd seen her picture the day before, and I recognized her the moment I saw her in the arms of the nanny at the orphanage. We held her, and counted her arms and legs to make sure she was all right, and cried. Then the nanny took her back, and we spent hours completing paperwork.

At last they brought her to us, to start our life together. The trip home, although emotionally exhausting, was easier than I had expected. Emma was ill, sick with bronchitis, and the antibiotics combined with Tempra and all the food she wanted (and she wanted a lot of food) resulted in a quiet baby for the long flights home. Once home we got more antibiotics, checked her pooh for evil things, and got an all-clear from the doctor. We had a great party a week after we got home to introduce her to all the friends who had tried so hard to help us adopt. Everyone was pleased for us, and with her. She was very willing to be with people, to be passed around adults. But we knew that there would be trying times to come.

Emma wasn't used to being held. She would hold her own bottle, grabbing it from our hands and looking after herself as she had learned to do. We had to work with her independence and gradually accustom her to our touch. We started slowly at first, holding her while she ate, bringing her to our bed to roll and move. Playing little games, pattycake, touching toes, beeping noses, anything which encouraged touch. She responded slowly, and we let her set the pace. It was difficult not to reach out and wrap her in my arms, to give her the physical affection I craved, but we were sure that she would come around in her own time.

Luckily my husband Brian had about four weeks' holidays and was able to stay home, and we could work together to get settled in. It helped. The jet lag and lingering exhaustion were incredible. I don't know how I would have coped at home alone those first few weeks.

I remember when I had to take Emma for her blood tests. Watching two adults hold my child down to draw blood was horrible, and waiting for the test results was just as bad. Thankfully every test my doctor ran, HIV, hepatitis B and C, syphilis, and a whole bunch more, came back negative, but it was hard to wait.

Then we began to experience nightmares with Emma. The first time was after a reunion party, a house full of Chinese babies. Emma woke in the night screaming, thrashing, lashing out at us. We had never heard that type of sound from a child. All we could do was hold her, rock her, keep her from hurting herself. It happened many more times, usually after situations where Emma was separated from us. My body was bruised from her thrashing, kicking at me, fighting with me. We found that one of the best things we could do was to show her the house, the dog, the cat, her toys. We had to make a nonverbal child understand she was at home, and that her world, which had been turned upside down and inside out, was now safe, secure, and unchanging. Somehow we managed. Emma sleeps nights now, cuddled under a comforter, surrounded by stuffed toys.

Christmas brought new challenges. All my starry-eyed dreams of our first Christmas together went out the window when three days before Christmas I woke to the sound of my daughter gasping for breath. Racing to emergency at 6:30 A.M. was the right thing to do. Emma was admitted to hospital with an infectious respiratory virus and kept in for two days. We had to fight with her to medicate her, two of us holding her to put a Ventalin mask on her face, to hold her down for a nasal tube. It was horrible, and I cried, for her fear and pain, and in fear that all the work we had done at getting her used to being held would be undone. But I was wrong, because when my husband sent me home from the hospital for a shower and a change of clothes Emma kissed me goodbye. It was the first time she had reached out to me, and I cried again as I drove home.

January brought swim class, an exercise in sensory stimulation and holding onto Mommy or Daddy. We used this to build up a lot of trust fast, and it worked for us.

My birthday last summer was like a dream come true. There was my daughter, all dressed up and smiling, carrying my birthday present across the room. It was a scene I had imagined for years. Once again I cried my eyes out and loved every minute of it.

We get lots of questions about our daughter. We have comments on her hair, her cheeks, her eyes. We get a lot of questions from people in mixed-race couples. They seem to smile a lot when they see us. Some people just look from one to the other of us and don't ask anything. We're learning what to say to people and when not to say anything at all. We don't owe our life story to anyone, and Emma's story belongs to her. We've learned it's important to tell the difference between racism and stupidity. There are a lot more stupid people around than racist people.

The days have moved quickly this year. We've had teething (yuck!), shots, fevers. We have more laughter in our home than we've had for years. We step over toys, and the house is a mess. We're tired, and our marriage needs time to get back on track after the years of hard knocks. We decided that I would stay home (an unexpected choice), so we have no money, but we sure spend lots. Shoes, clothes, toys, books, sand box, diapers, milk. The list is endless, but we manage. Life is different from before, but that is what we wanted.

Emma grows and changes every day. She walked before she was a year old, and ran soon after. Child-proofing the house is an ongoing issue. She loves to go fast in friends' boats and runs everywhere she can. She uses the dog as a speed bump or a step stool, depending on where she is going. She wakes up laughing, and goes to bed smiling. She is a joy in our lives.

I remember an American woman I met at an airport in China. She looked at us, smiled, and said, "One long journey ended, another just begun." Both our journeys have been hard, exhausting. But this one, our journey with Emma, is fun, filled with love, laughter, smiles, and hope. Worth every moment of the journey to get her.

A year and a half ago we had no child. We were unhappy, lost in the life we had, which wasn't the one we had planned for or wanted. Now we are a family.

Laura Cowan, Brian Smith, and Emma live in Scarborough, Ontario. This article appeared under the title "It's Been Quite a Year" in *Adoption Helper* (Oct. 1995).

Hannah's Story

Diane Kramer
FCC-Baltimore

Hannah, her caregiver explained as she smiled and handed a grinning baby to me, was "very active." And she wasn't wrong! Unlike the descriptions of many developmentally delayed infants I had read about and expected for months, Hannah turned out to be a whirlwind of energy: standing, tumbling, crawling, with incredibly strong back and leg muscles. Hannah was just short of nine months then and had been in the orphanage in Yangzhou, Jiangsu province, since two weeks after her birth. On the surface, our child didn't appear that different from U.S. babies at the same age. Even her weight and height were right on target according to U.S. charts.

But Hannah did not know anything about "cuddling," and relaxing her by either massage, holding, or loving words was close to impossible. We had been committed as a family to the "family bed" concept; it is something we use successfully to this day with our almost five-year-old. But sleeping with Hannah was impossible for all concerned. It wasn't so much the thrashing about, but rather that Hannah is an unusually light sleeper and comes awake to play and talk with the slightest sound.

After about three weeks of struggling with sleeping together, sleeping next to her bed, sleeping with her bed in the same room, and never more than two hours of steady sleep for Hannah or us, we bought dark shades, put up the crib, moved it into her bedroom, and all of us now sleep soundly through the night (usually in bed by 9:30 P.M. and up by 7:30 A.M.). It wasn't what we wanted ideally, but it is what works for Hannah and the rest of the family. (We also have a baby monitor and keep her door ajar all night). The only night disturbances we have now are teething related, one night out of two weeks.

So what about cuddling? I have learned to "cuddle" Hannah by combining the tumbling play she loves so with lots of hugs, kisses, and really short massages. Usually I take off everything but the diaper and have her either at eye level or we both sit face to face on the grass or rug. Hannah absolutely *loves* to suck on my nose, so that too has become "cuddling" (although the tooth coming in is making this game a little dangerous for mom!). Sometimes I put massage oil on, sometimes not. The important thing is the touching and the skin contact, even when they are in motion. Right now we have a new game called hugs, kisses, and tickles: hugs are always bear hugs with grunts, kisses are sloppy nose sucks, and tickles are thrown in to keep the game lively. Hannah gets a fast-paced and interesting game; Mom gets to be close.

We also use "holding time" several times a week to kind of break down the distance barrier. While Hannah protested very vigorously the first couple of times, the sessions now resolve into ten-minute periods of crying followed by ten minutes of intense eye contact and "almost cuddling," where Hannah will suck her thumb and sort of rest her head.

Winding down to bed was also a major problem that is beginning to resolve itself. Hannah could only get to sleep by sustained and intense face rubbing, frantic thumb sucking, and throwing herself back and forth in your arms, like you were a pillow she just couldn't get comfortable with. We added a darkened room, Mommy or Daddy rocking and singing, with some gentle rubbing. The intensity of the "get to sleep" ritual is fading, and Hannah is able to relax in our arms and let us know, by leaning backwards, that she is ready to lie down.

Playing with toys was also difficult in the beginning. When I first handed Hannah a small stuffed animal in China, she looked at it as though it was a tissue or a piece of paper. For several weeks, she would pick up and drop toys with almost no interest, but excitedly stand at our knees ready for more somersaults or head stands. Play for Hannah was crawling and jumping on people. We did little to push toys on her, but made sure the play area had a number of interesting things (rubberized blocks, pop ups, balls, animals, nesting boxes, beads on wires, etc.).

Slowly, proceeding via advanced toy sucking, Hannah has arrived at the point where she will now play intently on her own for about 30 minutes and will even play ball with me (using a big soft orange ball that she can both grab and roll). I will never forget the night she seemed to finally "connect" with play animals. I was doing my usual pretend stuff, and something must have clicked. All of a sudden, she saw that little animal as "alive," and her face lit up with incredible delight. It was magical.

Everyone keep in mind that, books and experts aside, each child is different. While I have used some of what I've read, other things I have had to abandon, and go out on a limb and solve the problem by working with my daughter and learning her needs and wants from her reactions. Undoubtedly many of Hannah's adjustment difficulties come from being in an institution. At the same time, her birth personality underlies the institutional experience, and how Hannah "experienced" orphanage life was undoubtedly colored by who she is.

I believe my daughter's strong muscles and facility at gymnastics comes in part from her caregivers' perception of the kind of child she was and how they then interacted with her. Active children get active play. For Hannah, loving care came to mean active play. We now are trying to broaden that definition, so that Hannah can learn about the pleasures of slow and gentle touch, cozying in someone's arms, etc. Again, I dreamed for months about holding and cuddling in the traditional way with my new baby. Instead, I am learning there are many ways to be close and show love.

In eight weeks (counting the time since we met), Hannah and her new family have come far. Today as I sat and pulled weeds in the garden, Hannah stood behind me, resting her chin on my shoulder and watching intently. She seems to love to be outdoors, in the grass and dirt, and I would even say it is somehow "easier" to be close to her in such a setting (although I don't know why).

Hannah now understands basic things we say ("Where is Daddy?" "cat," "your diaper," "Hannah come," "no," etc.). Just two days ago she finally noticed the sounds coming out of the radio and the TV picture (I am guessing this is because English is finally making some sense to her). All of us seem to be better able to read each other's sign language too. While it will take many months, I think, before Hannah understands that we are more than great caregivers, she is learning about kinds of human closeness that are probably very new to her.

What I have learned from this experience is to be very open to the unexpected in your new child. While these children undoubtedly mourn for their old life, they are also learning about and joyously exploring a strange, exciting, and initially unintelligible new life. Don't assume that your child will be just like what you've read about. Watch her, learn from her.

Diane Kramer lives in Gaithersburg, Maryland, with her husband Michael and their two daughters, Hannah (three) and Katie (seven).

Pass It On!

Jean MacLeod
Metro Detroit FCC

Lily was seven months old when we adopted her in Nanchang, China, in July 1996. She was a bright, alert, and very happy, outgoing baby. On our third morning at our hotel's breakfast buffet, Lily was spirited away from my arms by several of the young Chinese waitresses who loved to fuss over and amuse our babies. From 20 feet away I watched our tiny daughter suddenly look around her in dismay and begin to sob. I rushed to pick her up, she clung to me, and the cries stopped. Lily had quickly and fiercely decided we were hers, and bonded to us with all her heart.

For the next five months she went to no one else (except her older sister) willingly. Our baby had spent the first several months of her life in the orphanage, and the past couple in foster care. Her strong attachment to us was healthy; we respected her deep need to be close to us physically and protected her from well-meaning adults who didn't understand her issues. A loving but insensitive uncle tried to carry her away from me in a playful manner—as she screamed and cried and reached for Mama. He handed her back at my request with the comment, "You'll be sorry you're spoiling this baby one day!"

We were confident we were not spoiling Lily, but giving her what she needed. And it has paid off. She is becoming more relaxed and interactive with friends and relatives with each passing month. She is choosing her independence, and it has given her confidence.

Lily's initial attachment process was quick and definite, but there was some other minor socialization that we worked on with our baby. Lily didn't like the intensity of a lot of direct eye contact, or having her face kissed. We played a lot of peek-a-boo, patty-cake, and tickle games, and held her closely while she fed, with the bottle positioned so that she would look into our face. To accustom her to our "mushing" over her we would blow raspberry kisses in her neck and whisper in her ear, which made her giggle. Then we'd sneak in a quick kiss! She went from grimacing and turning away from kisses, to bored acceptance of them, to active slobbery participation in a few short months.

Initially, when Lily would get hurt she would cry but refuse comfort from us. We were diligent about responding immediately to any real or perceived "boo-boos" and would shower her with kisses and sympathy. Lily had to learn that we were there to meet all of her physical and emotional needs and that being a little soldier was not nearly as satisfying as having Mama or Daddy make "all better"! Lily has also become a very empathetic child.

So what if it's not this easy? What do you do if you are faced with post-adopt problems that can't be solved with cuddling and games? Where do you go for information if you find yourself dealing with attachment problems, post-institutional behaviors, passive, aggressive, or autistic-like disturbances, or developmental delays and learning disabilities?

Your home study case worker may have the information to refer you to local resources. Another truly impressive resource is the Parent Network for the Post-Institutionalized Child. The Parent Network was created in 1993 by a group of parents whose Romanian adopted children were diagnosed with attachment disorder. "We are attempting to create a network of parents to share information on medical centers, doctors, psychiatrists, psychologists and therapists who recognize the unique disorders created by an infant history of privation," the Parent Network introductory newsletter states. They have planned several conferences, have a wonderful suggested reading list, and are a huge clearinghouse for information and videos on a wide range of topics, including "Tips on Parenting Children with Attachment Problems," "Theraplay," "Hepatitis," "Cleft Palate," "Speech and Language Disorders in the Sensorial and Maternally Deprived Child," "Adopted Children from Institutions: Myths and Reality." The Parent Network also offers a "Pre-adoption Package" which includes information on "what parents need to know before adopting internationally." A Parent Network newsletter and order form can be requested from the Parent Network for the Post-Institutionalized Child, Box 613, Meadow Lands, PA 15347, USA.

When we left for China last July we went prepared for every possible minor and major medical difficulty imaginable. No one ever told us what to do if our daughter wouldn't meet our eyes. Lily's avoidance behaviors were not complicated; we were able to draw on previous parenting experience and some excellent advice from the internet, but I know we would have been very grateful for the Parent Network if our problems had been serious or had persisted.

On our return from China I was puzzled by the lack of personal conversation on the adjustment of newly adopted children. I knew that we were not alone—why weren't people talking? As adoptive families we have a powerful collective knowledge, and as Families with Children from China members one of the most important things we can offer each other (and especially new parents) is honest advice and support. We have experienced a unique, extraordinary parenting journey, and have accumulated a lot of hands-on information. Pass it on!

Jean MacLeod, the newsletter editor for Metro Detroit FCC, is married, works as a flight attendant, and lives in Michigan. She is the mom of two extraordinary girls, Molly and Lily Tie Lu, from Nanchang.

A Sign of the Times

Valerie A. M. Demetros
FCC-Arizona

At the age of 14 months, our Julie Anna's vocabulary had grown by leaps and bounds. She arrived in the United States at the age of 11 months with a vocabulary of one word—*Mama* (my personal favorite). In just three short months, the list had grown to include *dog, horse, frog, cookie, eat, fruit, potato, cheese, drink, bird, ice cream,* and *food.* By 16 months, she's added *gorilla, again, please, more, thank you,* and the all-important *I love you.*

How did she learn all of these in such a short time? It's simple. She says them all with her hands. Julie is speaking American Sign Language (ASL), the official language of the deaf population of the United States. After reading about ground-breaking studies where toddlers were taught ASL before they learned to speak, I decided that our China-born child was the perfect candidate. ASL is, in effect, a foreign language just as are Chinese, Spanish, and French. And research has suggested that children learn second and third languages easier when they are younger.

Of course, not everyone follows that viewpoint. Many people, upon learning that Julie Anna is signing, remark on what a crazy idea it is. Or ask, "Why would you want to teach her that? Is she deaf?" The answer is in response to a question many parents ask themselves, "How can I ease my child's frustration while she is learning to communicate?"

Julie Samota asked herself the same question about her daughter, Laura. At the age of five months, Julie began to teach Laura simple signs. "We taught her so that she could communicate with us before she could speak," Julie says. "We wanted to make mealtime easier for Laura."

It worked. Laura's first signs were *all done, please,* and *eat.*

The same works for Julie Anna. When she wants a cookie, she makes the sign. (Cup the right hand in the shape of a C; place the right hand, fingers down, in the open palm of the left hand and turn back and forth a few times, like you're screwing on a lid.)

The first step to teaching ASL is to find an easy book on the subject. *Baby Signs: How to Talk with Your Baby—Before Your Baby Can Talk,* by Linda P. Acredolo and Susan Goodwyn, Ph.D., addresses how to teach sign language to a young child. The book details observations of more than 100 children signing between 7 and 30 months old. Some of the findings in the book include:

All babies can, and often do, use some kind of sign language to communicate.

Signing may be particularly good for boys, who typically learn to talk later than girls.

Signing requires eye contact, which is good for communication and bonding.

Signing does not delay the process of learning to talk. In fact, when the children studied had reached the age of two, they were better at expressing themselves and understanding what was said to them. On average, they had mastered a larger vocabulary, some 350 words, compared to 300 for their nonsigning peers.

For a good signing dictionary, try *Signing for Kids,* by Mickey Flodin. It's a simple introduction to ASL with basic words only. Keep the book on the table and read through it each morning to find just a few new words for the day.

Of course, when I began to teach Julie Anna, she didn't catch on immediately. First, she had to figure out just what the heck I was doing each time I handed her a cookie. It took awhile before she finally put the two together. Late one night, about a week after I had begun signing to her, I sat in her room, rocking her back to sleep at about 2:00 A.M. With her eyes closed and head resting on my arm, Julie made the sign for cookie in her hand and then brought her hand to her mouth. She was talking in her sleep without saying a word.

Of course, you don't want to overwhelm a child with too many signs. Read your child's response to signing and follow her clues. Some children may pick it up more easily than others. Julie Samota and her husband, John, began teaching Laura, now 17 months, very slowly. Laura picked up the signs after repeated introduction.

"It took a while," Julie says. "You have to start out slowly with just a few signs, then add new ones as they learn."

For Julie Anna and Laura, learning to sign has made it easier to communicate, with fewer frustrating moments. The whining and pointing has been replaced with signing and smiling. After her first word, Julie Anna was learning new words in just days, sometimes hours. It took only one hour for her to pick up on the sign for potatoes. (Hint: start with words for food and animals. These are the most important things to them at this age.)

Each morning, I read through *Signing for Kids* and find a word of the day. Some are easier than others; some of them Julie Anna has modified if they are too difficult.

The bottom line is simply trying to make life easier for both you and your child. A child who can communicate her needs is happy and confident. And a parent who can curtail just a little whining is a parent with a big grin.

A Few Tips for Teaching American Sign Language

1. Start as early as possible. The sooner they see the signs the better.

2. Remember to always use the word as well as the sign each time. This will ensure that speech development will progress with the signs.

3. Learn the signs for *good* and *thank you*. Use them often.

4. Praise your child each time she uses a sign. Say the word aloud and repeat the sign.

5. Acknowledge a sign just as if a child had spoken. For example, if she makes the sign for cookie at bedtime, you may respond with, "Oh, you want a cookie?" Make the sign for cookie. "Mama will give you one in the morning. It's time for bed now."

6. Start out slowly. Don't try to do too much.

7. If babysitters and/or relatives spend a lot of time with your child, make sure they are aware of the signs and can recognize your child's modifications. The frustration begins anew when your child is signing for a drink and is ignored because nobody in the room understands her.

8. Have fun. She'll learn more quickly if it's fun.

9. Don't push it if your child doesn't pick up ASL right away. Some children may not want to learn, and for others it may just take a little longer. Be patient.

Valerie A. M. Demetros is the mother of Julie Anna, age two and a half and adopted from Hunan province in October 1996. She and her husband, Jim, are anxiously awaiting approval for their second child from China.

Night Terrors and Nightmares

Kathe Henke

Families of the China Moon (Virginia)

Several families in Families of the China Moon have expressed some concern that their children appear to experience "night terrors" more often than children born in the United States. To address this issue, let's talk about nightmares and night terrors, what they are and what to do about them.

First of all, nightmares and night terrors are not uncommon in young children. Nightmares can begin as soon as your child is old enough to realize specific fears or concerns. The nightmare content will reflect your child's level of emotional development. For example, a one-year-old may dream about a recent scary event like falling and hitting her head. A toddler may be more concerned about Mom or Dad leaving her and this may be reflected in her dreams. Dreams and nightmares occur mostly during REM sleep, and most of our REM sleep occurs during the early morning hours. So, the first clue about a nightmare versus a night terror is the timing. Nightmares are more likely to occur toward morning. Children who have nightmares will generally also awaken fully and be able to describe the nightmare. They may be upset and crying, but they will want you to comfort them and hold them. This is the best approach for handling a nightmare. Offer comfort and reassurance that you will not allow anything bad to happen to them. If your child is five or six years old and still has frequent nightmares, then it may be a sign that your child has some significant concern or possibly more serious problems.

Night terrors are different from nightmares in appearance, cause, and best response. Night terrors are actually in the same class as sleep walking. They occur as the body transitions from our deepest sleep to lighter sleep. Because these occur after deep sleep, night terrors more often occur in the early portion of the night. A night terror is a partial awakening and can occur even in infants. In infants, however, it may just look like a simple nighttime crying episode. In slightly older children, the child may cry or moan, sit up, and open their eyes. In more severe cases, the child may scream loudly or run around the room.

It is very important to understand several things about night terrors. First, your child is not awake, and if you do not awaken her, she will fall back to a calm sleep eventually with no recollection of the event. Second, if you try to intervene or awaken your child, you will not only prolong the event but will likely frighten her as she sees your reaction. The best thing to do during a night terror is to be watchful. Make sure that if she is thrashing about or gets out of bed, she cannot hurt herself. Other than that, there is not much else to do.

Discussing the event in the morning may only frighten your child. It should be cautioned that night terrors are not normal developmental events in older children (older than five or six years). In older children they may reflect underlying emotional problems, and you should speak to a professional.

I hope this helps. If your child has any kind of sleep problems or if you have any questions about sleep and making some of those important transitions, I strongly recommend *Solve Your Child's Sleep Problems*, by Richard Ferber, M.D., a pediatric sleep specialist. It has all kinds of helpful information. You can get it in local bookstores.

Kathe Henke is the director of the Sleep Disorder Center of Virginia. Since writing this article, Kathe has been joined with her lovely daughter, Debra.

What About Us?

Missy Shen Ming
FCC-Chicago

Lately, I've been looking at the make-up of our FCC group. Each time we get together, we oooh and aaah at the little ones, we celebrate Chinese traditions, we support waiting families. But there is a group of people who don't seem to get as much attention. Have you noticed them? They are our children's non-Chinese-born siblings. How do they feel about all of this adoption-in-China stuff? Recently I asked several of our children to comment on this subject. Here is what they had to say.

What Was Your Family Like before Adopting a Sibling from China?

Jess Dunn-Reier (14 years old, from Geneva, Illinois, big sister to Malia) said that she found the first question "very humorous." "Our house was always very neat and tidy. Everything was in its place, and there were many little knick-knacks out. Not anymore! As for my feelings, I must admit I was very spoiled! After all, I was the oldest grandchild and the one and only child. I was the star of the family. If I wanted something, it was given to me on the spot. Everything was planned around my schedule."

Pablo Jones (12 years old, Libertyville, Ill., big brother to Tia Ming, Shan Mei, and Benjamin Wu) wrote, "The kitchen table wasn't crowded and neither was the house before they came. The only people I got to play with were my friends around my neighborhood, and when they went home, I got bored."

Kaylin Krashesky (9 years old, Naperville, Ill., big sister to Kiera, who had been home about seven weeks) told me, "My Mom and Dad used to spend more time with me. We used to be able to go places on the spur of the moment."

Joe Bouchard (28 years old, Storrs, Connecticut, big brother to Mei-Mei) said, "Before we adopted Mei-Mei four years ago, we were just a house of adults; no toys around, no one to baby-sit. And it smelled different; no diapers, none of that mushy baby food. I had been an only child for 24 years, so it was kind of interesting to have to think about sharing my Dad with someone else."

Alex Braatz (8 years old, Naperville, Ill., big brother to Elizabeth, who had been home about seven weeks) said, "We used to be able to go somewhere anytime we wanted. I didn't have to share my time with Mom and Dad."

What Is Your Family Like Now?

Jess: "My whole life has now turned upside down! When Malia first came home, everything was great. Little did I know how hard it really was to be a big sister. She took up so much attention. Even though I am 14, I went through my jealous stage. In addition, I now have opened my eyes to prejudice and how ignorant people really can be. My family 'suffers' from what we call 'M.J.S.': Michael Jordan Syndrome. It seems everywhere we go, people look at us funny or just stare. While my parents take it all in stride, at first, it was really hard for me to get used to. The hardest part for me was when people asked about China killing their little girls. I got to a point one time where I just wanted to scream. These strangers think that they know everything. They don't care that my parents have been to China and that I, as a 14-year-old, might know more about it than they do. I have always tried to patiently answer their questions and correct the rumors that they are spreading. After all, they only know what they hear through the media. It just seems that they only want to believe the bad."

Pablo: "The house is crowded except for when my Mom goes out somewhere with the little guys. I also have to baby-sit sometimes. And, with all the chairs in the kitchen, I stub my toe on them a lot. And I don't get bored as often."

Kaylin: "Now, when we go somewhere, we have lots of stuff of Kiera's to bring along. I know they need to spend more time with her right now, but I miss the attention I used to get. She gets more attention when she cries. I'm understanding, though. I love my little sister a lot, and I'm glad we adopted her."

Joe: "Well, since I'm an adult and out of the house now, I don't feel the impact as much. Dad always makes time for me when I need him. He's very good at giving to both of his children. It's so much fun now during the holidays with a little sister around. When I lived with them (until Mei-

Mei was two years old) I had to baby-sit her at least once a week. I had never been around babies before so I just had a talk with her and asked her not to do a poop diaper when I was baby-sitting—and she never did! It was also fun to take her to the mall to go shopping because she's so cute she would attract lots of single girls for me to meet."

Alex: "We can't just go somewhere spontaneously. When we go out to eat, we have to bring lots of stuff for her to eat and bibs and bottles. It's not easy to just pick up and go. It's fun to have a little sister. Mom and Dad have to spend a lot of time with her, but they also spend time just with me. If I get enough of being around so many girls, like at Chinese parties, I just go off by myself for a little while."

What Are the Advantages of Being a Multicultural Family?

Jess: "When we decided to adopt a Chinese baby, we realized that we were not only adopting her, but the whole Chinese culture! I have learned more about China in the past year than I have learned about the United States in the past four years. Before Malia, China just seemed to be a huge, different country with too many people; but I have now realized all the beauty it has to share."

Pablo: "Having Chinese in the family means that you get to celebrate two New Years."

Kaylin: "I always wanted a little sister. It's really interesting to learn more about China." Kaylin traveled with her parents to China to adopt Kiera. Kaylin enjoyed seeing Kiera's hometown and can tell her all about it when she is older.

Joe: "Good to learn more about Chinese culture. I'm glad Mei-Mei is growing up with such an international focus."

Alex: "Just fun learning about China."

What Are the Not-So-Wonderful Aspects?

Jess said that always being stared at as a family gets annoying. "I also have had to deal with a couple of people at school calling Malia a 'chink.' I will never forget the first time it happened. I came home crying and crying because of that. I was so mad I wanted to hit the person, but at the same time, I just wanted to cry. I didn't realize how mean people can be. Malia seems just as American as anyone else to me. My Mom told me that it wasn't going to be the last time, so we talked about ways to deal with the issue. It's so hard for me to accept that though. Now, instead of getting upset and angry, I try to educate the people who say those things. Anyone who makes those comments needs a reality check!"

Pablo: "Some of the bad things are that we go to Chinatown a lot, and I don't really like Chinatown very much. And I also have to lay the table for six people and that gets pretty boring."

Kaylin: "The only bad thing is I worry that people might tease my little sister."

Joe: "Nothing really. The only thing is when really insensitive people ask incredibly stupid questions about my sister, like 'How much did she cost?' or (this is a really good one!) 'Are you going to tell her that she was adopted?'"

Alex: "Nothing bad—except that I don't really like eating Chinese food."

How Has Your Life Changed?

Jess: "I have really had to grow up taking care of my little sister and dealing with all the stares and comments that have been said. I have always been someone who has expressed how I feel about different topics. This has been a *great* topic that I am more than willing to discuss with many uneducated people. In addition, I know that I do not want to have a child until I'm much older, and I certainly don't want to be a teen parent—it's just too hard. My parents keep telling everyone that Malia's been the best investment in preventative birth control for me that they've ever made. My eyes have been opened up so much, in fact, that I have decided that I want to be a social worker and work with adopting families. I want to go over to Asia and help all the children get homes and hopefully try to speed up the adoption process so that more children can come home. Not only children in China, but children in Korea and Vietnam also. It's the least I can do."

Pablo: "Just more people in my family."

Kaylin: "Not as much time with my parents; sometimes I want more attention from them and it makes me mad. But I understand and I'm coping OK. I'm learning how to share Kiera with Mom and Dad."

Joe: "Just more fun around the house. She adds so much positive excitement."

Alex: "She cries and makes a little noise, but it's not too bad."

What Advice Would You Give Another Child?

Jess: "Having a multicultural family has been really a great experience. It's really scary having your parents way across the world for two weeks, but the end results are awesome. You really become more aware of different cultures and peoples' differences. Of course there are the ups and downs of the experience, but the ups outweigh the downs by far! Malia has probably been the best thing that has ever happened to me!"

Pablo: "Some advice I would give to other kids who are going to have Chinese kids in the family is to think that they are just part of the family even though they are adopted. I like having them in the family because they're so cute."

Kaylin: "If you're an only child, start getting used to having to share Mom and Dad before the little one arrives. I would definitely recommend it. Also, watch out for when the baby is in jet lag when you come home from China—they can be pretty grumpy!"

Joe: "Learn a lot about China, its people and customs so that you can talk to your sister or brother about their home country. Always show respect for China around the house. And coach your friends on the right adoption language to use—like 'birth parent' not 'real parent' and not to make racially charged jokes."

Alex: "Don't be too scared when your Mom and Dad are in China to get the baby. It's pretty scary knowing they are so far away and you can't really talk to them."

Thank you to each of the young people who shared their thoughts and feelings with all of us. The next time we are all together, pay close attention to this special group of our children. They are terrific older brothers and sisters. They are terrific people!

Missy Shen Ming, the author of *For Mei-Mei: A Love Story of Four Parents and Their Child,* is the pen name of Missy Bouchard, who resides in Maple Grove, Minnesota, and Longwood, Florida. The Bouchards took on Chinese middle names, given to them by Chinese friends, after they adopted Mei-Mei.

Health and
Development

Handle the difficult while it is still easy.
Cultivate the great while it is still small.

Laozi (trans. Tolbert McCarroll)

An Open Letter to Pediatricians on Medical Issues Relating to Adoption from China

Deborah Borchers, M.D.
FCC–Greater Cincinnati

Dear Doctor:

In June 1994 I returned from China with my daughter Anna, who was then 19 months old. I again traveled to China in April 1996 to adopt my second child, Sara, then 5 months old. During that trip I was fortunate to visit a pediatric children's hospital. Both trips were made viewing China and its medical care delivery system through the eyes of both a mother and a pediatrician. It is my wish to communicate to you the conditions from which your future patient may come.

Both Anna and Sara were from orphanages in remote towns. There were about 30 children in Anna's orphanage, most of whom received little stimulation. I saw very few toys, and there were 4 to 6 children in each large, table-sized bed. The children were bundled warmly despite outside conditions in June of 80-plus degrees Fahrenheit. In Sara's orphanage and in the children's hospital there was no central heat, and the outside temperatures were 40 to 50 degrees. Many of the children had rashes, and lice were evident. Despite the reports in the media, however, it was obvious that the caretakers cared for the children in very loving ways, meeting their basic needs of warmth, food, and changing diapers.

I examined all four of the children from Anna's orphanage after arrival in the hotel. Three of the four had ear infections, all had clear rhinorrhea, all had some degree of scabies and lice, and one had extensive eczema. The children from Sara's orphanage did not have the lice and scabies, but ear infections, impetigo, and skin infections were rampant. All of the children showed significant improvement with "Western medications" not obtainable in China, including Elimite, Nix, hydrocortisone cream, and antibiotics as I prescribed. These children had been seen by a local physician only because they were being adopted by Americans. Because we had the medications appropriate for the treatment of their medical problems, they improved rapidly, and the adults in the party did not contract the scabies.

While in Guangzhou both times I also examined other children from other orphanages. Some of these children also had scabies, and quite a few had impetiginized areas on the back of their scalp. One child had a perforated eardrum due to a delay in starting antibiotics after three days of a fever. One family had taken their child to a Chinese physician, and a Chinese medicine (one not used in this country) was prescribed. The child worsened, and we were also able to treat appropriately once I examined her and changed courses. It was evident that these families, all of whom were first-time parents, had many medical issues regarding their child's health, but they were unable to appropriately address them.

Since my journeys, two families in my local area have had children that became quite ill prior to their journey home. One had seizures with fever due to pneumonia, and the other had pneumonia. Both were hospitalized at Chinese hospitals. The mothers said that the hospitals were quite antiquated by our standards, and the decision to treat with antibiotics was a decision reviewed each day. Thus, these children received only three days of medication for problems routinely treated in our country for ten days. Fortunately for one child, a physician also adopting a child was able to counsel the mother to continue appropriate medications and prevent rehospitalization. Both mothers were concerned that the children would actually contract illnesses from their hospitalization, as they were not able to be reassured that sterile needles and technique, as well as blood and body fluid precautions, were being used.

My visit to a children's hospital revealed doctors trained in Western medicine, but very limited in the technology and ability to provide care as we know it in this country. IVs were not as sterile as they are here, and the trauma room had very limited equipment and lighting. Even the required physical examination done on all adoptees before obtaining the visa necessary for entrance into the U.S. was quite limited in its scope, with no blood work for HIV, hepatitis B, or syphilis, no PPD, and no monitoring for stool infections. Some children had received immunizations, but there was no guarantee that the vaccines had been stored or administered properly. Thus, there were questions as to their efficacy.

It was evident to me while in China that medical care is much different from here in the States. There was *no* access to physicians who could diagnose otitis media (headlamps were used for the immigration physical, and otoscopes were simply not available), and the style of medicine practiced there varied from our accepted norms.

For the sake of your future patient, please consider setting up criteria which may be used by a family for starting antibiotics that you allow the family to take with them to China. These may include three days of a fever less than 103 degrees, irritability with fever, pulling ears, thick rhinorrhea, or other symptoms you outline. If you are hesitant, then think about giving the family phone numbers to call you from China to discuss the child's symptoms and see if antibiotics are necessary. Giving the family information (and perhaps even a picture if available) about scabies and a prescription for Elimite should also be considered, given the ease with which skin mites spread and the low toxicity of that medication.

The adoption of a child is a very special time for a new family, and the transition is made worse by having a sick child for whom the family cannot obtain adequate medical treatment. Many of these families have already dealt with the issues of infertility and disrupted adoptions. Their helplessness in feeding, sleeping, and emotional concerns will only worsen their own feelings of inadequacy if they are unable to help their child through an illness and to adjust to her new life.

As a physician I continue to be quite concerned about the overuse of antibiotics, and I rarely phone in medications, particularly for patients who have not been examined. The adoption of a child from China (or other third world countries, for that matter) is one instance where an adequate examination of the child may not be possible for one to two weeks. Most families will be anxious to see you upon their return to fully evaluate all of their child's medical needs with appropriate treatment. Making it clear to the family that you do not intend to phone in medications in the future will help them to understand that this episode is the exception, not the rule. Please weigh your hesitancy to prescribe medications for a child you have not yet seen with the risks encountered in a delay in obtaining appropriate medical care.

117
An Open Letter to Pediatricians on Medical Issues
Relating to Adoption from China

Please contact me if you have any questions about this information or the medical conditions of children adopted from China or other countries.

Sincerely yours,

Deborah A. Borchers, M.D., F.A.A.P.
Eastgate Pediatric Center
Cincinnati, Ohio
(513) 753-2820
e-mail: dborchers@pol.net

This article has been updated to include the current recommendations of the International Adoption Clinic at the University of Minnesota.

Medical Items to Take to China for Your Child

Deborah Borchers, M.D.
FCC—Greater Cincinnati

It is helpful to take at least a ten-day supply of antibiotics. Several do not need refrigeration, namely, Cefzil, Lorabid, Suprax, and Trimethoprim-Sulfa (also known as Bactrim or Septra). My personal preference is Cefzil, as it covers ear infections, skin infections, and pneumonia. With a prescription, the dry powder of any of these may be obtained from a pharmacist. Upon request the pharmacist will also put the correct amount of sterile water in a separate bottle to mix with the powder. Pharmacists often state that this must be refrigerated, but according to the manufacturer this is not necessary.

Ask your doctor to write down the dosage range based on weights. (You may be able to estimate your daughter's present weight by looking at growth charts and plotting known weights, then using the curve to estimate up.) Optimally antibiotics should not be used without an examination by a physician. Chinese physicians do not look in children's ears the same way that Western physicians do, so you should discuss conditions with your physician that are acceptable for you to start antibiotics without an exam by an M.D. Such symptoms may include a child with a fever for three days, a child with persistent thick discharge from the nose, or an irritable child who is pulling her ear.

If your doctor is reluctant to give antibiotics, ask if an arrangement can be made for you to contact her or him at home or office (remember the time difference!) to discuss if antibiotics are needed. Often there are physicians traveling with other adoption agencies to adopt children, so an exam by a U.S. physician *may* be possible. They will not have access to medications as they do in the States, so your physician's assistance in supplying the prescription will expedite care for your child.

A syringe calibrated in cc or ml (identical) is needed to mix and give antibiotics. If you do not have water premeasured in a separate bottle, you may safely use the boiled water provided in the rooms once it has cooled down. That water may also be used for making the baby's bottles. If your child has feeding problems and will not suck on her bottle, the syringe may be used to slowly feed your child fluids and prevent dehydration.

Nystatin cream (prescription) or Lotrimin cream (over the counter, in the athlete's foot treatment area) may be used for diaper rashes that are red and weepy, often caused by yeast infections. These often occur when children are on antibiotics.

Desitin cream, Daily Care cream, Balmex, or A & D Ointment are useful in small amounts for irritant diaper rashes. You do not need to put any medication on your child's bottom if there is no rash. Check with your child's doctor or nurse practitioner to see if he or she recommends the routine use of baby powder—many do not.

Elimite cream is a prescription medication used to treat scabies. This condition, caused by a skin mite (and highly contagious) is characterized by small red bumps that are very itchy. Consider this diagnosis if all (or most) of the children in the orphanage have a rash, especially on their faces, heads, hands, or feet. Scabies should be diagnosed by a doctor if possible. Apply the cream from head to toe everywhere (not just where there is a rash). Leave it on for 8 to 12 hours, then bathe. All bedding and clothing should be washed after treatment. If your daughter has scabies, also wash or dry clean your clothing that came into contact with her. You may wish to put her clothing from the orphanage into a plastic bag or two, and wash them in hot water when you get home.

Nix cream rinse is the best (and unfortunately the most expensive) treatment for head lice. There are now generic versions of Nix (permethin 1%) available in many discount stores for a lesser cost. Lice are little hopping bugs about an eighth of an inch long. Often you can only see the nits, the cases of the eggs, which are concentrated behind the ears and at the hairline. Nix is safe for all children. After washing the hair you put on the Nix for ten minutes (just as you would a cream rinse), and then rinse the hair. There is a comb enclosed. You can use it to comb out the nits. Often they must also be removed by hand-picking them out. Once you have treated for lice, your child is no longer contagious, even if nits still remain. Some physicians now recommend re-treating in one to two weeks to make sure that the lice are gone.

Baby shampoo is useful for washing your child's hair, as well as to treat mild cases of cradle cap. At the start of your daughter's bath, put a small amount of the shampoo directly on the area of dried, crusty scalp, which is most commonly over the soft spot on the top of the head. Wash her as usual, then work in the shampoo with a damp washcloth to loosen the scaly area. Using the rough side of the washcloth will provide the necessary friction to loosen the dried, crusty area, but if that doesn't work after a day or two, use a moist toothbrush (often provided in hotel rooms in China). More severe cases may need to be addressed by your child's doctor upon returning from China, as fungal infections such as ringworm of the scalp will be less responsive to this treatment.

Acetaminophen drops or syrup (best known as Tylenol, but generics are just as good) is helpful if your child is irritable or running a fever more than 101 degrees. The dose is 40 mg (½ dropperful of the infant drops or ¼ teaspoon of the children's syrup) for a child under 12 pounds, 80 mg for a child 13–17 pounds, and 120 mg for a child 18–23 pounds. You can estimate weight from kilograms to pounds by multiplying kilograms by 2.2. Your physician may have a dosage chart for acetaminophen to help you be more accurate with the dosage for your child.

Take a rectal thermometer, either glass or digital. Ear thermometers are convenient (and expensive), but many doctors question their accuracy when used by inexperienced caretakers or on younger children. To take a temperature, lubricate the rectal thermometer with Vaseline and insert less than one inch into the rectum while your child is held over your knees. A glass thermometer should be held in place for five minutes, a digital until it beeps. If your child has a fever (usually defined as a rectal temperature more than 101 degrees), it lets you know that you should watch your child for other signs of infection. What is also important when your child has a fever is the way that your child feeds, sleeps, and interacts with you and the environment. A low-grade fever without other symptoms is not harmful. If your child has a temperature of more than 104 degrees, the fever itself is not dangerous, but you may wish to seek medical care to evaluate the reason for the fever, particularly if your child is not responding normally or is acting ill. With any fever your child will require an increase in her fluid intake to prevent dehydration.

Any over-the-counter cough and cold medicines are helpful if those symptoms are present. Many children have some runny nose and a dry cough after leaving the orphanage. Most doctors only recommend treating these symptoms if they interfere with sleeping or eating. Often children with nasal congestion will "feel" like the congestion is "in their chest." This is merely the sound of the nasal congestion being transmitted into the chest cavity and is not necessarily a sign of bronchitis or pneumonia. You should be concerned about these illnesses if your child's breathing is labored and fast (more than 10 to 15 times in 15 seconds of counting). Medical consultation should be obtained if those symptoms are present, especially with a fever of more than 101 degrees. A safe dose of cold/cough medicines for a child over six months old is one-quarter of the dose recommended on the bottle for a six-year-old child. Consult with your doctor before leaving for China to see if he or she recommends these medicines for children younger than six months old.

Saline nose drops (such as Ocean, Nasal, or Ayr) and a small ear (not nose) syringe are also quite useful for nasal congestion. They may be safely used in children of any age. Put one drop into each nostril with a dropper before each feed or prior to sleeping, then suction the nose once (not repeatedly) with the ear syringe. You do not have to obtain mucus when suctioning for these to help.

Hydrocortisone 1% cream may be useful for rashes due to bug bites or irritation from new clothing or soaps. This cream may be used for any rash that remains after treating scabies or for rashes with very dry skin. Do not use it with any rash that looks infected, namely, with blisters, pus, or significant redness, as it may worsen infections.

Benadryl (generic name, Diphenhydramine) is an antihistamine with the most potent side-effect being sedation. It is safe to use ¼ to ½ teaspoon every six hours on the flight home if your child is inconsolable. Be warned, however, that some children may become more irritable with Benadryl. It is suggested that you try Benadryl some afternoon before you leave China to see if it will have this undesirable effect on your child.

Babylax or glycerin suppositories are useful to have in the event that your child has constipation. Constipation is usually defined as hard, infrequent bowel movements (less than one every two or three days). Normal bowel movements for infants are soft and mushy (usually requiring two to three baby wipes to clean up). Some children have problems with constipation in the change to different baby formulas. The suppository or Babylax should be put in only about 1 to 2 inches using your finger. Do not push further into the rectum if resistance is met. If your child has severe abdominal pain with drawing up of the legs, vomiting, or bloody bowel movements (more than just a small streak of blood), obtain medical care IMMEDIATELY. It may also be helpful to take one or two small cans of apple juice to help keep your child's stools loose if a suppository is needed. Ask your pediatrician about her/his recommendation, but a good mix is 1 ounce of juice to 1 to 2 ounces of water, given once a day.

Pedialyte or KaoLectrolyte is a helpful formula substitute to use in the event of diarrhea, defined as frequent (more than two or three) water-loss bowel movements. Pedialyte comes premixed; KaoLectrolyte is a new formulation that comes in premeasured powder packets, takes up less luggage room, and is cheaper. If unavailable in your home stores, you can take rice cereal and salt to make up a substitute for these water-based solutions. Use 2 cups of water, add ¼ teaspoon table salt (the amount of salt in two packets from your favorite fast food place), and dissolve the salt into the water. Gradually add ½ to 1 cup infant rice cereal to the water until the mixture is as thick as is drinkable. Mix well. Give this solution or the Pedialyte or the KaoLectrolyte solution to your child after each diarrhea-like stool, giving infants a half cup and older children a full cup. The rice cereal solution should be discarded after six to eight hours. If your child is vomiting, offer the mixture in amounts of 1 teaspoon or less. If your child fails to urinate, a medical evaluation is needed.

This information—revised May 8, 1998, to include the current recommendations of the International Adoption Clinic at the University of Minnesota—was written by Deborah Borchers, M.D., a general pediatrician in Cincinnati, Ohio, and the mother of two daughters adopted from China. It is not intended to be a substitute for medical care if there are any concerns about your child's health. Dr. Borchers strongly recommends that all families traveling to China or other countries schedule an appointment with their child's physician or nurse practitioner prior to traveling to review these recommendations, as well as others they might have. If you have any questions about these recommendations or the medical care situation in China, please feel free to contact Dr. Borchers for more information and assistance. She can be reached at Eastgate Pediatric Center, (513) 753-2820; at home, (606) 331-7026; or via e-mail, dborchers@pol.net.

The U.S. Visa
Medical Examination

Jerri Ann Jenista, M.D.
FCC–New York

"The visa medical examination said she was normal!"

"If hepatitis B is a contagious disease, why doesn't the U.S. Embassy require a test for it before they give visa approval?"

"My child doesn't need any tests now that he has arrived home because he was already checked for his visa."

All of these statements show common misconceptions about one of the most poorly understood aspects of international adoption. For parents who travel, the visa examination is just the last hurdle of the obstacle course that will finally allow them to leave with their new child. For children who are escorted, parents may not be aware that a medical examination was ever a part of the visa process, since no paperwork must be done for it in the U.S.

Why a medical examination for a visa at all? The visa exam has only two purposes: to protect the public health of the citizens of the U.S. and to exclude mentally or morally defective persons from the U.S. who might become public charges. In other words, the Public Health Service wants to protect the people who already live in the U.S. from two threats: exposure to a contagious disease and the burden of supporting persons who might never become law-abiding, self-supporting members of our society. If you think about these guidelines, you will realize that the concern is not for the health of the immigrant, it is for the health of the people already in the U.S. The U.S. government has no particular interest in assuring the well-being of people who are not citizens of this country. Thus, it does not undertake to determine that all persons applying for a permanent residency visa are healthy or well. It only cares that those persons are not threats to the safety and well-being of its own citizens. Thus, a visa medical examination does not assure an adoptive parent that his child is physically, emotionally, or developmentally normal.

What does the law require in a visa medical examination? Any person applying for a permanent residency visa (students, tourists, and other temporary visitors are exempt) must undergo a physical examination by a medical officer approved by the U.S. embassy or consulate. The examination must look for these excludable conditions: sexually transmitted diseases including chancroid, gonorrhea, granuloma inguinale, lymphogranuloma venereum, and syphilis; active leprosy; HIV infection; active tuberculosis; mental retardation, insanity, narcotic or alcohol addiction, or sexual deviation; serious or permanent physical defects, diseases, or disabilities.

In addition, persons 15 years and over must have blood tests for syphilis and HIV infection and a chest x-ray looking for signs of tuberculosis. Children under 15 are not required to have these tests unless the examining physician feels the history or physical examination indicates a possibility of exposure. Notice that many contagious diseases such as hepatitis B, chicken pox, measles, intestinal parasites, and malaria are not on this list. They are missing because either the conditions are already very common in the U.S., they are not spread by casual physical contact, or the conditions needed to spread the diseases are not found or are rare in the U.S. (So why is HIV on the list? For purely political reasons, of course.)

As of 1997, an additional requirement for immigrants is documentation of complete immunizations to U.S. standards. Adopted children under 10 years of age applying for an orphan visa are exempt from this rule. Adopted children age 10 and older must have proof of disease or immunization for polio, tetanus, diphtheria, measles, mumps, rubella, hepatitis B, hemophilus influenza type B, varicella, pneumococcus, and influenza. Exemptions are granted if the vaccine is not available or is contraindicated by age, season, or certain medical conditions. Religious or philosophical exemptions may be granted through a special waiver process that takes several weeks.

What do these regulations mean for the internationally adopted child? Most children will have a brief physical examination including a medical history (if there is any information to be obtained). If the child does not have any obvious abnormalities and there is no reason to particularly suspect one of the listed infectious diseases, no other tests or examinations will be required. The officer will fill out the medical form, which is then sealed into an envelope to be delivered to the U.S. embassy. There, after all other documents have been approved, the medical examination is reviewed and the visa usually granted. The actual medical report goes into a sealed packet which is left with the immigration officer at the point of entry into the U.S. Thus, if the parents are not present at the visa examination, they are likely never to receive the results of that examination and may not realize that it ever took place.

What if the examining physician feels there is a problem? He may order any tests that he wishes to rule out any of the conditions on the above list. Although these are usually as simple as a syphilis blood test, he may request psychological or IQ testing if he thinks it is necessary. In some areas of the world, certain tests are done routinely, regardless of the condition of the child. Thus, you will almost always find that the officer will require syphilis testing in infants in Latin America or HIV testing in children in Haiti or Uganda. The parents cannot protest the request for the test. The officer will just give an unfavorable medical report, and the visa will be denied.

The parents can request extra testing themselves; they are paying for the examination. Such testing may not be readily available, may not be accurate, and almost certainly will delay the granting of the visa. However, in some circumstances this is the only reasonable approach, as in HIV testing in Romania. Obvious conditions such as a missing limb, a cleft palate, or a known disability such as epilepsy, thalassemia, or cerebral palsy will often merely be noted on the examination report without any further evaluation as to the severity or repairability of the condition. The quality of these kinds of notes is extremely variable. In Seoul, which has granted more orphan visas than any other office in the world, even simple birth marks or hernias will be listed. In other offices which see few children or which frequently process children in very poor nutritional or developmental condition, only severely disabling conditions will be noted. Thus, a parent cannot rely on the visa examination as an absolute assurance that the child does not have anything on the list of excludable conditions. The quality of the exam depends almost entirely on the experience and thoroughness of the person performing it.

What if the examining officer issues an unfavorable report, that is, he finds a condition on the excludable list? Parents can appeal almost any decision, following certain courses of action. If the child has active tuberculosis or another untreated infectious disease, the condition can be reclassified after the child has begun treatment. If the condition is a mental or physical disability, the orphan visa officer may interview the parents, if they are present, to assure himself that they realize the extent of the condition and that they are capable of caring for the child. However, for most severe disabling conditions and for HIV infection, the parents will have to undertake a "waiver process." To obtain a waiver, the embassy or consulate forwards the visa medical report and any supporting evaluations or tests to the Centers for Disease Control and Prevention (CDC) in Atlanta. There, the Office of Quarantine contacts the family who must then provide the following:

An affidavit explaining that they understand the extent and severity of the condition and giving a compelling reason to allow the child to enter the U.S. (Adoption is considered compelling for most children!)

Proof that they have adequate financial resources to care for the child. This may include proof of health insurance and sometimes even an advance approval from the insurance company guaranteeing that the child's condition will be covered.

An affidavit from a physician stating that he will provide care to the child after arrival in the U.S.

This information is forwarded back to the CDC, where a panel of physicians reviews the material and makes a determination that the child will or will not likely be a threat to the health of others or become a public charge. This determination is then sent back to the embassy or consulate. Only then, the material is again reviewed and, if all appears appropriate, an orphan visa granted. The waiver process typically takes three to six months to complete; however, it can be accomplished in as short a time as a week if the medical condition is life-threatening or there is some other compelling reason to move quickly. Most waivers applied for by adoptive parents are approved, probably because the parents have already had plenty of opportunity to review the child's condition and their own financial resources.

General questions about the medical visa examination can be answered by any INS office or the CDC. Specific questions about a particular child or about local requirements are best answered by the embassy or consulate where the visa will be obtained. The best advice to keep in mind is this: The visa exam is just another bureaucratic step in the immigration process. Parents should not depend on it for any medically valuable information. If there are concerns about a particular child, ask questions of the agency or lawyer or get a second medical opinion. Visa approval provides no guarantees of the health of your child.

Jerri Ann Jenista, M.D. (551 Second St., Ann Arbor, Michigan 48103, tel: 734-668-0419), is a pediatrician specializing in pediatric infectious diseases and the medical problems of adoptees and immigrants. She is the mother of five children adopted from India.

Medical Tests to Be Done upon Return Home from China

Deborah Borchers, M.D.
FCC–Greater Cincinnati

It is suggested that you make an appointment with your pediatrician, family practitioner, or nurse practitioner within one to two weeks after your arrival home from China. This will allow you to have your child examined for any contagious illnesses and evaluated for any conditions that need additional medical referrals (chronic problems) and will allow your child's physician to review your child's immunization status.

Some physicians may see your child, in her clean, middle-class attire, and tell you that testing is not necessary. This is not true. Children adopted from other countries may have any or all of the following illnesses with absolutely no symptoms, namely, no cough for TB, no diarrhea for parasites, no jaundice for hepatitis B, and no growth failure for thyroid dysfunction. Please ask your physician to look at your child as if he/she were with birth parents in native attire in the country of birth. Most physicians would not balk at evaluating for these medical problems in this situation.

A good reference for your child's physician is a book that should be on the desk of all pediatricians, the *Red Book*, a publication of the American Academy of Pediatrics. This book has a chapter which details the testing for all children who have been adopted from other countries, particularly with reference to infectious diseases. All of the tests listed here are in this book, as well as others now recommended by the International Adoption Clinic in Minnesota. Since medicine is an evolving science, new recommendations for evaluations may be forthcoming even after the publication of this article.

Recommended Blood, Urine, and Screening Tests

Your child should have several blood tests after she arrives home. These will help to evaluate for medical conditions that have been seen in internationally adopted children.

A hepatitis B profile is needed to evaluate your child for acute or chronic hepatitis B. This should include the hepatitis B surface antigen, hepatitis B core antibody, and hepatitis B surface antibody (HBsAg, anti-HBc, and anti-HBs). These basic tests will show if your child has hepatitis B, has been exposed or has had the vaccine, or is a carrier of the disease. If they are positive, your doctor may recommend further testing to delineate the extent of the illness. If you have a question about the interpretation of the testing, contact the Hepatitis B Coalition (612-647-9009) or Hepatitis B Foundation (215-489-4900) for more information. Since the incubation period of this illness is three to six months, it is recommended that your child be retested six months after his/her arrival home to reassure you that s/he does not have this illness. It is necessary to do all of the tests listed above (and not just the hepatitis B surface antigen, commonly done by most doctors as a screen), as up to 60 percent of children with hepatitis B may be missed with only doing the usual blood screen. All children with hepatitis B infection should also be examined for hepatitis D. In addition, all children with either acute or chronic hepatitis B infections should be referred to a pediatric liver or infectious diseases specialist for long-term care.

Hepatitis C has also been seen in some Chinese adoptees, and the International Adoption Clinic at the University of Minnesota recommends that all children born in China be screened for this virus infection.

HIV testing by ELISA for HIV-1 and HIV-2 is recommended for all children. This illness, although rare in China at present, is recommended for parental peace of mind and for early identification of HIV. If your child is less than 18 months of age, it is recommended that she also have an HIV PCR if the HIV ELISA is positive. This will identify any false positives (giving the diagnosis of HIV because of maternal antibody being present). Even though HIV still has a low incidence in Chinese adoptees, it is now recommended that this test be repeated six months after the child's arrival in the U.S.

A stool examination for ova and parasites, giardia antigen, and bacterial infections is recommended for all international adoptees, particularly those with diarrhea. You will need to contact the laboratory that will process the stool specimen to see if special handling instructions are necessary with collecting this specimen. Children living in impoverished orphanages are at a higher risk, as are children who are significantly malnourished. It is not necessary for your child to have diarrhea for her to have illnesses diagnosed by these tests. In asymptomatic children, a single stool examination will identify 85 percent of infected children. Some physicians will recommend that three specimens be obtained, particularly if your child has diarrhea. These need to be collected 24 to 72 hours apart. If a parasite is found, it is recommended that the stool examination be repeated after treatment. Some parasite infections found in international adoptees will resolve without any treatment, so do not be alarmed if your child's physician does not recommend medication.

A complete blood count to check for anemia is recommended. A hemoglobin electrophoresis is also recommended for children of Chinese descent to identify thalassemia, a blood condition similar to sickle-cell anemia, that has been seen in some Chinese adoptees. It is also recommended that all children have lead levels tested, as several international adoptees have had elevated lead levels leading to anemia. Behaviors associated with lead poisoning include pica (eating dirt and other nonfood items) and irritability.

A blood test for syphilis (usually an RPR or VDRL) is recommended to evaluate the child for syphilis, likely passed to the child from his/her birth mother. If this test is positive, further testing is recommended. A spinal tap to check for neuro-syphilis, which could cause developmental problems, may also be recommended. If your child has a medical history that states "syphilis treated in child," make sure that the child has a full evaluation anyway and do not assume that the treatment was adequate.

A screen for hypothyroidism (at least a TSH) is recommended specifically for children adopted from China. Low thyroid disorders have been diagnosed in a significant number of international adoptees, and the reason is not yet known. Symptoms may include a low resting heart rate, fatigue, and being overweight (gaining weight easily). Most birth children born in the U.S. are screened for this disorder at birth.

A PPD test should be placed on your child's arm to screen her for tuberculosis. Many children born in China have received a vaccine called the BCG. This vaccine is supposed to protect against tuberculosis, and the children may have some reaction to the PPD after receiving this vaccine. However, it is still strongly recommended that *all* international immigrants be screened for exposure to tuberculosis, regardless of whether they have received the vaccine. The only exception to this is if the vaccine scar (similar to the old smallpox scars) appears to be freshly healing. In this case, the PPD test should be done at one year of age. This test can be done on children safely as young as five or six months. It should be read in 48 to 72 hours by a health care professional, not just a parent. According to experts at the University of Minnesota, a positive result is one where the injected area is raised above the skin more than one centimeter. This interpretation of the test is different from that of children born in this country, who are not considered to be children at high risk (as are children born in China).

A dipstick urinalysis should be done on a specimen of your child's urine to evaluate for any blood, protein, or infection in your child's bladder.

Other Recommended Evaluations

In addition to blood and urine testing, it is strongly recommended that your child have other medical screens that may yield diagnoses difficult to make in these children.

A hearing screen by audiometry or BSER (terms your doctor will understand) is recommended for all children being adopted from other countries. In many countries (China included), the health care for these children is marginal. Many children have had ear infections diagnosed after arrival in the United States, and it is assumed that these children may have previously had (undiagnosed) infections while still in their orphanage. Early intervention with children with hearing impairment is necessary to ensure proper language development and hearing augmentation, so it is helpful to have this screen done soon after arrival home (within one to two months). Better results are obtained if all ear infections have cleared (if this is possible).

Likewise, a vision screen and evaluation by an ophthalmologist is recommended. Crossed eyes are a common problem in institutionalized children. In China there is no knowledge of birth history, so it is not known if the birth mother had any infections that could compromise the child's vision long term. These infections could include toxoplasmosis (a parasite infection often passed through cat feces) and rubella (German measles). Similarly, a family history of eye problems is not known, so the ophthalmologist should screen for any hereditary eye problems.

A developmental screen is recommended to evaluate your child's developmental level at the time of her arrival home. In some states this information may be useful in helping your family to qualify for a special-needs adoption subsidy. This can be done by your physician or nurse through a test known as the Denver Developmental Screening Test (DDST), easily administered in the doctor's office, or through agencies in your county. These resources, through your local county Board of Mental Retardation and Developmental Disabilities, include a program known as Early Intervention. This program is available (free of charge) to all children less than three years old who have developmental concerns. Despite the name, a referral to this program does not mean that your child is retarded. In most parts of the country, a parent can initiate the referral. Most children born in China qualify for at least some services by being at risk, namely, by being previously institutionalized in an orphanage. The therapists in the program will help you help your child by working with your child in your home or in a school setting. Referrals may be made at any time you have a concern about your child's development, not necessarily at the time of his/her arrival home.

Immunizations

Some children in China will have received immunizations prior to their adoption. Others may receive immunizations at the time of their medical evaluation for their U.S. visa. Generally, the timing falls into one of three categories:

1. Immunizations given to children while in orphanages in China should be repeated. Questions have been raised about whether the vaccines are stored and administered properly, as well as whether the records are even accurate. Blood testing has been done on children in institutional care in Eastern Europe, and despite records that reflected a full set of immunizations, children were often found not to have full antibody protection against the diseases for which they had been immunized. If your child received three or more DTP vaccines, then s/he should have antibody to those illnesses. Your physician can order a simple blood test to see if your child is immune to diphtheria and tetanus, indicating that only booster shots of those immunizations are needed. Most of the vaccines used these days have such low side effects that it is safe to repeat them, even if your child received the vaccines overseas. The one exception to this is the DTP, as the diphtheria and tetanus portions should be limited to four vaccines by the age of four. Again, if antibody testing is done, this will show if the DTP vaccines were actually given or were effective. All live virus vaccines, such as the MMR (measles, mumps, rubella or German measles) and chicken pox vaccine should be repeated. Blood testing should also include testing for the hepatitis B antibody (as mentioned earlier), as this will show if your child has antibody to hepatitis B. Even if your child has antibody to hepatitis B after two shots, s/he should be given the third in this series to ensure life-long immunity. If s/he

has antibody believed to have been acquired from the birth mother, then the hepatitis B immunization is not necessary.

2. Immunizations given to children in foster homes are thought to be more reliable, and probably do not need to be repeated. Again, it is completely safe to repeat all vaccines if you desire with no risk to your child.

3. Immunizations given to children at the time of the medical evaluation for the visa are considered to be the safest and most reliable of the vaccines. The record needs to be presented to your doctor so that s/he can then time the administration of future vaccines using that information.

Families adopting children from China should feel free to share these recommendations with their child's physician. The information is obtained from the *Red Book* (a resource book published by the American Academy of Pediatrics), the physicians at the International Adoption Clinic at the University of Minnesota Hospital and Clinic (800-688-5252), and *Adoption Medical News,* a medical newsletter for professionals providing care for children who have been adopted. This article was revised August 22, 1998, to include the current recommendations of the International Adoption Clinic at the University of Minnesota. Deborah Borchers, M.D., is a pediatrician in general pediatric practice at the Eastgate Pediatric Center, Cincinnati, Ohio, (513) 753-2820; home: (606) 331-7026; e-mail: dborchers@pol.net.

Hepatitis B

No Guarantee

Jerri Ann Jenista, M.D., Dana E. Johnson, M.D.,
Laurie C. Miller, M.D., Dennis L. Murray, M.D.
FCC—New York

Hepatitis B is the most prevalent chronic virus infection worldwide, affecting an estimated 800 million people. The disease is found globally, with the highest rates in Asia and Africa and lower rates in the Americas. Local conditions, however, may lead to a high rate of infection in a particular region or institution.

Although most people with hepatitis B will never show any ill effects of the disease, a significant proportion will go on to develop serious complications including cirrhosis, liver failure, cancer, or death. Treatment but not cure is available for some affected persons. Prevention by immunization is a major public initiative in many countries around the world.

Chronic hepatitis B infection is the most common serious infectious disease affecting children adopted internationally. Approximately 5 percent of all such adoptees to the United States have active infection at the time of arrival. A somewhat higher percentage of children show evidence of immunity from past infection or from immunization. Exposure to hepatitis B is found in children of all ages and from all countries. Since the blood tests for hepatitis B are simple to perform, relatively inexpensive, and available in most areas of the world, adoptive parents may, quite reasonably, ask that their prospective child be screened for this infection. Many parents are dismayed to discover, however, that such pre-adoptive screening may not answer their concerns.

1. Hepatitis B screening tests (usually hepatitis B surface antigen or HBsAg) done in the countries from which most adopted children arrive are frequently unreliable. Often there is a lack of appropriate reagents, clean equipment, or adequate training in the laboratory.

Even if the test is run under good conditions, there may be difficulties with the actual blood sample itself. Common problems include mislabeled specimens, blood contaminated by unclean collection tubes, and cross-contamination in the laboratory from other positive specimens. Occasionally, no blood or an inadequate amount was drawn from the child to run the tests supposedly done. Unfortunately, there is no accurate way to predict for any individual child whether or not the reported result is correct.

2. Reported results are frequently uninterpretable. Sometimes the wrong test has been done. The result may be interpreted incorrectly, indicating that the child is immune when he is infected or vice versa. The result may be translated or reported in such a way that it is unintelligible. Occasionally, reported results are entirely fraudulent.

3. Drawing blood for the test may actually expose the child to hepatitis B or other blood-borne infections. Re-use of needles is very common in other countries, especially when there are limited resources. Sterilization of needles can be particularly difficult when hepatitis B is involved.

4. The test may be run too soon to indicate the child's infection status. Since the incubation (the time from exposure until disease) can be as long as six months for hepatitis B, it is possible that a child tests negative when he actually has incubating infection. This is particularly a problem for infants less than three months of age with infection acquired from mother-to-baby near birth. Older children may have been exposed through a medical procedure, transfusion, or other blood contact.

5. Some children will accurately test negative before adoption but will show positive results after arrival in the adoptive home. As long as the child lives under orphanage, institutional, or other nonoptimal conditions, he remains at risk for hepatitis B. So, until that child is at least six months from the last possible exposure to hepatitis B, a parent cannot be absolutely assured that the child does not have infection. Although most hepatitis B infections are detected at the arrival evaluation, there are a few children in whom infection is not found until months after adoptive placement.

6. Testing for hepatitis B raises the cost of and may delay adoption. Although the screening test may not be expensive, there are many other hidden costs including personnel time to get the child, draw the blood, transport the specimen, and collect, translate, and relay

the results. All of these steps cost money and take time. If the result is uninterpretable or unexpected, more time is lost in repeating the testing or counseling all the parties involved.

7. Test results may label some children as "unadoptable." Although many families are willing to adopt children with unknown hepatitis B status or even known chronic infection, adoption agencies and authorities in other countries may feel that such children should not be placed for adoption. Some children will incorrectly be labeled as infected based on inaccurate laboratory tests, and others will be denied the opportunity for adoption, even though hepatitis B is a manageable condition in the U.S.

8. There are no guarantees in adoption. Even though hepatitis B is a well-defined and apparently easily resolved issue, it is not the only, or even the most common, condition affecting internationally adopted children. Focusing resources on screening for hepatitis B may decrease the efforts put into more important assessments such as the developmental and emotional health of the prospective adopted child.

9. Pre-adoption education of adoptive families is the most efficient way to deal with hepatitis B. When families thoroughly understand the issues, they can make an informed choice about whether to proceed with an international adoption, whether or not the child has been screened. Hepatitis B must always be viewed within the context of all the medical, social, and emotional conditions affecting adopted children.

Adoption agencies, orphanage authorities, physicians, and parents must consider all of the above factors in determining whether or not routine hepatitis B screening should be obtained in all children prior to adoption. Although there will always be circumstances in which such screening is essential for a particular placement, in many circumstances, parents may find themselves falsely reassured by an unreliable pre-adoption assessment.

This statement is copyright free. The authors—Jerri Ann Jenista, M.D. (*Adoption/Medical News*), Dana E. Johnson, M.D. (University of Minnesota International Adoption Clinic), Laurie C. Miller, M.D. (New England Medical Center International Adoption Clinic), Dennis L. Murray, M.D. (Michigan State University)—encourage agencies and social workers to reprint it in newsletters and educational materials. Questions about the statement itself may be directed to Dr. Jenista at 551 Second Street, Ann Arbor, MI 48103, USA (734-668-0419 or jajenista@mem.po.com).

Hepatitis C

What You Should Know,
Why You Should Test

Bonnie Garmus
FCC-Northwest

Some of you may have seen an article that recommended against testing your child for hepatitis C (HCV), a viral illness that affects the liver and that, at present, is incurable. While much is still unknown about HCV (especially pediatric HCV), I'd like to change your mind about testing for this virus for five important reasons:

1. There is no vaccine for HCV, and because of the virus's ability to mutate, it's safe to say a vaccine isn't coming down the pike any time soon. That means that, as the American Liver Foundation says, "prevention of transmission is the best form of treatment."

2. If your child tests positive, it's your responsibility to teach him/her some simple transmission prevention techniques: no biting or scratching, and no sharing his toothbrush, bottle, pacifier, or nail clipper. These are things all children need to learn anyway, regardless of whether they have a transmissible blood disease. But in your child's case, consider them mandatory.

3. You'll need to avoid specific over-the-counter cough and cold medicines that stress the liver (especially things like cough syrup made with alcohol) and, at times, Tylenol.

4. Though risk of transmission is very low in the daycare setting, you'll need to notify your child's school or caregiver to ensure "universal precaution" guidelines are in place (i.e., the teacher dons gloves whenever helping *any* child with a blood injury; all blood spills are cleaned up using a solution of bleach and water). Whether or not you decide to tell other parents is up to you; just make sure

they understand that HCV, while sharing a few HIV-like characteristics, *is not* HIV! All HCV-positive children deserve to be treated
the same as any other healthy child.

5. Even if your child tests positive, you and your physician may decide
not to treat your child at present. But ongoing monitoring of the
health of your child's liver is essential to understanding the progres-
sion of the disease and to future decisions regarding treatment.

What Is Hepatitis C?

HCV, formerly called non-A, non-B hepatitis, is a specific virus that
infects and causes inflammation in the liver. Symptoms are typically
nonexistent, although a few individuals complain of mild flu-like symptoms. At least 50 percent of those infected will develop chronic liver disease. Approximately 20 percent of those with chronic HCV will eventually
develop cirrhosis and are at substantially increased risk of developing liver
cancer. Currently there is no way to predict which chronic cases will
progress to cirrhosis or cancer.

In the U.S. alone, over 3.5 million people are HCV-positive, most picking up the virus through blood transfusions or dialysis before 1990, or
through shared contaminated needles. While it is possible to give a child
HCV in utero, in the case of our children in-utero transmission is unlikely
based on low Chinese HIV rates. (For some reason, HIV-positive mothers
have a much higher risk of transmitting HCV to their child than do mothers who are HIV-negative.)

What Are the Symptoms?

Hepatitis C is marked by a "silent" and unpredictable course, starting
gradually and progressing slowly over 10 to 40 years. Often asymptomatic,
many patients will have no idea they have it—even though the virus may
be actively creating inflammation in the liver, scarring and even destroy-
ing liver cells. In general, doctors use liver blood tests to track disease
activity (the tests tend to elevate when more active damage is occurring),
although in many cases these same liver test results may be inconclusive,
with levels going up and down, or showing mild elevation over the course
of time. In fact, it is the virus's ability to "hide" from the immune system
that makes HCV so difficult to treat.

While liver blood tests can tell us whether or not the liver is being
injured by HCV, only a liver biopsy can present an accurate picture of the
liver's disease state. In general, biopsies are unnecessary unless tests such

as HCV-PCR and HCV-branched DNA give cause for concern, or unless recommended by your child's pediatric gastroenterologist. The biopsy, used to measure liver scarring, is usually done while your child is under general anesthetic.

How Is It Treated?

Patients with hepatitis B or C appear unable to produce normal amounts of interferon; therefore alpha-interferon is currently the treatment of choice—but with fairly limited success. The usual course of treatment involves injections three times a week for 6 to 12 months, with side effects ranging from nausea to depression to marked weight loss. Unfortunately, interferon only clears the virus permanently in about 15 percent of cases, and recent research indicates the reason may lie in the virus's multiple genotypes.

The Hepatitis C Genotype

Today HCV is characterized by several different genotypes, including at least 6 main types and 11 or more subtypes (with a number of recent candidates for new types originating in Southeast Asia). Some show some response to interferon, others present a mild disease course, and still others appear highly infectious, with no interferon response. Therefore, it's important to determine your child's genotype before considering interferon treatment. It's also important to note that some researchers believe interferon is less likely to perform well on the Asian populace owing to the DNA makeup of the drug.

While there is much controversy over which patients should be treated with interferon, when treatment should start, and how long it should last, the good news is, promising new therapies are currently in clinical trials. One new drug called Amantadine appears to be outperforming interferon in about 50 percent of cases, and with few side effects. The current study group is small (about 20 patients), and at present it has not been tested on children.

For those patients reaching end-stage liver disease or cirrhosis, liver transplants are recommended. Unfortunately, HCV will more than likely reinfect a new liver. If all treatments fail, HCV will ultimately result in death.

Is Hepatitis C Common among Chinese Children?

Of all the hundreds of children who have come home from China, only a handful (that we know of) have tested positive for hepatitis C. It's significant that some of these children come from the same orphanage—it may mean that injections are given with shared needles, or that an infected worker is unknowingly spreading the infection to her wards. In any case, it's important to let your agency and orphanage know about the infection so that they can take whatever measures they can to stop transmission.

What Tests Should I Ask My Doctor to Perform?

Tell your doctor to add a screen for hepatitis C to your regular battery of child's blood tests. This test, called Anti-HCV, determines whether your child is producing HCV antibodies. False positives do happen, so test twice to be sure.

Many pediatricians are completely in the dark when it comes to HCV—and some may even tell you "it's nothing to worry about." They may be basing that opinion on the disease course of one specific HCV genotype. What they don't know is that hepatitis C disease course varies between genotypes, and as we know, some genotypes are uglier than others. A gastroenterologist or hepatologist will understand these issues and will probably want to track your child's infection with periodic blood tests—and if those tests warrant, go further with more decisive tests—before treatment can be considered. Because hepatitis C is still fairly rare among pediatrics, there are no statistics to tell us how children do over the long term.

Your best bet following a positive anti-HCV test is to ask for a referral to a pediatric gastroenterologist—even if your child's liver levels are normal. Remember, liver function tests can often appear normal, despite inflammation. Chances are good a gastroenterologist will follow up with a RIBA-anti-HCV test to determine chronicity.

If your child is a chronic carrier and her liver level tests are elevated, your doctor may want to consider the next tests, called HCV-PCR and HCV-branched DNA, which measure both the presence and amount of hepatitis C virus in the blood. Based on those test results, they may decide a liver biopsy is necessary in order to determine the actual state of the liver. At the same time, they should perform an HCV-genotype test to determine which genotype your child carries.

Current Research

If your child tests positive, don't panic! Today researchers worldwide recognize the threat of hepatitis C and are busy working on treatments, cures, and vaccines. Although research dollars in the United States are few and far between, as famous people bring the threat of HCV to the limelight (Naomi Judd's personal battle, Mickey Mantle's death), research may expand accordingly.

Interestingly enough, the Chinese have treated liver disease for thousands of years with milk thistle (silymarin), a homeopathic treatment thought to strengthen the liver. Researchers at Harvard have recently discovered that blue-green algae appears to have strong anti-viral properties, and still others believe specific thymic vitamin therapy can be effective. In general, however, effective research begins by studying the disease course. And to do that, researchers need to track those infected. So, next time your child needs a blood panel, ask them to throw in the anti-HCV test. Should your child test positive, please contact me so that we can pool our information and test results. Thanks!

For more about hepatitis C, contact Bonnie Garmus at bgarmus@msn.com; the National Institutes of Health, (888) 644-2667; or the American Liver Foundation, (800) 223-0179.

The Asian American Donor Program

Helen Archer-Dusté, R.N., M.S.
San Francisco Bay Area FCC

If your Chinese child is diagnosed with leukemia and you are not of Asian descent, there's little chance that you will be a suitable bone marrow donor. Where on earth can you turn?

In 1989, two Asian leukemia patients, a nine-month-old baby and a 32-year-old woman, were in desperate need of bone marrow transplants. Both patients were unable to find a match within their own families. Turning to the National Marrow Donor Program (NMDP) Registry, the patients' families hoped to find unrelated marrow donors. With only 123 Asian donors listed in the registry, they were told that they had virtually no prospects of finding compatible donors. A campaign by the families increased the number of Asian donors in the registry to 2,000. Despite these heroic efforts, no matches were found. The unfortunate deaths of these two people led to the establishment of the Asian American Donor Program. Today, the NMDP Registry has 187,776 individuals of Asian American ethnicity.

What is bone marrow transplantation, and why is ethnicity an issue for matching? Marrow is a tissue found in the large bones of the body. It produces vital blood components, such as white blood cells (which fight infection), red cells (which carry oxygen), and platelets (which prevent bruising and bleeding). Any disease that attacks the marrow may eliminate the body's ability to protect itself. Marrow transplantation is the proven cure for patients with aplastic anemia as well as some leukemias, lymphomas, and diseases of the immune system. Leukemia and other diseases affect all peoples. However, marrow transplants are more complicated than matching blood types for transfusions because they require matching tissue types, and tissue types are characterized by complex genetic traits often unique to a particular race.

Initially, marrow donors were sought among family members. However, approximately 70 percent of patients needing a transplant do not have a family member who is a compatible donor. Obviously, for those of us who are transracial adoptive families, the probability of a match is even lower. Through human leukocyte antigen (HLA) typing, nonrelated compatible donors can be identified and successfully used in marrow transplant. HLAs are markers on the white blood cells. These antigens are inherited characteristics. In a tissue transplant, the closer the match in HLA type between the donor and the recipient, the greater the chance that the transplant will be successful. Because of these genetic factors, patients have the best chance of finding a donor among people of the same racial background. As of April 30, 1998, the NMDP has facilitated unrelated marrow transplants for 159 Asian Americans.

The Asian American Donor Program (AADP)—an NMDP recruitment agency that provides education regarding the issue of unrelated marrow donation—needs our support and assistance. Because of the critical need in ethnic minority populations, AADP is funded to encourage everyone, specifically in minority communities, to be HLA-typed. The program would welcome our participation in the following ways:

1. Parents of Asian descent may want to consider serving as donors.

2. Direct monetary contributions will help the AADP with their recruitment efforts. AADP is currently seeking funding for the costs of translating a recruitment video into multiple Asian languages and dialects. Donations are tax deductible.

3. People of all ethnicities are encouraged to volunteer at community events, at recruitment events, at donor drives, and in the speakers bureau.

For more information and to volunteer or make a contribution, contact the Asian American Donor Program, 7700 Edgewater Drive, Suite 265, Oakland, California 94621, USA; tel: (800) 59-DONOR.

Helen Archer-Dusté is a registered nurse and the 1997–98 president of the San Francisco Bay Area chapter of FCC. Her daughter, Emma, adopted from Wuhan, is four years old.

Facing Delays Head On

The Promise of Early Intervention

Priscilla Scherer

FCC–New York

Before Jung and Piaget, before Freud, even as far back as Plato, wise people knew that early experiences influence a child's development. So why
did it take me so long to realize that our Elisabeth wasn't catching up as
well or as fast as almost everyone said she would? And why did it take me
until she was almost two and a half to do something about it?

All of her friends from our 1994 Hefei adopting group seemed to zoom
through their delayed developmental stages as if they had simply been
waiting for the starting gun. Elisabeth proceeded a bit like a mule, moving
forward only when she was sure about what lay ahead. She studied each
new skill as if she needed to understand the physics of the movement
before she would even think of attempting it. Sure-footed, I told myself;
not impulsive, a good thing not to be. Her speech followed the same deliberate pattern. Words, even proto-words, never tumbled out in a rush.
Repeating and mimicking were not her style. From time to time, I'd catch
her looking at my mouth, trying to form her mouth into the words I
spoke, but as soon as she saw me watching, she would look embarrassed
and stop trying. Shy, I decided. She had been shy from the moment we
met.

I had plenty of support for my denial. Lots of well-meaning friends,
including our pediatrician, recounted stories about themselves, their children, their best friends not uttering a word until age two, three,
four,…and now she's a litigator for a big law firm or something equally
dependent on stellar language skills. I happily held onto these stories. Elisabeth was clearly a bright girl, a little comedian, she understood everything, but seemed stubborn or shy about speaking. Still, questions about
her development—particularly her speech—nagged at me.

When we first met, Elisabeth's motor skills were severely delayed. At eight and a half months, holding her head up for more than a few minutes was a struggle, and her legs and feet were little more than a curiosity to her. She smiled, giggled, and babbled, but mostly in the privacy of our room. And even then, she seemed to tune out easily, to go off into her own head. I knew this was probably a way she had learned to cope with the minimal stimulation available at the orphanage.

I read lots of books about early childhood development, and all the experts reassured me. In her deliberate way, Elisabeth did pass the milestones, if only just within the "normal" time frame. Naively, I didn't consider the first eight and a half months of Elisabeth's life and the influence they probably had on her thinking and consequently her speech. Stupidly, I hadn't consulted the early childhood experts on adopted children.

A variety of intrinsic and extrinsic factors will influence later speech development. For abandoned infants (as well as some other adopted children), the genetic tendencies, prenatal nutritional deficiencies, and gestational age at birth (prematurity) are simply unknown. Other, extrinsic, factors are also unknowns, but we can speculate. Iron deficiency anemia, early exposure to lead, and severe malnutrition (conditions suffered by children in orphanages everywhere, including China) can slow down cognitive development in the young brain and cause speech and other delays. A possibly greater influence, however, is the problem of multiple caregivers and inconsistent or limited care and the impact these have on the baby's intellectual development. When an infant doesn't have a consistent, attentive person to attach to, she is at risk for a variety of later problems, including speech delays, learning disabilities, difficulties integrating and processing sensory stimuli, and poor impulse control.

This makes sense. If a baby doesn't have someone she can depend on, can listen for and respond to, she has no need for depending, listening, or responding. I can well imagine that Elisabeth, with her somewhat independent temperament, might have thought, "The hell with this, I'm not paying attention anymore," and tuned out all the unrewarding talking, crying, and cooing going on around her. (By contrast, another child from our adopting group, who is about the same age as Elisabeth and came to the same orphanage at about the same time, talked early and talked a lot. She was an outgoing baby and very likely soaked up whatever stimuli came her way.) I can speculate about other factors that might have contributed to Elisabeth's speech delays: perhaps she had ear infections and didn't hear the language around her, or maybe she was so healthy she didn't need any extra attention and thus didn't hear much directed speech.

At a workshop entitled "Adopting from an Orphanage," held at the Spence-Chapin Agency on May 8, 1996, I was struck (and comforted) by the numbers of parents who reported that their children were in early intervention programs for some of these problems. Perhaps the topic drew mostly parents of children with problems, but I wish I had gone to something like this sooner, not only for the support but also for the awareness it would have given me. Language is the way we perceive reality. The way we use it and understand it helps us interpret the world and what happens in it. It is the means by which our intellects develop. Any delay will affect confidence, personality, and relationships with others. The early intervention programs aim to establish or redirect the patterns by which very young children process what's going on around them. For Elisabeth, such a program might make it more rewarding for her to pay attention and use speech than to tune out and wait for her needs to be met, or to grunt and point.

As soon as I started talking about getting Elisabeth's speech evaluated, I began to hear about other children from China with speech and other delays. One of the girls from our adopting group—four months younger than Elisabeth—was already receiving speech therapy. But hearing about children now older than Elisabeth and their parents' regret at not insisting on intervention earlier finally pushed me to do something.

Armed with the names of several pediatric speech therapists, I called our pediatrician to tell her what I was doing. She had always been positive about Elisabeth's development, following her closely but not anxiously, taking a wait-six-months-and-see attitude, always certain that Elisabeth would catch up (and she did, for the most part). This time, she humored me, giving me the telephone number of the early intervention program at the New York Hospital. Because this program offered comprehensive, one-stop shopping—behavioral, physical, hearing, and speech evaluations—I decided to go with that rather than a private speech therapist.

The experience of Laura Handlin and her daughter, Emma, was far different. Because their pediatrician had seen a number of children adopted from orphanages in various parts of the world, he took a proactive approach to their development. Emma also came home at eight months with significant motor delays, and she was referred immediately to the LifeStart program at Lenox Hill Hospital. Now 11 months old, Emma receives physical, occupational, and speech therapy at home through the federally funded early intervention program.

"I compare it to what actors go through for their careers," Laura says. "Actors take dance and movement, elocution, acting, maybe singing classes. Emma has the same sort of regimen, but hers will prepare her for the rest of her life."

We're waiting for final recommendations from the panel of specialists who saw Elisabeth. Their individual, preliminary impressions were no surprise, though. Her hearing and understanding of speech are normal. Her attention span is a bit short, and speech output and physical functional levels are about six months behind. In the grand scheme of things, this is probably relatively minor, and she may well catch up on her own. I admit, however, to hoping that they recommend some kind of special help for her. Right now, the delays are easy for everyone, including Elisabeth, to overlook. This won't be the case when she starts kindergarten, a notoriously cruel, confidence-shattering time for children.

Early intervention programs are mandated nationwide to head off developmental problems and give children a boost well before they have to confront school. Early Childhood Direction Centers (ECDC) provide information and referral services for children from birth to age five who have known or suspected developmental problems. In New York, these centers are funded by the state education department and are available throughout the state. The centers will refer you to various agencies that provide services, including diagnostic evaluations; preschool special education programs; speech, occupational, and physical therapy; and parent education programs. All services through this program are provided at no cost, regardless of the family's income. Your pediatrician probably also has information about the programs in your area. Many large hospitals participate through their pediatric or speech and hearing departments.

Priscilla Scherer is an editor and medical writer who lives on the Upper East Side of Manhattan with her daughter and husband Oscar.

Nurturing Speech Development in Very Young Children

Priscilla Scherer
FCC–New York

Among the stack of photographs that didn't go into our memory book is a snapshot that pretty much sums up what I didn't know about how to nurture language in our young child. It was taken not long after I brought my daughter home from China. She was about ten months old and not yet sitting up without support, so she was in one of those hammock seats on top of the kitchen table. In the picture, I'm sitting at the table next to her, my elbow resting on the side of the hammock, bottle of milk in my right hand, bottle in Elisabeth's mouth, *New York Times* spread out in front of me. What do you think I was looking at? If you said the baby, you'd be wrong. In my defense, it was nap time and I was trying to encourage sleep rather than speech at that particular moment, and, a month and a half into parenthood, I was newspaper-deprived and sneaking quick shots of news analysis whenever I could.

I know, I know.

But the point is, I really didn't know then.

Now, some of you are reading this and saying, "I did the same thing, I have the same snapshot, and my daughter's speech is just fine," and some of you are saying, "Stupid woman, everyone knows you have to talk/read/play with your child." It all seems obvious in revelatory hindsight.

Don't get me wrong, I don't imagine that if I had been reading *The Cat in the Hat* aloud to her instead of the newspaper silently to myself she would have had no delays in speech. But I do wish that two years ago someone had sat me down and told me that language interaction with babies is more than just an optional, nice thing to do occasionally, that it's

147

really important, and even if it doesn't come naturally to you, it may help in the long run.

For most children adopted from China, speech and language will develop normally and, in some cases, will outpace the speech of many others in their age group. But a minority of children may need an extra boost. Regardless, the strategies outlined here can't hurt and can be implemented whether or not your child has a delay, or while you're waiting for an evaluation or for services to begin.

To start, in children who began their early months in institutions or without a single consistent caregiver, speech delays don't usually come in isolation. In fact, you will commonly find other, albeit subtle, developmental problems intertwined with the speech delay. This is because the brain centers responsible for the various sensory, motor, and cognitive processes develop interdependently. And the brain receptors in all of these centers need to be stimulated, especially early in life when the brain is preoccupied with development. Stimulation comes when the child is touched and caressed, spoken to directly, and shown pictures, people, and other objects in the environment. When the neuronal pathways are ready, the child begins to interact actively with her environment and, eventually, she talks.

In her book *Childhood Speech, Language, and Listening Problems: What Every Parent Should Know* (New York: Wiley, 1995), speech-language pathologist Patricia McAleer Hamaguchi outlines the processes that must take place before a person can speak:

The brain creates an idea it wants to communicate, sends it to the mouth, and "tells" the mouth which words to use and which sounds make up those words. Then the brain sends signals to the tongue, lips, and jaw muscles, which, in turn, must have the strength and coordination to carry out the brain's commands. The lungs must have enough air and the chest muscles enough strength to force the vocal cords to vibrate. We must be able to hear the words we speak—to assess whether we are saying what we intend to say and to help us to imitate other words and build up our vocabulary. Another person must be interested in what we have to say and eager to respond to it.

Clearly this is a complicated process that could easily be sabotaged by inconsistent physical, emotional, and sensory experiences during the early months of life. Just as clearly, the answer lies in going back with the child and helping her work through her development to smooth out the neuronal kinks.

Step by Step

The brain creates an idea it wants to communicate, sends it to the mouth, and tells the mouth which words to use and which sounds make up those words.

Start talking to your daughter (or son) as soon as you meet her. This will help her to begin to know and love the sound of your voice and to hear and distinguish patterns of speech and intonation. Talk as if she understands every word and as if you expect a response. Then, respond for her. ("What would you like to wear today? This red romper? Do you think it's warm enough? You can wear a T-shirt under it. How about a hat? You don't like hats? But this blue hat will keep the sun off your face.")

If you're not a talker, you'll feel stupid doing this. Do it anyway. When you're peeling potatoes, raking leaves, pushing the stroller up Broadway. Drive yourself crazy. Notice everything out loud. Narrate your day together. At the end of the day, talk about what you did together. Use fairly short words and sentences, especially for younger children.

Take a few simple, colorful books to China with you and start reading to your child right away. Hold her on your lap, point to the pictures, explain what's happening. And while you're holding her and talking, stroke her arms or back, if you can. This not only introduces speech but also provides visual and tactile stimulation. If your child resists the stroking, try smaller doses with firm pressure (as if giving a massage). After a few days, she will likely begin to tolerate it and then even enjoy it, but you have to persist a bit at first.

If your child is older or you start reading later, she or he may resist sitting still and following along as you read. In this case, you might want to begin with very short interactive books (*Arthur's Neighborhood* and *Elmo's Big Lift and Look Book,* by Random House; *Who's Peaking?* and *Who's There?* by Price Stern Sloan) or books that tie in with videos the child knows. Random House publishes videos based on Richard Scarry's Busytown books that children seem to adore and, of course, there are all the Walt Disney stories. I also found that my daughter better tolerated being read to when she was sitting in her high chair than when we were in her room with lots of distractions.

If your child is easily distracted and pulls all the books on the shelf without ever deciding on one or two favorites to read, limit the selection to eight or ten books (you can rotate them every month or so). I'm not sure why this helps a child become more open to having a book read to her, but it does. Perhaps it is because some children don't organize sensory input well, and so too many choices add to the confusion. Having fewer choices may also enable your daughter to become more familiar with and more interested in the books that are available.

Recite nursery rhymes (see Mother Goose); sing simple children's songs ("Twinkle, Twinkle Little Star"; "Ring around the Rosie"; "Happy Birthday"). In children with speech delays, use tapping and clapping along with the melody and words to establish the rhythm and distinguish syllables.

Children who avoid reciting familiar nursery rhymes or who cannot repeat simple, familiar nursery songs may have speech or language delays. At three and a half, Elisabeth still has trouble with songs. I think that the melody and rhythm are competing with the words because of some auditory processing snafu that she's experiencing (see the section about hearing, below). However, when the words and song are accompanied by gestures ("Open, shut them; Open, shut them; Give a little clap! clap! clap!"), her ability to repeat improves. This is called "visual cueing" and is an important learning technique for children for whom language is not a strength.

The brain sends signals to the tongue, lips, and jaw muscles, which, in turn, must have the strength and coordination to carry out the brain's commands. The lungs must have enough air and the chest muscles enough strength to force the vocal cords to vibrate.

Until they have teeth and can feed themselves, many institutionalized children in China are bottle-fed formula and the ubiquitous rice cereal. To enhance motor and sensory development of the mouth, start feeding your child foods with a variety of textures and flavors as soon as you can. Encourage her to try chewing with her back teeth sometimes.

As you use the bottle less and less, remember that a straw (the thinner the better) stimulates the mouth muscles more than a sippy cup. Drinking out of a cup without a straw or spout stimulates other mouth muscles. If your child uses a straw, gradually introduce thicker and thicker liquids (from juice to milk to milkshakes or oatmeal) to make the mouth work harder.

Blowing bubbles, noisemakers (sorry), and toy instruments (recorder, clarinet, trumpet, harmonica) not only stimulate the mouth and cheek muscles but also help strengthen the diaphragm and increase lung capacity. Upper-body weakness may also influence the way the jaw, throat, tongue, and mouth are used. Exercises to strengthen arms, shoulders, and back include lifting or pulling somewhat heavy objects, mashing, squeezing, and stretching clay. (Play-Doh makes a toy called the Fun Factory that requires the child to use firm pressure to push the clay through certain molds, or she can squeeze clay through a standard garlic press. The Great American Backrub sells a small yellow smiling-face ball called My Friend that can be squeezed and stretched and then draws back into shape.)

We must be able to hear the words we speak, to assess whether we are saying what we intend to say and to help us to imitate other words and build up our vocabulary.

Many of our children had lung and ear infections before their adoptions. The first, most important, thing we can do to ensure normal hearing is to get rid of such an infection if it exists. You may have to remind your pediatrician of your child's pre-adoption history to get him to pay special attention to her ears. You may want to consult a pediatric otolaryngologist upon return from China for a second opinion. If you have any doubts at all about your daughter's speech development, I cannot stress enough how critical it is to ask that her hearing be evaluated as early as possible.

That said, a normal hearing test does not necessarily mean that the child is processing what she hears in a normal way. Hamaguchi calls children's processing disorders "listening problems," and they include a spectrum of complicated receptive language disorders. A child with central auditory processing disorders has difficulty distinguishing speech from background noise; the child with auditory memory problems may forget much of what she hears soon after hearing it; and the child with language processing problems may have trouble understanding what is said to him.

It doesn't take much of a leap to see how an auditory processing disorder could be related to the whole issue of sensory integration and how we interpret all the visual, tactile, and auditory information around us every minute of every day. In addition, children who have had recurrent ear infections are at greater risk for these disturbances. Because some of the behaviors associated with these listening disorders are also common to three- and four-year-olds (easy distractibility, tuning out), and because these problems sometimes disappear as the nervous system matures, a firm diagnosis is difficult to make until the child reaches school age or older.

If you suspect that your child has a listening problem, there are a few straightforward strategies that are useful for all auditory processing disorders. Reduce the noise level in your home. I used to listen to National Public Radio in the morning while I was getting ready for work. My ears would tune it in and out, but I realized that, for Elisabeth, the background radio was turning our family breakfast table conversation into a jumble of not very meaningful words. Now the radio goes off as soon as Elisabeth gets up. If I want to have a conversation with her, we do it in a quiet room. I try to make sure she is looking at me when I'm talking to her. If she's involved in another activity, I wait to speak with her until I have her full attention.

Carpeting or area rugs improve acoustics and reduce the noise level in a room. If you want to talk to your child and the environment is noisy, raise your voice; if necessary, stop what you're doing (pushing the stroller, raking the leaves), and put yourself in a place where she can see what you're saying. Speak slowly, pause between thoughts, and repeat and rephrase what you want to get across.

Repeating words into a tape recorder, especially the kind with a microphone that amplifies the sound of the voice, helped Elisabeth get over some of her shyness about speaking. She avoided the microphone at first, and then would only blow into it, but as soon as she heard the sound of herself saying a word, she rather enjoyed it. This has also helped her to distinguish syllables when she speaks.

Another person must be interested in what we have to say and eager to respond to it.

This may be the most important step in the process of learning and using speech. Having an active listener will give your child confidence, help her expand on ideas, and increase her stockpile of words. This kind of listening can begin as soon as the baby starts to babble.

Mimicking is one of the first ways to encourage speech in a child. You mimic the sounds she makes and later, believing that this is what's done, she'll begin to mimic what you're saying. By the way, if she doesn't babble or, later, mimic you, this may be a sign of speech problems.

When she begins to point and grunt at objects or activities she wants, respond by telling her what she would say if she were talking. ("You want juice. I'll give you some orange juice. Mmm. Does the juice taste good?") Use short, simple sentences and repeat new words over and over, whenever you have the chance. When she begins to talk, continue with this strategy by repeating and expanding on what she says. ("Want juice? Would you like orange juice or apple juice? Does Elisabeth like apple juice? Mommy likes orange juice.") Praise her speech; blame yourself and your hearing if you don't understand her. By the time my daughter was about two and a half, she was acutely aware of and bashful about speaking. No matter how loving my approach and intentions, saying, "I can't understand you," made her clam up most of the time.

Play is an enormously useful way to have a conversation with your child and help her expand her ideas and vocabulary. Children who actively engage in imaginary play and conceptualizing (pretending a glob of orange clay is a tiger or a straw is a snake) also have an easier time learning to read later on. Take on roles, act out real and fairytale scenarios, lead her along to the next level of the play story, but do it all out loud. She'll soon take on all the roles herself, and you'll hear her chattering away as she plays alone with her toys. This all comes naturally to some kids, but others need a little coaching.

After Elisabeth's first session with her "special instructor," I remember thinking about how obvious most of these strategies were and wondering why I hadn't come up with them myself. I also remember feeling exhausted after an hour of concentrated play. I think I needed to have someone with experience say, "This is what works. Do it."

As for feeling exhausted, yes, I am, but I'm also exhilarated. At the risk of sounding too earnest, it's a heady feeling to watch her blossom and realize that I am actively influencing the way she's growing. After only five months of therapy, she's become a creative little chatterbox. I'm still the only one who understands most of what she says, and we have more work to do with focus and frustration, but getting to know this emerging person, my Elisabeth, is nothing but pleasure.

Priscilla Scherer is an editor and medical writer who lives on the Upper East Side of Manhattan with her daughter and husband Oscar. She would be happy to speak with FCC parents concerned about their children's speech development and can be contacted by e-mail at priscilla_scherer@scp.com.

The Special Needs Question

Our Experience with Stephanie XiaoJin

Sue Behnke
FCC-Chicago

Everybody wants a healthy, happy baby. But this does not always happen with biological children or, as we found out, with children adopted from China. Maybe if we had started our paperwork six months earlier we would have been referred a healthy baby. But then we would not have our daughter, Stephanie XiaoJin, the sweetest, most loving and wonderful child. She is the child that everyone falls in love with on first meeting, and we were no different. We adopted a wonderful little girl who happens to have a special need. It is the child that is important, not the special need.

When we began our quest in October 1995 to adopt a child from China, we were told that we would have to accept a special needs child because we already had one daughter. The agency assisting us in our adoption indicated that parents who had other children had been receiving basically healthy babies with a diagnosis of malnutrition, rickets, or something else listed as a special need. But when these babies were taken to doctors upon their arrival in the States, these conditions were not found. This was not the case with our daughter Stephanie XiaoJin.

We completed our paperwork early in 1996. There was a delay when our fingerprints were lost in the FBI during one of their shutdowns. Our dossier was sent to China in April 1996, and we planned to wait up to four months for our referral. We got our referral on June 21, just two months later. When the agency called, I told them they must be joking and to call back in two months because we did not think it would happen so fast. The social worker told us that she had some unexpected and surprising news for us. They were very concerned because our daughter was almost two years old and had a diagnosis of malnutrition and rickets. She was also listed as being only about 14 pounds and 27 inches at 20 months of age

154

(*minus* 20 percent on the Chinese growth chart). They told us we would have three days to decide whether or not we would accept her. After seeing her picture, we decided that we already loved her and it did not matter what her problems might be. For the next four months, we waited and wondered how much of a special need our daughter had. We did not find out until later that China had started being more strict about referring children with special needs to parents with other children.

On November 6, 1996, we took a train from Hong Kong to Guangzhou. We checked into the White Swan Hotel and started to see little Chinese babies all over the place. We completed our visit to the Civil Affairs Bureau that afternoon. The next morning, we took a van ride 45 miles to the Sanshui Welfare Institute to meet our daughter. The orphanage was nothing like what we had been led to believe by our popular media. While the building was old and worn, it was clean and appeared to be well kept. The room where the babies and our two-year-old daughter slept had a wallpaper border, an air conditioner, and ceiling fans. Each of the children had at least one toy in their crib. All four of the children in our travel group were clean; there were no skin problems, parasites, colds, or infections.

When they handed our new daughter to us, we had several surprises. First, she called us Mommy and Daddy when prompted by the orphanage director. Second, she was already potty trained. Last, she did indeed have rickets and her legs curved out by her ankles. Rickets is a softening of bones due to lack of or nonabsorption of calcium and/or vitamin D. Long weight-bearing bones curve because of the softening. Even then, we felt that our daughter would need surgery to correct the curve in her legs. The doctor we spoke to at the orphanage said that our daughter had been scheduled for surgery to straighten her legs, but it had been canceled when we agreed to adopt her. We were also told that she did not walk until she was about 20 months. We still wonder if this was because of the rickets or too much time spent in a crib.

We do not know much about Stephanie's early life. We were told that she was abandoned near a public security office on August 28, 1995, and that her age was estimated to be about one year old. She was given a birthday of September 20, 1994. It was assumed that she had been kept by her family or someone who loved her until they could not keep her anymore for whatever reason. She came to the Sanshui Welfare Institute in September 1995. After we accepted Stephanie for adoption, the orphanage assigned her an individual caregiver from one of the elderly ladies living at the welfare institute. Madame Ho took care of Stephanie for four months. We assume that she taught our daughter quite a few things and helped to prepare her for adoption. Stephanie became attached to both of us immediately and is especially fond of older people.

When we got home, we took Stephanie to our family doctor. Our doctor felt that although she was on the small side and had rickets, she was basically a healthy little girl. We have since found out that Cantonese tend to be smaller then people in other regions of China. In seven months, Stephanie grew three inches and added six pounds.

Our family doctor referred us to a pediatric orthopedist. The orthopedist confirmed that she did have rickets in her lower legs and discovered curving in the upper bone of each arm. The curving in her arms will straighten out as she grows. We also noticed that she did not move her upper body normally. Now she goes to occupational therapy each week to strengthen her arm muscles and learn how to use her upper-body muscles correctly. Both of her legs will have to be surgically broken and straightened sometime between the ages of four and five. The good news is that the rickets are not involved in either the ankle or knee joint, so that after surgery Stephanie has a good chance of having straight legs. After surgery, she will receive physical therapy. Until that time, any physical therapy she needs is taken care of by Gymboree, gymnastic classes, and chasing after her older sister.

We did not adopt a "healthy baby" from China. We did become the parents of a wonderfully loving, sweet, adorable toddler. Stephanie has a great sense of humor; she is always laughing or getting us to laugh with her. I cannot take her anywhere without somebody commenting on how adorable or cute she is. She has adjusted to her new surroundings, her new family, and Western food. She is never going to be very tall, but she has a mighty personality.

For those of you trying to decide whether or not you want to adopt a child with a special need, please seriously consider doing so. During your home study, you and your social worker will determine what type of special need you are able to handle, and this information will be included in your dossier. China loves these little girls and wants to see them matched up with loving and supportive families. One of the other children in our group was also identified as having a special need. She had a hernia, which was corrected within two weeks of her arrival home. She in now a very healthy toddler. I think that China knew what it was doing when it matched Stephanie with us. I spent two years in rehab after an accident, so we know what long-term treatment is like. We got through it once, and we will get through it again. This time, we will go through the process with a wonderful child.

Always remember, you are adopting a loving child, not a special need.

An Update on Stephanie

Stephanie has been making great progress. As of March 17, 1998, Stephanie completed her occupational therapy. She had been going once a week for about a year to "play with Sandy," as she told everybody. Her therapist was very good, and Stephanie thought that it was only playing.

She looks like a new kid. Her shoulders do not round forward, and she moves like a normal child. She can still hyperextend her elbows, and this will probably not change.

On June 11, 1998, Stephanie had her third appointment with the orthopedist. This new set of x-rays showed that her knee joints were parallel to her ankle joints—her leg bones are positioned correctly now. The doctor said that she would not be needing surgery. He wants to see her again in two years, when he will release her from treatment. Her leg bones will always have a curve to them, but at this point it is only a cosmetic problem.

After about 20 months, we finally have our "healthy" child from China.

Sue Behnke and her husband Ed live in Downers Grove, Illinois, with their two daughters, Kristy and Stephanie. For more information on rickets, see *Adoption/Medical News* 3, no. 6 (June 1997), or call (407) 724-3044.

Would You Do It Again?

Dianne Holdaway
FCC-Toronto

Would you do it again, knowing what you know? That was the question we were asked by a couple interested in adopting. As they sat in our living room we answered the general questions about adopting from China; then they asked about our adventure. We began by telling them that the problems we encountered were rare.

Our daughter Leanne (Jiang Le) was adopted from Bengbu, in the province of Anhui, on July 25, 1995, at the age of 18 months. We did not see the orphanage. (If anyone has pictures we would be interested in getting a copy.) Leanne was presented to us at the hotel in early morning. She was quiet and afraid. Normal behavior, we thought, considering the circumstances. Within an hour she was asleep in my arms. As she slept we noticed she had bug bites all over her arms, legs, and back and one of her toes was infected. Nothing that time would not heal, we said.

When she awoke, it was like we had a different girl. Leanne started to scream all the time. During our meals, if we tried to touch her food, bowl, or spoon, she would bite us. Leanne also had diarrhea; on average, we were using ten diapers a day.

Over the next few days the screaming continued, and she started to bite out of frustration when we tried to comfort her. Not only was she crying all day, but she was also waking up five or six times in the night.

We knew something was wrong, but what? She was supposed to be a healthy girl. We wondered, is it a health problem, a hard time adjusting, or both? Was this going to stop when we got home?

Our flight home was quieter with the help of children's Gravol, but it did not stop the diarrhea. When we arrived home, black and blue from all the biting, tired from the lack of sleep, and soiled from Leanne's diarrhea, we were exhausted. Our older daughter Jenny (then four years old) was waiting for us at the airport to finally meet the sister she had been praying for. Jenny fell in love with Leanne as soon as she saw her, but Leanne wanted nothing to do with her. During the four-hour drive from Toronto to Sarnia, Leanne cried the whole trip. This was not the beautiful beginning I had dreamed of.

We took Leanne to see the doctor. The results came back. Leanne had camplybacteria, cerdia, shigella, and a couple of parasites—all intestinal bacteria. We now knew why Leanne had cried so much: she was in a lot of pain.

Over the next few months Leanne was put on different antibiotics, which managed to cure everything except the shigella. The crying decreased as each illness went away. However, Leanne was still waking up several times in the middle of the night, screaming and kicking.

Shigella is infectious, so we had to keep Leanne away from children, and only casual contact with adults. We were told that in time the shigella would work itself out of her system. Just wait and keep your hands washed, we were told. Finally, at the end of November, Leanne received a clean bill of health. However, one week later Jenny was hospitalized; the diagnosis: shigella. Again different antibiotics were tried with no success. Time and prayer were the only answers.

With Jenny being isolated for three and a half months it would have been easy for her to blame Leanne; but she doesn't. The truth is this illness has caused an inconvenience for us. However, you make the best of what you have. Our time of isolation has allowed us to become a closer family. Leanne is now mentally and physically like a Canadian child her age. Her smile is the only thing contagious now.

Like birth parents who experience pain bringing their child into the world, the problems we had with Leanne could be considered our labor pains. Both birth and adopted parents soon forget about their pain and see only the blessing of their child. Leanne is truly a blessing to our family; and yes, we would gladly do it all over again knowing what we know today.

The Holdaway family resides in Sarnia, Ontario.

The Folly of Pursuing the Perfect Child

Christine Kukka

Maine Families with Children from Asia

Several years ago, when I was just starting the China adoption process, a friend asked, "Can you be sure the child will be healthy?"

"Oh yes," I assured her. "They say all the children put up for adoption are healthy, and you get a medical report." For all we had gone through to try to create a baby, surely fate could play no more tricks on me. I would have this reassuring medical report that would give me a small sense of control over the adoption process that left me feeling wildly out of control.

Despite her clean bill of health in China, my daughter has hepatitis B.

Today, I am profoundly thankful that three years ago the medical evaluation failed to pick up that minuscule virus in her body. If offered a child with hepatitis B, I might never have adopted her, never have known her, and never have loved her. My loss would have been unspeakable. I think about this sometimes when a prospective parent asks me in great detail about the chance that his or her future child from China might have hepatitis. I think about it when I hear someone has turned down a referral from China because the child lacked a finger, or had a cleft palate.

Now don't get me wrong: there is nothing wrong with wanting a healthy child. But set aside some quiet time to think carefully about what your hopes and expectations are. Clearly, you must have plenty of financial, emotional, and physical resources to raise a child with a severe disability. Some of us have it and some don't.

But now venture into a gray area: Consider a child with a missing finger or eye, or one who experienced malnutrition or lack of stimulation that may cause long-term developmental delays or lower IQ scores. Think of a child who has hepatitis, which can remain asymptomatic for years and against which Asians seem to be quite resilient.

What is acceptable and what isn't, and why?

As a prospective parent, I folded up like a cheap lawn chair under this scrutiny simply because I didn't want to experience the pain of watching my child endure ridicule, special challenges, and problems. As a parent-in-waiting, I wanted a near-perfect-as-I-could-manage-it parenthood experience, and my future parenthood world required a perfect child, at least at the starting gate.

But the world is full of surprises and sharp corners; they are what give us humility, strength, and appreciation of those fleeting moments of sunlight and happiness. In parenting, whether by birth or adoption, joy is often just a few small steps from sorrow.

Despite our desire for a smooth and easy path in life, all of us must be our children's advocates, warriors, and role models when the going gets tough in the neighborhood, at the day care center, or in school. Those skirmishes can be over cultural, racial, or educational issues, and, no doubt about it, those challenges become more frequent when your child has a health, learning, or emotional issue. But all children, I've learned, come with problems as well as great joy.

When I adopted, I wanted a child whom I could fill up with love and who would hopefully love me and need me as much as I needed her. I got what I wanted and more. I learned love becomes all the more powerful when there is no pretense of perfection and no guarantees—just blind love for the child fate has given you.

Christine Kukka, her husband John Roberts, and daughters Jinqiu and Molly live in Scarborough, Maine. Chris maintains a directory of adoptive parents of children with hepatitis B/C (e-mail: ckukka@deepriver.com).

Adoption after Infancy

My little pine tree is just a few feet tall.
It doesn't even have a trunk yet.
I keep measuring myself against it.
But the more I watch it, the slower it grows.

Wang Jian (trans. Minfong Ho)

I Don't Know
Her Name,
But I'd Like to Enroll
Her in Preschool

Patty Cogen
FCC-Northwest

Last April I began looking for a preschool for my hoped-for Chinese daughter. I called schools recommended by friends to find out about available space.

"Hi, I need some information about preschool," I would begin cheerfully.

"Yes, of course," the friendly voice on the other end responded. "How old is your child?"

"I don't know. We're adopting, and she hasn't been assigned yet."

There was a long pause as the school person recovered her poise and tried to figure out this unusual situation. "What is her name?" was the next question, letting me know that this person was unfamiliar with the adoption process.

"I don't know that either," I would confess, my confidence beginning to erode. Internally I began to feel dizzy. Why was I calling to reserve space for a child I'd never seen, whose name and age I did not know? I was entering the twilight zone.

Just Because She's Chinese...

This was late April and I was finishing up my adoption paperwork, hoping to travel to China in late June to pick up a three- to four-year-old girl who would become my daughter. I was still a month away from having a child assigned to me. However, I realized that if I didn't move quickly, all the preschool spaces would be filled.

Infertility and adoption can make us feel as though we have little or no control over our lives and the lives of our children-to-be. I wanted to be

164

able to choose a preschool for my daughter, not just accept what space was left over at whatever school would take her. I learned this lesson ten years ago when I went to enroll my birth son and discovered I should have gotten in line when he was born. So I began calling when my daughter was just a hope and a prayer plus a huge stack of paperwork.

I discovered that the reaction of school directors to my situation of adopting a child from China was a good indication of how experienced they were with adoption issues. All of them were thrilled at my prospective parenthood; however, from there they divided quickly into two types of responses.

The first type contained many value judgments: they praised me for being so *generous* (substitute any glorifying adjective) and told me how *lucky* (substitute any adverbs dealing with fate, God's will, etc.) my daughter was to be *rescued* (substitute any words that imply that death or worse await every orphan in China).

The second type was professionally oriented and focused on what their school had to offer a child who was internationally adopted as an older child. I ruled out several quite nice schools purely because I learned in our initial phone conversation that my child would be their first experience working with an adopted child.

If the reaction to the word *adopted* was revealing, the reaction to the words "she's Chinese" was even more telling. These very nice directors made it clear that my child was "different," and in many cases desirable (almost like a commodity) because she would help the school's "diversity." Although they had not met my child and knew nothing about her, the fact that she came from China generated a different reaction to her as opposed to a child who was Caucasian and Protestant. Initially I was delighted to think I could get into schools that otherwise might be closed, but gradually the broader reality began to dawn on me. I didn't want her to be seen as "different," even if that was a ticket to admission. I wanted her to be seen for herself.

I decided to call a friend who's been involved for nearly 30 years with questions of cultural diversity and education. Byrd Jones is a professor of education at the University of Massachusetts. I told him about my experiences with the preschools. "To the degree that people in power [in this case the preschool directors] react to skin color, or race, it becomes a construct [an idea] that has meaning," Byrd said. "It's not so much that people *are* different [intrinsically], but when they are *treated* differently, then they become different *because of that treatment*."

I could see that happening already. My yet-to-be-identified daughter was being offered a slot in a preschool purely on the basis of the "idea" that she was "different." I wondered what impact this would have on how the teachers and parents would view her. Would they also have the same construct, that being Chinese made her "different"?

Becoming a Multiracial Family...in Advance

Many years ago, when I looked for preschools for my now 12-year-old birth son, I hoped to find a school that had some children of color. I quickly discovered that looking for a school for my daughter was a completely new experience. Examining preschool classes, I imagined my Chinese/American daughter in each group of children. I began to see children and their "differences" in a new light. Suddenly the nonwhite kids weren't "nonwhite," they were "like my daughter." I looked for how many Asian Americans there were. Would my daughter be the only one (the "token"), or would she be part of a group?

My perceptions were changing. If the class were a meal, the children of color had shifted from the position of garnish to the status of entrée. I remembered a Mexican American woman who told me her experience of going to her first all-white school. "I was nine," she said, "and everyone looked like an angel with blond hair." I knew, and she knew, how she felt: she looked different, and not in a positive sense.

I noticed that in a class with just a few children of color, each child became unavoidably a representative of an entire racial or ethnic group. However, in a class in which there were several children of the same racial or ethnic background, each child was an individual within both their ethnic group and the larger class.

Several schools were willing to make room for my daughter *because* she was Chinese. But I felt uncomfortable having her carry that burden. Was I becoming overly sensitive? Was I imagining problems before they were real? I knew that adoption makes additional emotional demands on children, and I didn't want to add any more.

I was getting skittish. I felt myself changing. This was different from being a liberal and (hopefully) nonracist white person. I felt our family changing from the inside out. Pregnant women have a space the baby inhabits, but our daughter was taking up psychic-emotional-social space as surely as if she were present.

As it turned out, I chose a school that had a high population of internationally adopted children, a school that incorporated teaching about adoption as part of their curriculum about families. Although I knew I could have helped any school attract more internationally adopted children and develop a similar curricular program, I was grateful not to have to do so.

What Else Did I Look for at School?

I determined through my readings on Chinese child development and Chinese education that my daughter would come from a highly structured living and learning experience. So I viewed the open style of many preschools as "overwhelming" or "confusing," as I imagined how it would seem to my daughter's orderly Chinese mentality. Therefore, I looked at Montessori schools and other, more structured, types of settings.

I looked for schools that provided many opportunities for verbal interactions between teacher and child, knowing she would need lots of language practice. At the same time, I also wanted a school that understood the uneven process of language acquisition by a foreign child and had plenty of opportunities for nonverbal play and learning.

I sought out classes that contained a range of ages (as broad as two and a half years through five years) because I knew that there are cultural differences in terms of development. In addition, moving from one country to another and entering into family life for the first time would be likely to cause regressions.

Separation is a major issue for adoptive families, and I explored each school's policy about it, and in particular the initial steps for helping a child become accustomed to the school setting. I looked for a school that set clear limits that would help parent and child separate, rather than letting the separation drag on. There is a confidence that such limits instill in both parents and child.

Originally I thought I would have most of the summer for my daughter to become comfortable with the routines of our daily life. Now it appears she will be arriving in the U.S. just three weeks before school begins. I am grateful to the school for being flexible about how and when my daughter can begin school.

How the Past Informs the Present

Several years ago our family suffered two major "adoption miscarriages." This past grief made my task of making plans for an unassigned child even harder. When anyone, school personnel included, began to gush with joy over the new child about to join our family, I found myself withdrawing. I'd watch the other person's thrilled face from deep inside myself and think, "Well, it could fall through; it has before. You never know." I was cold, numb; I didn't want to get goosebumps and all that happy stuff. I remembered how long it took our whole family to recover from the pain of losing a hoped-for, but unassigned child because Brazil closed adoptions. Then there was the even more painful experience of having the birth mother decide to keep her baby a month before it was born—after we had persuaded her to get regular medical care and eat well-balanced meals.

Having to go to a preschool and "pretend" that the adoption was really happening ranked with getting teeth pulled, or worse. I felt stiff and awkward. After leaving each interview, even the most positive ones, I felt drained and dizzy. My world was turning upside down and my emotions were in turmoil. The same dizzy feelings followed each step of the way: making the application out, paying the first month's tuition, getting the invitation to the "new family potluck dinner," which we decided not to attend, even though by then we had a faxed photo of our little girl.

Although my daughter now has a name, a birth date, and a face, I don't think these feelings will depart completely until we as a family of four depart from Guangzhou and begin the journey home to Seattle and the rest of our lives.

Patty Cogen, her husband Larry, their son Robin, and their daughter Sun-Jia live in Seattle. Patty is a child development specialist who works with children ages birth to five years and runs the First Year Home Group, a support group for internationally adopted young children and their parents.

Teacher as Parent, Parent as Teacher

What I Learned from a Chinese Toddler

Susan Matson

FCC–Los Angeles

Over 16 years ago I stumbled into a profession that I quickly fell in love with: teaching English as a second language. Armed with that love, I eventually found myself dealing with almost every audience possible: adults in college preparatory programs; semiliterate refugees; high school students in Eastern Europe; unruly teens here. My grip on teaching was sound enough that I ended up doing teacher training and, currently, administration. However, none of these experiences prepared me for suddenly being responsible for the language development of a post-institutionalized Chinese child.

Josi was 14 months old when she was first placed in my arms. I was staggered then not only by suddenly becoming a full-time parent, but also by the shock of realizing that she was an infant in a toddler's body. Repeated illness, malnourishment, and neglect—the orphanage only had one caregiver for every 25 children—had taken their toll. Only 15 pounds, she was unable to walk or even stand. Certainly there was no eye contact, and language—*any* language—was out of the question. The offer of milk was the only way to get her to stop banging her head against the crib bars. My doubts were overwhelming. On the other hand, her powerful cry when food was withdrawn gave me hope: here was a survivor, fully determined to make it.

For the first nine months, I had many lessons to learn about child development, and I had to learn them from Josi. Somehow I had forgotten "Maslow's hierarchy of needs," learned ages earlier in a graduate school class, The Psychology of Learning. Basically, the hierarchy reminds us that the need for food and shelter must be satisfied before an individual is ready for love, and the need for love must be met before intellectual needs, like learning, come into play. I knew that intellectual and language development build on each other (see *Raising Your Child,* by Penelope Richardson). And so I was anxious to have language start, to trigger learning, during the critical "learning window" of early toddlerhood—maybe too anxious.

Josi, however, had other ideas. She had never read Maslow, but she agreed with him completely. She wanted first and foremost to make sure, really sure, that food would always be there when she needed it. Until she was sure, she was going to stay silent. And while she was silent, I had no way of recognizing her real needs; I was caught in a Catch-22.

How to break the vicious cycle? It was obvious that when she had first started to babble and vocalize, as all infants do, there had been no reinforcement, no emotional payback. She had learned to live as a passive object: acted upon, at the whim of others, and never given a "voice" of her own. For almost a year we were quite the odd couple: the silent Buddha on the one hand, the would-be-psychic parent on the other.

In time, I abandoned the teacher role for that of mother. Parenting books and magazines offered little guidance to someone like Josi. But I did discover some keys by lucky instinct: having food easily available in the first months, whether she seemed to need it or not; hugging, but knowing when to back off when she resisted; demonstrating how humans use smiles and laughter—all of these seemed to wear down her resistance to me.

A breakthrough came when she was around 20 months. I began imitating random noises she had begun to make while staring at a wall. She repeated and then tried other sounds to see my response, still avoiding eye contact. Before long, we were having call-and-repeat "conversations." Not much, but a first meltdown of Josi's obvious fear and mistrust.

Walking was another major goal affected by fear. After the first few trials, she gave it up altogether rather than deal with falling. Finally I gently forced the issue, taking her by the hands to keep her upright while praising her. This brought out the first hint of a smile (directed at the wall, of course). Josi finally walked alone just short of her second birthday because she was tempted by a peanut butter sandwich at arm's length. My mantra grew simpler: feed the body, *then* the mind.

This approach—in which I thought less of the brain and more of the stomach—finally gave me leverage for language teaching. I stopped giving her milk automatically at mealtime. Instead, she got it (and praise) only when she produced a sound. "Luh-luh" had to do for starters; it was the only thing she was capable of at two. "Muh" came after she'd had a lot of modeling, and today, as her third birthday nears, her "milk" is just fine. She has about 300 other words as well.

Did I "teach" these to her? Unfortunately, I did "teach" in some cases and am still working to undo the results. Because I had insisted that she repeat much of what I said, and she was still such a passive learner, she took everything as gospel. Even questions came back to haunt me. For example:

Me: Do you see a car?

She: You see a car.

Me: Josi, do you see a car? Say "yes."

She: See a car, say yes.

Another lesson learned. Asking for faithful repetition helps with adult language learners. With very impressionable children, who are trying to bond through language, this technique can spell disaster. These days I'm working to honor whatever Josi says that I can understand, and I rarely correct her mistakes. I give her options and try to respond to whichever option she chooses, getting better results.

My roommate Joy, who is not an educator, instantly got it right. Josi had never asked her own questions. Joy had her toy penguins romp through a picture book, "talking" to each other.

Penguin A (high voice): What's this?"

Penguin B (low voice): It's a motorcycle!

Today Josi dashes from object to object in the house, asking, "What's dis?" in a high-pitched penguin voice. It's her first real tool for managing language herself. And she's becoming a constant vocabulary collector, not because anyone told her to learn it, but because she wants to imitate her penguin models.

Here are a few other techniques, some researched, many graciously given by other parents, that might help other language-delayed children:

Lots of singing (God bless Barney and Big Bird tapes).

Altering lyrics of kids' songs to fit the child's everyday lifestyle. (Josi loves "Rice, rice on the stove," sung to "Home on the Range.")

Commenting on everything and anything around you. (*Parenting* magazine reminds us that verbal parents produce verbal kids.)

Repeating, repeating, repeating.

Showing real pleasure and pride in every response your child manages, responding to the content rather than the form.

Photographing *any* interesting event you shared (parades, zoo visit) and using the photos to review the vocabulary and "plot" involved.

In the same way, using bedtime stories about real, shared events, with strategic pauses in which the child can finish the sentence. (Adult: "We went to the river and we saw a…?" Child: "Duck!")

Using rhythm (toy drums help) and dance to reinforce songs and talk. If communication is fun, your child will want a double dose.

Reading to your child while she is on your lap. If communication is loving, your child will want a triple dose!

Recognizing that every child has plateaus of little progress followed by upswings of improvement—and accepting it fully.

These days, Josi is near the top of her special education preschool. (They don't quite seem to know what to make of her, but love her enthusiasm.) Her thinking skills are coming along, too, and even include making analogies (she compares swallowing noodles to food in the sink going "down da dwain.") On her own, Josi has moved up the hierarchy of needs, each day ready for more autonomy.

As I teach Josi a bit, she teaches me more. She is the best student I have ever had: nonjudgmental, joyous, optimistic, and unworried about mistakes. With her, my various roles have finally merged, just as we have merged as family.

Susan Matson, a member of the Steering Committee of FCC–Los Angeles, lives in Culver City, California.

How Old is She?

Sylvie Doyon
FCC-Toronto

In August 1994 we left for China to meet our new daughter, Fu Lu Lu, who was 16 months old. We pictured her walking and running, with long black shiny hair. We made sure to pack baby slippers and barrettes. Her 11-year-old sister was part of the decision and thought that a toddler in our home was just perfect. We just couldn't wait any longer when the call finally came. Andreanne couldn't come to China with us. Rumor had it that peanut butter and Kraft dinner were in short supply in the land of the Great Wall.

The hotel in Changsha had been selected to be the location where we would be united. At noon on Wednesday, exactly two and a half days after we had left Canada, we heard the squeaky noise of the elevator announcing the arrival of the nannies with our adopted daughters. Here they were, babies in arms, carried down the hallway in what was to be one of the most memorable days of our lives. And there she was, Fu Lu Lu, in her nanny's arms—completely bald! Not even a brush cut or shaved, just bald. She wasn't wearing shoes either because she couldn't walk or crawl. We're not sure what thoughts came first through our minds: what a cute baby, can't believe we're finally able to meet you and hold you, God she's completely bald, or, man, what are we going to do with all the barrettes we brought over?

Back in our hotel room she sat on our bed and stared at us. She couldn't move. She just didn't know how and didn't have the muscle tone to do it. Fu Lu Lu was far from behaving like a typical toddler of that age. She smiled, and for us, looking into her eyes was enough to bring us joy and confirm that the long wait had been worth it. It took more than two weeks for Lou to feel comfortable with her new mommy. We figured that despite the good care she received from her last nanny, Lou had probably been exposed to other female figures. Her hesitation came from wanting to ensure that this new woman in her life was going to be here for a while and that she could trust her. Perhaps Lou felt daddy was fading of exhaustion and that maybe she ought to give this new mom a chance while he was still alive. Time, patience, and love seem to solve all problems. Lou finally accepted her mom.

Back home in the land of mosquitoes, friends, relatives, and neighbors couldn't wait to see our new baby. Was it the fact that our hairless baby wasn't walking, not crawling, or that she wasn't moving much that made people ask the same question, "How old is she?" Sixteen months, you say. "Oh, I see." "Oh, that's nice." We learned to smile and nod. We sure got used to those age-related questions and had all the right answers, the lack of stimulation and her difficult start; you know, the usual stuff about comparing North American developmental stages. Sure we had some of our own questions and did not have all the answers. Was she really 16 months old or younger? We knew she was our baby, and that was just fine with us.

Lou's revenge was to demonstrate a steep growth curve and to show off four months after she had arrived that she could walk and that crawling had already come and gone. That Christmas she even had some hair. Still not enough for barrettes!

Lou is now three and a half years old and right on target for her age, taking gymnastics, riding her bicycle (with training wheels), and wearing pig tails. Over two years have now passed since our return, and we don't need to answer those initial questions. People continue to ask questions, but different ones. We're quite happy to answer and share with them the joy that Lou has brought to our family. Questions will never stop, but it appears that age is no longer at the top of everyone's mind. The answer is that time, patience, and love will move mountains. Even Andreanne has learned to enjoy Chinese food!

Sylvie, Pierre, Andreanne, and Lou Doyon reside in Campbellville, Ontario.

Adopting a Toddler

Susanna Porter
FCC–New York

After an hour's wait in the hot sun outside our hotel in Hefei, my husband and I finally saw the white van pull up filled with the women and babies from the orphanage. Although we were supposed to be waiting up in our room we were too anxious to sit still, so we kept a nervous vigil that turned out to be worth the effort. As one by one each woman stepped from the van holding a baby in her arms, we kept looking for a match between each small face and our photograph. No luck—until the final pair descended. The last young woman climbed out alone, then reached behind her, and lifted out a toddler dressed only in a white T-shirt, too-large underpants, and pink plastic sandals. She put the little girl down on the pavement, took her hand, and the two walked side by side into the hotel as we stood by, speechless. We recognized our daughter immediately—not only from her photograph, but because at 19 months, she was the only child in our group of eleven adoptees old enough to walk into her new life.

My husband and I had not expected or, to be honest, even wanted to adopt an "older child." In fact part of China's appeal had been the fact that we qualified for an infant in spite of our relatively advanced ages. At 57 and 42, we were able to just sneak in under the wire with a combined age of less than 100, which meant we could expect to adopt an infant of under a year. Our agency, Spence Chapin, warned us that they'd heard the rules were about to change but believed we were far enough along in the process to be grandfathered. But last April, while we were waiting for our referral, the combined parental age for an infant suddenly dropped to 90, and we were told that we now qualified for a child aged two to three. We were very upset, and when we calmed down and asked ourselves why, we realized it was because of our fear that a child who had been in an orphanage that long would suffer irrecoverable developmental delays. When we really thought about it we agreed that what we most wanted was a healthy, normal child. Her age was much less important.

And so we decided to wait for our referral and then find out whatever we could about her. As it happened she was only 18 months old, younger than we qualified for, and indeed only one of the two ministries would approve us as a result. And so we waited while Spence Chapin's marvelous Beijing-based operative, Xiong Yan, argued our case. The baby's picture was waiting for us in the agency's East 94th Street offices, but we didn't want to go see it in case we were turned down. After a tense few weeks Xiong Yan got us approved and managed to send us answers, by fax, to most of a list of questions we'd sent her about the baby's developmental milestones and past history. It turned out our daughter had lived with her biological family until she was one, then stayed at the orphanage for only a few days before being sent to live with a foster family. Relieved by the information we'd learned and thrilled by the photograph of a darling though sad-looking toddler, we decided to go ahead. Nevertheless it was a little difficult, changing our sights from baby to toddler, telling our friends (amazing how many people said to us, "Oh, I thought you wanted to adopt a *baby*," as if an 18-month-old was in an entirely different category), reshaping our expectations…When all the other families in our group were packing formula, booties, and rattles, we packed cups, sneakers, and crayons.

Alex was nearly 20 months old when we first met her in China. She was walking well, talking baby-talk Chinese, eating with a spoon, and drinking from a cup. She was almost potty trained. Although the orphanage had taken care to remove her from her foster family a few days before she met us, she was clearly sad from missing them. She recited their names again and again and kept talking, calling for "Mimi," which we were told is the local Chinese word for "little sister." As the only toddler in our group, she was the only child old enough to miss her past life and be afraid of the new one. The best piece of advice we got to help her over the transition came from our pediatrician, who suggested we bring a doll for her to hold and bond with, as it would be a while before she'd feel comfortable doing that with us. From the first moment she loved the Madeline doll we brought, hugging and talking to her and refusing to be separated from her. In the beginning our daughter would hold our hands only when she needed help, and never try to hug or touch us. The best way to reach her during this early period was through humor—tickling and laughing made her respond in kind. Only slowly did she begin to take comfort from touching us and being held, and we let her take it at her own pace. Last of all came eye contact. She didn't really look me straight in the eyes for several months, and after eight months she is still shy about it.

So the toddler's adjustment to you is undoubtedly slower—I'd say that's the aspect of Alex's adoption that demanded the most patience. But the immediate rewards more than made up for it. She was such fun from the very first day. While other parents were thrilled with a gurgle or a small smile, we were thrilled when Alex spoke her first English word, "okay," on our second day together. Several new words followed every day thereafter (I remember "Madeline" was another early one), and at two years and four months she's extremely articulate, showing no sign that she spoke her first English word only eight months ago. From the very beginning she has slept through the night, and after a little lapse in toilet training due to our different Western practices, she is now almost finished with diapers. Maternity leave is more fun and certainly more active with a toddler—we swam, went to the playground, and took bicycle rides with Alex-in-helmet behind me—than I imagine it can be with an infant. And when September came I enrolled Alex in a nursery school, and although she had been in America only two and a half months she was already on a par with her peers, both socially and verbally.

So as China's age restrictions get tougher, don't be put off by the idea of adopting a toddler, especially if you can get enough background information to reassure yourself about the child's development. As one adoption expert advised us, it is much safer to adopt over the age of one, as one is able to tell so much more about the overall health of the child. I know if we have the opportunity to adopt again we will request a toddler—and this time it will be our choice.

Susanna Porter is a senior editor with Random House, Inc. She lives in Manhattan with her husband and their daughter, Alexandra.

Bringing a Toddler Home

Sarah Young
FCC-Northwest

Our family grew again this past fall. My husband and I adopted a two-year-old girl from a village in Jiangsu province. I traveled solo to China while Mark stayed home with our three-year-old son, Nathan, whom we had brought home from Hangzhou as a five-month-old baby.

Leaving Nathan was the hardest part of the trip. We had never been apart for more than a work day, and I felt apprehensive and guilty leaving him. Mark and Nathan tracked the trip—and my absence—on our kitchen calendar by placing a sticker of Nathan's choice on each of the squares as the days passed. I left Nathan with a kid photo key chain with snapshots of him and me, his little friends that he wouldn't be seeing for a few weeks, and his sister-to-be, named Jiang Lan. As it turned out Nathan quickly adjusted to bachelor life with Dad—lots of pizza dinners and apple juice, not to mention the wonderfully messy house!

In China, the plan was to have the children escorted from their orphanages to Nanjing, where we would meet them. When the eventful day finally arrived, the children filed into the Nanjing hotel room, each in the arms of her nurse, where we expectant parents had waited all afternoon. In minutes the babies were either cooing or crying in the arms of their brand new parents. Jiang Lan, the "big sister" of the children, sat in the lap of her nurse, looking away from me, as I sat next to them on the bed we shared. Her nurse followed suit and also looked away from me. Minutes later they were still resolutely looking away from me. I took turns patiently waiting…tentatively holding my hand out to Jiang Lan…venturing a few words of Mandarin…and trying to engage her attention nonverbally with a toy. After five minutes, I felt foolish, nervous, and, although I didn't realize it until much later, even annoyed. I don't know how long this kept up—both their posture and my feelings—but finally they each cast a synchronized, tentative glance at me, and the ice was broken!

For the next day or two, Jiang Lan was very withdrawn, apathetic. She would not make eye contact with me. I set her in her crib to get her a comfort bottle, and she slumped over with no effort whatsoever to hold herself up. She hardly ate or drank. The toys I placed in her hand fell to the floor as her limp hand hung open and she stared vacantly off into space. The following day I stood her up, and she slumped over again. I began to think there was something very wrong with her. Was she retarded? autistic? I agonized, and I felt very alone. I tried to be brave and mature about all this. After all, I had read a lot about adopting older children. I had already adopted once before in China. But this was a leveling, grounding experience. I had been emotionally prepared for both clinginess and anger, but not this silent rejection. It was powerful.

Slowly and tentatively Jiang Lan opened up. A few days later, she was looking at me, "cruising" around the room, holding my hand to walk a few steps, occasionally smiling, and eating like a horse. I believe she often ate more than I did at meals. Her breakfast routine was a large bowl of congee, two eggs, and other abundant breakfast fare. I always stopped breakfast before she stopped, out of anxiety that her stomach would not be able to handle the vast quantity of food she was eating.

A few days after that she was walking on her own, playing ecstatically with everyday chopsticks, hotel toothbrush, and food wrappers, and continuing to eat voraciously. She stopped pocketing food in her cheeks after meals. She began to cry at night and to allow me, sometimes, to comfort her. She objected when I left her side. She said "mama" and "paper." By the end of the trip, she hummed and sang to herself on our tour bus. She let her "extended family," that is, the other parents in our group, hold her. She constantly pointed at things with a look that said, "What's that?"

Jiang Lan has been in fast-forward development since those first few days. Little of it came easily. I challenged her. I persistently doted on her and persistently stuck out her bouts of rejection. I urged her to walk, to hold me, to look at things around her. I initiated and sustained more eye contact than I would have ever imagined. I deliberately put my own feelings and needs on hold.

We arrived home, and both Jiang Lan and Nathan regressed. Jiang Lan became wary of adults all over again, slept poorly for a few nights, and had temper tantrums. Nathan elected to sleep in his crib instead of his big-boy bed, and he became very distressed over Jiang Lan's tantrums. But Jiang Lan and Nathan have recently hit a stride. They still struggle over territory (toys, floor space, and Mom and Dad), but they also make each other laugh infectiously, and they are mischievous "partners in crime." Nathan is quite protective of her and comforts her as only a three-year-old can—ironically it's often his own misbehavior that prompts him to offer her a toy or stroke her hair and ask, "Are you all right?"

Jiang Lan is sturdy and self-reliant, and she's developing at an astounding rate. Her language comprehension is amazingly sharp, considering how short her exposure to English has been. What she lacks in physical strength she makes up for in energy and curiosity. She still eats enormously. She still occasionally has bouts of inconsolable moodiness, but the emotions are less intense. She is very sociable with strangers and downright playful with us, but prefers to interact without a lot of holding, hugging, or close eye contact. Her attachment to us, her parents, is slowly and steadily developing. One of these days, I believe, she will cry when she sees the baby-sitter arrive.

Sarah Young edits *Little Treasure,* the newsletter of FCC-Northwest, where this article first appeared in 1995. She lives in Issaquah, Washington.

She Likes Me!

Francine Campagna
FCC-Arizona

As if the entire 16-month adoption experience wasn't scary enough, I'm at what I felt was the end of the journey (adoption success at last). I'm sitting in a Holiday Inn lobby in Urumqi (it only looks like "a room key," but it's pronounced "wooloomoochi") in the northwest corner of China with a two-year, nine-month toddler glaring at me. She doesn't like me. She likes the almond cookie I gave her, but she doesn't like me. She doesn't like me touching her or holding her. She doesn't even like me looking at her.

Oh, boy. This could be a long life ahead of us.

I've read that this is normal and that it will all work out. The experts say there's nothing to worry about even if she loves my sister-in-law, the other families we're traveling with, any stranger on the street, the government officials, the orphanage staff, the waiters at the restaurants…just not me. I tried to keep it all in perspective. How long could the next 20 years be?

Well, after many tantrums (hers, not mine), lots of crying (both of us), my sister-in-law leaving to go back home, the passage of several weeks…I can proudly say that we're buds.

She knows I'll protect her from my 75-pound golden retriever who just wants to endlessly lick her and steal food off her plate. She's figured out there is an endless supply of food if she wants it. She knows she looks as cute as a button in the color-coordinated outfits with matching headbands I put on her. She knows the glasses I bought her have expanded her world beyond the half meter she could clearly see. She knows she feels better, although she wouldn't understand it is due to her diminishing anemia and lowered lead levels.

I'm not saying we don't have a very adversarial relationship at times; we do. She is, after all, a toddler who is a survivor with a very strong will. I can see the determination on that little face—that she will learn the language, that she will figure out preschool, that she will conquer the latest changes to her ever-changing world.

I can see she's also determined to come to terms with the lady she has called Aiya ("auntie"), Mama, and Mom-Mom. Now, should any other toddlers come too close to me, she physically places herself between me and the toddlers and with a jab of her elbow their way, says, "No, my mommy!" Trust me, they get the point. And so do I.

Waiting parents anxiously ask me, "What's it like to adopt a toddler?" My answer is simple, "Heaven."

Francine Campagna adopted her daughter, Allegra Xiu Hong Campagna, in September 1997 from the Wulumuqi Welfare Home in Xinjiang Autonomous Region.

What We Learned from Our Older Girls

Barbara Knapp
FCC-Northwest

These are the experiences of four families who have adopted girls aged six to eight years (at the time of adoption) from the Hangzhou Welfare Institute. At the present time, all are well-adjusted and wonderful little girls. The following observations may help you plan for your older child.

The children are generally smaller than you may imagine. My seven-and-a-half-year-old wore size 4 clothes and toddler size 10 shoes. Look at the 3–10 percent marks on an American growth grid, and that's a good starting place to guess your child's size. I had the exams filled out at the local hospital—my daughter was 5 pounds lighter and 4 inches taller than at her last physical (which was three months old)!

We traveled in the spring when it was 80 degrees Fahrenheit and very humid. People still admonished parents for not having their babies covered up. The older children wore shorts and sleeveless shirts, but I think it was out of obedience to us. By the end of our two weeks, even though the sweat dampened her hair, Laura was asking for long pants and long sleeves. At one point, the older children tactfully asked through the translators "if we had more clothes for them to wear when the weather got colder." After that I pulled out the lightweight hooded jacket that I had brought along, which she wore in addition to everything else. Meanwhile all the adults were huddled in front of the fans.

Toys

Again, think younger than your child's chronological age. If your child is right on target developmentally, she can still play with toys for younger children for the time you are in China. The Institute School at Hangzhou was poorly supplied. Our older children had no exposure to playing with most toys, crayons, balls, simple puzzles, etc. My suggestion is to bring coloring books of simple pictures and just a few colors of crayons. The children are very used to the physical play of running and chasing each other.

The cultural gap between the Institute and America is great. My daughter did not recognize pictures in books for weeks. She thought red hearts were apples, couldn't identify a house or the contents of one. I took along word books, even some in Mandarin, but they were of no interest to her. Even when we got home, she appreciated books, knowing they are important, but looked at them only for a few minutes before leaving them for toys. I kept telling myself, there is plenty of time ahead for books.

Bridging the Language Gap

Think about a few key phrases you absolutely need to communicate with your child, and use them consistently. Break down your language to simple words and associate them with hand or body movements. Some words like *shower, bathroom, hungry,* and a few key verbs like *go, eat, sleep* will be helpful. Use sign language. My daughter knew a lot of Chinese signs to speak with her deaf friends. She was open to using signs she knew or making up new ones for the things we did. The first signs I learned were for *bathroom, later,* and *eat.* After we got back to the U.S. she developed signs for new things like *going out in the car* or *gymnastics.*

Once we left China, it was almost impossible to find a translator for our girls. We now know that the translators in China did not understand much of what they said. One finally confessed they talked a lot of baby talk. The children were not raised to express themselves. In school they did songs and dances; otherwise they talked among themselves.

In only a few weeks, Laura and her lifelong friend adopted at the same time could barely speak Mandarin on the phone. And when her best friend arrived four months later, Laura could not communicate in her native language at all. The girls became completely immersed in learning our language and culture—as they must. We still go over the names of things in Mandarin in a book, but she does not have the sophisticated thoughts in her first language. Now she has more experiences in English that she knows no Mandarin words for. For all intents and purposes, she has no Chinese language skills now. However, it may be easier for her to pick it up as she gets older. If I had a nickel for every person who thinks I've missed the boat over keeping her first language, I could have paid off all my debts. She has saved many important Chinese values—honesty, kindness, a good sense of humor, etc. These may be more important to save—right now—than the simple Chinese she spoke.

Behavior

While we were in China, almost any kind of behavior was normal: kicking, hitting, biting, spitting, clinging, darting away, climbing all over a parent's body, temper tantrums, never sitting still, and crashing at the end of the day. They were up *very* early the next day (out of excitement) and were difficult to get to sleep at night (for fear of waking up back at the orphanage). Once they got to sleep, they slept very solidly.

They flicked every light switch and pushed every button. They went straight for the matches in the ashtray and the sodas in the hotel room refrigerator. I had only one mystery phone call on the hotel bill. If you are planning to keep in touch with any of the accompanying children in your group, it may be a good idea to have the children speak to each other on the hotel phone just to get the hang of phones before you separate.

Some children were not willing to go into the bathtub or hotel swimming pool. But Laura, who had no lice, washed her hair at least five times a night in the tub and loved the pool. We invited other girls over for tub parties. They had lots of fun. (And the bubble bath at the Hangzhou Dragon Hotel is the best!)

We parents all agree the older girls were testing their limits. We feel that harsh words and face slapping and spanking may have often been used as discipline at the Institute. A couple of us tried "time out" in the hotel. I turned a chair to the wall and placed Laura in it. Then I turned around and counted to 10. They are in such a fragile state that any longer could be really devastating. If you need further discipline, try repeating it a short time later rather than increasing the time at each session. It worked wonderfully. She comprehended the seriousness of her actions immediately. She was a changed girl, and we went on to do fun things.

Those children who do not cling and cry a lot usually don't cry at all. It was odd. Maybe it was because they never got any sympathy for hurts and scrapes. Sometimes they laughed inappropriately. It will really tear at your heart strings. Laura was not used to being touched. She couldn't go to sleep with me in the bed—instead she held my little finger until she was deeply asleep. A year later she still cannot fall asleep in my arms watching TV. And while she likes to be rocked before bed, she has to lie down on the bed to fall asleep.

Our girls had obviously been loved, as they all have bonded with their new parents and are doing well. It's a great adventure. Good luck, and know that the best is yet to come.

Barbara Knapp is the State Nutritionist for Meals on Wheels. Her daughter, Laura, arrived home in June 1994. They live in Juneau, Alaska.

Adopting Older Children

A Chinese View

Weihang Chen
FCC-Baltimore

Weihang Chen wrote these comments in response to the following questions sent to the post-adopt-China internet discussion list: "We wonder if you might be able to tell us how older children, in general, feel about adoption in China—especially to an American family? Also, do you know how the children are prepared by the orphanage to join their new families? Do most children have an opportunity to learn any English in school, and if so, starting at what age?"

Your deep concern about the fate of the older children that are still in the orphanage brought up a painful feeling within me. We believe that all children in the world deserve the warmth of parental love and care, but not all have it.

To know Chinese orphanages' general situation, one needs to know the general situation of Chinese society. During the past 20 years, China has been in a fast process of opening up to the world. You can call it industrialization, or Westernization. The general feeling toward Western countries has been very friendly, with a lot of admiration of Western material achievements. Chinese know their own problems well, but know very little of the problems in the West. What they see is that Western countries do not have the problems they have had for so long. They generally picture the U.S. as a happy and rich land.

With the development of tourism in the past decade, Chinese city people were impressed by the spendthriftiness and polite manners of American tourists. Because of the change in government policy since the end of the so-called Cultural Revolution, in the government-controlled media there have been less hostile criticisms of Western political and social systems. All this has helped to create a Chinese myth of a golden land of

America. When you are in China, you will feel the existence of this myth yourselves.

In such an atmosphere, it is only natural that people view the babies that are adopted by Westerners as lucky babies. Not all Chinese think the same, but I am talking about the general attitude. Chinese youths want to go to the West to further their study; thus we have a lot of Chinese graduate students in every good university here. Chinese view these students as lucky students also. For Chinese in general, they admire those who get the chance to go to the West.

Because of international adoption, orphanages are in the social spotlight, which is good because there will be more help from Chinese society itself. Since the early 1990s international adoption has brought many changes to those orphanages that have joined in the trend. All the changes are good, not only for the children there, but also for the staff, for the administration, and for the infrastructure. This means the changes are significant and will have long-felt influence. No Chinese who works in an orphanage environment could possibly retain any negative opinion toward international adoption. Thus, within an orphanage, there is mostly a feeling of admiration toward those children that have been adopted internationally.

For the older children living in the orphanage, this feeling is especially strong. A few among them were internationally adopted already. It was for them like hitting a lottery. There is some sadness in this mentality also. Actually the deciding factor for the life and the happiness of the adopted child is the adoptive parent(s). The admiration of the West overpowers and overshadows the much-expected parental love, for the latter the children have no way to choose. Can they differentiate the would-be parents and only choose those good-natured, kind, open, and warm-hearted ones? It is only in the orphanage administration's power to put those "good" children into the international waiting list. From that time on, to be adopted successfully will be the child's dream. For the cases I experienced, I believe that the older children were better prepared than the parents in this new adoptive relationship. They were more accepting, and more ready to love their new parents. They might not know exactly how to express their little hearts, but that eagerness was there. When they went to their new families, they knew that this was their only home and their last resort. They would never dare to damage it. Their horror was to be taken back to the orphanage again. Thus, most of the older children would shun any Chinese and Chinese things.

To speak about their education in the orphanage, that depends on the local situation. Generally speaking, Chinese orphanages cannot boast about their education facilities. Their most important task is to keep the children alive, and then, to be healthy, and then, to be disciplined, which is the most important part of the family education in Chinese tradition. Chinese orphanages are mostly run like a big family. Children there are like children of a big family. There are families in China as well as in other places in the world who treat children worse than the orphanages. Chinese orphanages are less like institutions in their nature than orphanages in many other countries. Social tradition is an important factor. The general situation of the orphanage older children is that they will be able to go to a regular school (like public school in the United States) at the age of six or seven. But they do not go to kindergarten, thus they usually miss the two years of kindergarten education most other Chinese city children have. But children living in the countryside also miss kindergarten, because there are few kindergartens in the Chinese countryside.

I don't think the older children have any chance to learn English in the orphanage or in the primary school. It is a heavy study load to learn the Chinese language in the early years of the primary school. They would have had some math also if they did go to school.

So much could be said about those lovely older children. It is really painful for me to think about them and to talk about them but to do nothing for them. I wish more families that have adopted older children would be willing to write so that others can learn from their experience. For ignorance always brings prejudice. It is up to you, dear parents and would-be parents, to give the most-needed love to someone among them and not to be affected by prejudice. You are their hope and their dream.

Weihang Chen is China Program Coordinator for Alliance for Children and adviser to the board of FCC/New England. He lives in Gardner, Massachusetts.

Attachment Problems

Jane Brown, M.S.W.
San Francisco Bay Area FCC

I thought that I might share with you a long-term perspective on attachment problems. I prefer the word *problems,* as opposed to the technical term *reactive attachment disorder* (RAD, often called simply *attachment disorder*), since so few children are actually struggling with the very handicapping challenge of RAD. Many adoptive families who speak of having a child with attachment disorder don't realize that there is a *major* difference between RAD and the more minor to moderate collection of behaviors that are symptomatic of children with attachment *problems,* which are less severe and entrenched, cannot be measured through brain scans (as RAD can), and are more easily remediated.

A child with attachment problems might be tough for families to recognize since his or her behavior isn't dramatically different from that of children without these problems, although the problems may grow and blossom in the teen years. A child with RAD is unmistakable, if one understands what RAD is.

I believe that children are at risk of attachment problems if they are adopted after the age of one year, although occasionally children who are adopted in infancy can have problems that don't resolve quickly and sometimes children who come older don't have any problems, as we all know. I think that age is one factor, personality another, and the number of moves is *the* most significant factor. Abuse, neglect, and fetal exposure to alcohol are also important factors in whether children have attachment problems. Although significant fetal exposure to alcohol would indeed be unusual in a child adopted from China, the other risk factors, I believe, are not. Yet I am concerned that two common misperceptions may lead parents of children at risk to assume, with all the best intentions, that their child cannot be affected.

First, as a social worker I have for years heard families claim that the children from *their* child's country don't seem as affected by institutionalization as children from other countries and therefore that the care must be much better in the orphanages that *their* child came from than anywhere else. I have heard this from families who have adopted from the Philippines, from Korea, from Guatemala, from Peru, from Vietnam, and so on. Although it is true that many more children from Russia and the Eastern Bloc countries are being diagnosed with the more serious RAD, I have to wonder whether this finding has something to do with the prevalence of alcoholism in those countries and whether some if not most of these children wouldn't be better diagnosed as having fetal alcohol effect (FAE). (Fetal alcohol syndrome is visible; FAE is not and is tougher to diagnose.)

I have a good friend who worked as a volunteer in a Chinese orphanage in 1994 through early 1996. That orphanage did *not* provide good care. In fact, every baby except one (who was lucky enough to be adopted quickly by a European family) died as a result of the poor quality of care.

China is a vast country with limited resources. There is no consistent standard of care throughout the country's orphanages. Also, as my friend reminded me, the workers are generally not there by choice but were assigned to work there by the government; as a result, not all of them value the lives of these children, not all understand or care that it is important to hold them, and yet all are paid the same whether they take good care of the children or not. Unless we know for certain about conditions in a particular orphanage, I do not think we can assume that *all* the children received optimal care. However, the orphanages that place lots of children probably do give good if not excellent care to the children in their charge. That is what attracts many of the agencies' facilitators to try to work with those orphanages in the first place.

Second, most of us miss or misinterpret symptoms of attachment problems, unfortunately, until our children blossom in late childhood. Suddenly those traits that we passed off as unique to our child and not really so serious a problem—things we thought our child would outgrow or traits we expected to soften and modify over time and with love or that didn't seem terribly problematic in the first place—become BIG problems. The teen years can be particularly trying, as children approach the time they are to individuate from us, and this scares the bejeebers out of them.

What many families experience is a child who has done quite well academically and hasn't had major problems, but who was rather superficial, who had a great need for control, who was bossy and particular, and who craved material belongings ("the more things I have, the more others will value me, and since I don't value myself all that much, this is *very* important"). The child with attachment problems also tends to be cut off from his or her feelings. The child usually refuses to discuss being adopted, birth parents, or cultural or racial differences—assuring parents that s/he is "fine" and doesn't need to talk about that stuff and frankly isn't interested and doesn't understand what all the fuss is about. These children are often quite charming, and others like them.

I will give you an example. A former client of mine has parented three biological children, a daughter who came from Korea at the age of three and a half, and a son, still at home, who was born in Korea and is now 17 years old. This son had been a model student, a super athlete, very social, very outgoing, and fairly undemanding of his parents up to this point. He had few problems and seemed to avoid attention in the family. He has always had to have the most and the best material things and is fastidious about how he dresses. He is popular with peers and teachers alike. He has never wanted to discuss being adopted and claims that he doesn't remember anything of his past, although he came to the United States at the age of six and was only in the orphanage for a few months. He doesn't seem to connect with his emotions, although this hasn't, up until now, been a problem. In short, he was not a problem child and seemed to like his family, but he didn't get close to anyone. As his siblings left for college and then got married or moved away, he seemed to have no feelings about that and never really wants to talk with them when they call or visit.

This year, all has changed. The boy is still doing OK at school, but he has been getting into all sorts of trouble. He has been arrested twice for drunk driving. He has become extremely defiant. He has informed his parents that they have no control over him and he will come and go as he pleases or he will move out. He has been arrested for shoplifting and he continues to shoplift, nonchalantly. He doesn't care any longer whether he is headed for college or not. He appears to have no feelings when he is arrested. He is quiet, but not particularly scared or upset or worried about his future. He becomes angry and then violent, traits he never exhibited as a younger child. When the family discusses his moving on to college, he acts out and gets in trouble, but cannot connect any feelings with his behavior. He blames everyone for his troubles and seems to have no sense of responsibility.

This is *not* a dysfunctional family. They are one of those families who seem to have the right balance of just about everything in their parenting. Their other children have done well and have met challenges easily, and they are a close, loving, warm family—just the kind of family that an agency loves to see come knocking on the door. The parents have a close, loving, balanced relationship built on mutual trust and a strong ability to work together. They are likeable, honest, open, and open-minded people who communicate easily with their children and are deeply involved in their children's lives. They are feeling, at this point, scared, inadequate, angry, worried, and overwhelmed by the behavior of this boy.

The child is struggling with attachment problems that were identified early on, but were never resolved because no one knew, years ago, what to do about them or pinned much significance on them. The problems went underground as the boy sought to fit in with his peers and not bring any notice to himself. He was superficial and skated along through life. Now it is no longer possible for him to do that as he approaches the time to leave another family, and he can't seem to handle that emotionally.

His inability to understand, express, and cope with feelings has created a situation where he instead acts on the feelings. In my opinion, he is acting out his "badness," his "unworthiness," and his fears that he is not a lovable, worthwhile, responsible human being. He steals because he believes that others will value him for what he has, since he himself is not of value. He is scared to leave his family, yet he can't let them get close and help him to uncover and deal with those feelings. He needs to be in complete control because he has *never* been in control of what happened to him: others decided for him that he couldn't stay with his first family, that he would be abandoned, that he would go into an orphanage, that he would be sent to the United States, and that he would land in his adoptive family. Now others can no longer push him around, and he is going to show everyone just how much he is running the show from here on out.

I believe that families who have parented children who were born to them or were adopted and did not have attachment problems are much more likely to be able to tell the difference when a child comes into the family and has attachment problems. They know how it is supposed to feel between parent and child within a reasonable amount of time, given that many of us don't feel *instant* love and deep connection with our children whether born or adopted into the family. First-time families have a more difficult time recognizing attachment problems because they don't have the same basis for comparison.

Stages of Attachment

Before we can recognize attachment problems in the early stages, we need to know what attachment is—and what it isn't. The "bonding" that people often extol is, I believe, mythological. "Bonding" is a pop psychology term for attachment, which is actually a process that occurs over time, not a wet glue that hardens instantaneously to bind parent and child forever after. We got the glue idea in the 1970s when social scientists were experimenting with baby monkeys, and it has been tough for us as a society to shake this erroneous notion.

Although there is a difference between the attachment process of mothers and babies who have a biological connection that begins before birth (but has to be readjusted after birth when the baby is a visible, breathing, behaving, separate being with the beginnings of a personality) and the process that happens with biological fathers and adoptive mothers and fathers (who meet only after the baby is born), there is, in the opinion of most psychologists and other professionals who work with families today, no instant bond that has to happen *or else*. Where pop psychology warns that if the mother and child don't "bond" immediately after birth their relationship will be impaired and perhaps damaged forever, most researchers now speak of the *process* of attaching.

Attachment, then, takes place over time. Sometimes it begins quickly. Sometimes it does not and has to be nurtured by parent(s) and sometimes even jump-started with the help of professionals who know something about adoption.

There are also stages of attachment in adoption, in my opinion. The early clinging and desperate looks when Mommy moves out of sight do not indicate attachment. They mean that the child now recognizes this new caretaker as familiar and kind and loving, and that the child is fearful of losing yet another caretaker or set of caretakers and being sent to yet another unfamiliar stopping place. A child who is insecure and fearful of being moved is not attached. (Usually we see signs of this insecurity at night when the child resists going to sleep or awakens many times during the night and cries out.)

During the next phase, the child begins to enjoy getting all that individualized attention and affection and to have some basic trust that this good stuff isn't going to disappear. She smiles, babbles, imitates, and responds so as to engage the caretaker/parent. As this continues, the child begins to trust that the new parent(s) will not go away and that it is OK to love back without fear of being hurt or losing someone significant again. Sometimes the process is not altogether straightforward. If the child has to cope with a fearful event—such as an illness or even rapid progress through developmental milestones—insecurity can temporarily undermine the child's attachment. Generally, though, the attachment process moves forward over time.

The age of the child at adoption is not the only factor that determines his or her ability to attach or even the pace at which attachment occurs. Another is how well the child was cared for before adoption and whether there was at least one person with whom the child could form an attachment early on (a deciding factor in whether a child can form basic trust or not, according to Erikson). Another is whether the child's needs for food, warmth, and comfort were met consistently or whether the child frequently had to wait for his needs to be met. Another is the child's basic personality and temperament. Is she resilient and flexible or rather rigid? Is he easy-going or rather intense and a bit difficult? Is she outgoing or shy (did she vehemently demand attention or, when someone didn't come right away, did she give up and turn to self-stimulating behaviors to soothe herself, for example)? Is he the type of child who makes transitions easily, or is he frightened and upset by change? Finally, the most significant factor is probably the number of times the child was moved. Did she stay with one foster mother or was she moved several times, leading her to believe that adults can't be trusted and that love is temporary? A child who has learned that giving love results in hurt when the loved one disappears, over and over, tends to put up barriers and not allow himself to want or need or love others. (This is when we see kids develop RAD.)

Children, moreover, are not the only ones who need to attach. For parents, lots depends on our expectations and whether the child we receive meets them or not. As a social worker who has presented many referrals to adoptive parents, I have seen some waiting parents taken aback by the photograph or referral information, while others are instantly joyous. The same happens at the moment of meeting: sometimes it is an instant flow of love from parent to child; sometimes it takes time and often a positive response from the child for the parent to see that sparkle and feel the beginnings of love.

When to Get Help

As many of you know, I participate in many discussions about adoption issues on the post-adopt-China internet discussion list. I think it is wonderful to support each other through this list and offer balance—encouragement to get help if a problem is suspected, but advice to be cautious about jumping to the conclusion that a child has a serious problem or set of problems. I am concerned, though, about giving advice when one does not know the child or family and when we do not have expertise in treating children with specific disorders, disabilities, or emotional problems. There is a great tendency for some of us to overreact and others, especially those who have never parented a difficult, troubled child, to minimize problems and pooh-pooh the advice or expertise of professionals. I think it is dangerous to say, as some do, that psychologists, social workers, and psychiatrists can find something major wrong with anyone and tend to pathologize everyone. I agree that mistakes can be made and that labels are sometimes applied unnecessarily. At the same time, a great many children and families miss the opportunity to have fulfilling lives when problems are not identified early, intervention is not offered when it can most help (in early childhood), and problems have a chance to grow and multiply simply because a family does not get help and encouragement to recognize the struggle early, when it is most treatable.

I would like to share a personal example. Our 17-year-old son, Matthew, has a difficult learning disability and is challenged, in addition, with sensory-motor problems. The temptation for us as parents was to ignore the signs and hope that he would outgrow the minimal problems we suspected when he was a toddler. They weren't, after all, too far off the norm. Part of the draw of minimizing was our deep desire for Matthew to be normal and have a happy, easy, trouble-free life. It is always overwhelmingly painful and scary to acknowledge that one's child, whom one loves dearly and protectively, might have a permanent challenge to cope with. Most of us practice a great deal of denial.

We decided, instead, to act on our concerns. We read, we researched, and we studied. We opted to receive testing and intervention very early. We worked with an occupational therapist who was knowledgeable about sensory-motor integration and could provide therapy. We stayed on top of the current and upcoming research. We taught teachers along the way. We sought private testing for Matthew rather than relying on the school districts to do the testing since it was in their interest to find him without too many problems. (They have to pay for the services when they identify a child as having challenges.) We worked with Matthew to help him understand not only his problems, but also his gifts that came as a *result* of and not in spite of having challenges.

Today Matthew is still a person with learning challenges. But instead of being a behavior problem, a poor learner, a child who lacks motivation, or someone who doesn't succeed in school, he is a terrific student. He has to work harder than most. He has to keep a sense of humor. He has to pay more attention to his organizational skills since this is a weak area. He is an A/B student in regular education classes (he just passed chemistry!). He is more determined than most and knows how to persevere. He is extremely responsible. He is also very talented. His challenges have given him the gift of seeing the world a little differently, and he is a successful and talented artist.

I believe that had we not recognized the problem and gotten help early, Matthew might have been in tremendous trouble later on. Lots of kids like him have poor self-esteem, fail in school, and deal with emotional and social problems and sometimes drug and alcohol problems as well. Had we acted on our concerns only to learn that we were overreacting and that there was really nothing at all wrong, *nothing* terrible would have happened to Matthew. Families who suspect that their child *may* have attachment problems do no harm when they seek assessment and help. If they suspect something, there is probably some basis for their concerns, and they can successfully help their child overcome these problems early. If there is no basis for concern, an honest, ethical professional will tell them so and send them on their way. I do *not* believe that the great majority of professionals make up disorders to recruit clients. On the contrary, those professionals who really know their stuff don't have enough hours in the day to treat all the clients who come to them.

How to Find Appropriate Professional Help

Finding a therapist who is knowledgeable about adoption issues can be challenging, depending on where you live. In some areas where many adoptions take place and agencies have trained therapists, there may be an abundance of therapists who can recognize and treat children and work with their families. In areas where there have been relatively few adoptive families, getting the right kind of help can be a struggle.

Often it is a good idea to contact your agency or an established adoptive parent group for a list of qualified therapists in your area. The therapist ought to be able to give the parent(s) an overview either on the phone or during the first visit of how s/he can help. Although it is best to find someone experienced with attachment issues in adoption, sometimes families have to be creative and ask a therapist whom they or friends know to be good, but not knowledgeable about adoption, to do a little research, especially when the choices are limited in their geographic area.

Act Now

Please pay attention to your young child's behavior and learn about the symptoms of reactive attachment disorder and the less serious forms of attachment problems. If you suspect that your child is at risk, get help. If a professional identifies your child as struggling with attachment problems, don't ignore the warning. Do something about it while the opportunity is open to you. A teen simply *won't* participate in therapy—it's too late. Even a school-age child may resist and be treated too late to make much of a difference. The earlier you seek intervention, the more likely it is that the problems can be eradicated and you and your child can have a happy, fulfilling life together.

Jane Brown is a social worker with over 20 years' experience in international adoption.

Single Parenting

I'd always wanted to be a mother when I grew up. Well, I finally grew up at about the age of forty....Sure of purpose, I decided to adopt a child.

Sheila Rule

What a Difference a Child Can Make

Rita Guastella
FCC/New England

When you get a group of single parents together, you'd better be ready for a rush of one-downs-man-ship. "I missed a mortgage payment!" "Hell, I haven't balanced my checkbook for a year." "Ahhh, what's a checkbook?"

It's the kid's fault, of course. She's turned our lives upside down—emptied our pockets, stolen our brain cells, nabbed our free time, and driven us to the edge, where we skate, most of the time, joyously, artfully, on a slim rim of resources.

This and more was the talk served up at a gathering of single parents—a potluck dinner held amidst tinkling Waterford glasses and pressed linens at Phoebe Morse's home in Cambridge, Massachusetts. The group consisted of four pioneer adopters (all with babies from Wuhan), two prospective adopters (with papers in China), one newly relocated mom who'd adopted a three-year-old, and a single dad. Conversations began with each of us telling our story and branching into areas of time management, money management (or the lack thereof), health management, and advice we'd give to those just starting out. The following is a taste of the evening's discussion.

Definitions

Single parenthood is not a placeholder for parenthood, it's its own immutable bond. "I used to think that if I became involved with someone before my child was three, I'd no longer be a single parent," said Valery Rockwell. "Now that I'm in a relationship, it's clear that the bond between my daughter and me has a unique intensity—one that doesn't change when another adult, however loving, is brought into the mix. I never thought 'once a single parent, always a single parent,' but that seems to be what's happening."

Dealing with Adoption Agencies

Single-parents-to-be are especially vulnerable to the vagaries of agencies. The group observed that singles, in the absence of a mate, often make the mistake of sharing anxieties and ambivalence with those processing their applications. "These can be 'hot buttons' for social workers," said one participant.

"When I sounded concerned about the age of my referral, I was summoned for a two-hour grilling by the head of the agency and told that I was 'obviously not ready for adoption.' The adoption went through by the skin of its teeth. And my concern could have been resolved with one short phone call." The group was emphatic about the need for singles to network with other adopters and to "process" emotional crises outside the agency.

Isolation

This was identified as the single parent's primary concern. (Managing fatigue ran a close second.) For some, the stress of parenting without a partner comes as a shock. One single said: "I thought the hardest thing was being flat-on-my-back sick while my 18-month-old looked worried and offered me her Winnie-the-Pooh bear. But it's much harder being the only one to laugh when she does something hilarious and have nobody to share the joy with."

The group's remedy: Network. Network. Network. Use the FCC directory. Join SPACE (Single Parents Adopting Children Everywhere). Do it, even if you only have time for one phone call a day. And lose the expectation that the cute couple next door will invite you over for coffee just because your kids are the same age. Maybe yes, maybe no. But singles must consciously build a support network, including their own private stock of baby-sitters.

Work

The cardinal rule for singles is: NEVER, NEVER, NEVER call in to say your kid is sick. (We said, NEVER!) Your boss will feel abandoned—irrational but true. Call in and say that *you* are sick (don't worry, you probably soon will be). Other tidbits: force yourself to get an extra hour's sleep a night (two hours occasionally); outfit your trunk for emergencies, including storing extra formula, disposable diapers, clothing, and over-the-counter children's meds. If you're hauling too much stuff, get a foldable grocery cart—and watch your back! (Physical therapy costs money.) Get a will, get life insurance (FCC members can recommend great deals), get disability insurance, find out about pretax set-asides that enable you to use pretax dollars for the first $5,000 of over-the-table daycare.

Little Things Make a Big Difference

When your infant sleeps, you sleep. When your body tells you to stop but your mind tells you to go, listen to your body. Move quickly to handle your own illnesses. Do your bills at work. Try grocery shopping by fax or internet once a month. Check out the buys at the food co-ops and price clubs: you can save a thousand dollars a year on stock items. Talk to your daycare staff; they can be a valuable partner to you in understanding your child's development. ("Yes, two-year-olds sometimes bite.")

Anticipate Father's Day or Mother's Day. Have a plan. Don't expect your friends to watch your kid; find your own baby-sitting solutions (and keep your friends celebrating your family, not resenting it). Understand that when you hit bottom, it won't last forever. Cut yourself some slack in the guilt department, and get yourself as much help as you can afford. (Prewashed lettuce? A minimum. Cleaning lady? Ideal!)

"I remember feeling," said one guest, "'oh, there goes another piece of my life,' and feeling quite angry about it. But as my daughter and I settle in, I'm getting my life back, piece by piece." Remember, many singles have only one hour of discretionary time a day; give it to yourself.

"You have to understand," Phoebe Morse told the prospective parents leaving the table (one of whom was sighing audibly), "this is the best thing I've ever done. The best! I've never laughed as hard, I've never felt as much joy, I've never been happier."

"Me too!" said another, grabbing her coat.

"It's redefined my life. There's no stopping me now!"

"I'm absolutely in love!" shouted a third from the door. And so, now in a tangle of love-ups-man-ship, the guests, like Keystone Kops, righted themselves and drove off happily into the night.

Rita Guastella chairs the Single-Parent Committee of FCC/New England and co-chairs FCC/NE's Foundation for Chinese Orphanages. She and her daughter live in Cambridge, Massachusetts.

Hua Jun Gets Daddy

Doug Hood

FCC–New York

At a dinner party recently I mentioned taking Suki to her first movie, *Pocahontas*.

Someone said, "Did you notice they really did up Pocahontas, push-up bra and tight skirt?"

I answered, "Actually, I found her girlfriend cuter, with her little bangs and all."

Another friend lowered his voice and said, "Doug, it's just a cartoon."

"Listen, you're not a single guy raising a four-year-old daughter."

I was 46 years old, decidedly single, and the details of my life were worked to near-perfection, weekends at a lake cabin, marathons, hopping planes to Paris or Buenos Aires. In a bizarre twist, the last thing I needed actually became my obsession—a child. I pursued adoption, was shocked I qualified, and dreadfully closed in on the ultimate commitment. I played out many of my concerns—would I give up my *New Yorker*s for Curious George, forgo running for coloring, tend to another's potty instead of my own quads, and put up with spittle on my shirt and spilled milk on my computer? I would, I thought. And was I willing to let a communist bureaucrat select my child from his orphanage?

A one-inch photocopy arrived from the other side of the earth, a puffy pouty face. For weeks I studied it, propped it up on the dinner table and over my speedometer, talked to it, and pretended I loved this girl named Hua Jun. I strained to imagine her smiling, one day pretty, and frolicking with me, splashing me with hugs and kisses. But lurking in my mind I could hear the future matter-of-fact voices of my friends detailing my near-breakdown in having to cope with a little ADD pyromaniac from China.

At Fuyang they handed over four-year-old Hua Jun, undersized and floppy, with only the shirt and bug bites on her back. She was a peasant, abandoned at a train station. I called her Suki and handed her an apple. Ten minutes later she tapped my arm and returned the stem. One inch of stem, nothing more. Her first word was the one I thought I'd never hear, "Papa."

There's no mama at our address. And I'm no substitute. Instead of folding her dresses, we stash them and flap our arms to Madonna in the living room. Instead of watching Sesame Street, we paint her face with Karan d'ache and ride the bike, waving and weaving through the neighborhood. I drop her off at preschool draped in old-fashioned jewelry and a Boston Red Sox cap. I put a number seven on her cheek when Mantle dies. Instead of making sand cakes, we grit our teeth, shiver, and swim across the lake. We park the truck and jog through the woods—get home after dark, down a thick shake, and trade burps. We wear sweats to bed, and one of her first words is "sweaty." All right, her buttons should be in front and my socks don't match—hey, you should have seen our soccer match in the backyard.

We'd love to have a mom, I could send her in my stead to some of the places I can't believe I go—Chuck E. Cheese, Jennifer's birthday party, and showers. Showers, and I don't mean the ones where Suki pulls open the curtain on me. The baby kind. I've racked up five. I'm hanging with mommies, wiping snot with my finger, and talking about Pull-ups, kindergartens, and spot-removers.

Mothers tell me there's more; take her to Discovery Zone, Dairy Queen. To the zoo, to the library. But I toss her a globe, point to Myanmar and Tegucigalpa, and tell her, anywhere, anytime. I pat the big ball and say, "Suki's." I've got four decades on her and a drawer full of maps. But I can't shake her off my thigh. I talk on the phone, and she's got me in a Peking neck twirl. I wake in the morning because her foot is in my face. I go to the bathroom, the door cracks, and I see an eye. Finally I see, she's got her world.

I talk to mothers. When I'm asked, "Where is the cutie today?" I slap my head and say, "Oh God, I left her in the car!" Or just today I was asked, "Have you decided on a school?" I said, "I'm thinking of Spring Glen, but I'm bugged by her walking the mile home alone in the dark." Just kidding, just kidding.

I talk to my new daughter: "Suki, get your hand out of there!" (urinal). "Don't pull that!" (fire alarm). "Don't turn that!" (ignition while we're on the George Washington). "Do you have Ultimate Fighter?" (us at Blockbuster). "Play hurt!" (she falls). Or: "Yukka!" (picks nose, wipes on Papa).

It's not the stuff of Spock.

But I'm not apologetic. When one mother gave her a plastic kitchen set-up, I told another that she only played with it for five minutes, mostly with the battery-operated faucet. She admonished me, "Oh no, you have to pretend you have company and sit down for tea time." I fired back, "Forget it." Bag the kitchen, let's shoot hoops, where's Big Wheel? Yeah you're right, her bangs are too long, she doesn't know Barney from Barbie. But one thing she does know—this is better than Fuyang.

Am I scared? I was at first, getting her—I feared I was going to China and returning with a She-Devil. Now—losing her. I'm afraid I'll slip up. Forget her typhoid shot. Leave her in Penny's. In the truck she chirps the alphabet, hits the wipers, unravels a cassette, yanks the steering wheel, points to every dog, "Doggie!" (Yes, I know, Suki, you never saw a dog in China.) I'm afraid I can't lean across the seat to retrieve her barrette and keep us on the road, 900 times in a row. I'm never sure when I'm between the lines.

And I'm afraid I'm not enough for her. I'm not mama. My repeating to her "I'm pa and ma" has lost it's umph. How many women greet her for the first time and Suki dashes, arms windmilling, across the room. I shudder that quicker than she can say, "Xie xie," she'd be sweatless, ears scrubbed, hair pinned up, and in pink.

I'm afraid alone. That's new for me. When she's gone I see Suki's spoon, her dog-eared Mao book, the lost bird caller under her bed, the red Z she made on my khakis, her yellow frog in the tub. I get a flash, if she were gone? What if? My blood stops—suddenly I can't believe I'm this close to devastation.

How's the old ex-champ doing? In the grocery store when I'm not looking she snatches something off the shelf—matzo balls, rubber gloves, hemorrhoid cream, anything, and slips it in my basket. Two aisles later I discover it and hold it up like a dead fish, and she hurls her arms up. We howl, I'm a kid.

You can feel the eyes of other shoppers, mothers, peering eyes, envious eyes. "God, you are lucky." How many times have I heard that? In China it was, "Oh, she is a lucky girl." But little do they know. In my home study my social worker said, "Man, this guy did his homework!" And in Fuyang, Hua Jun was always the last to go in from the courtyard—she knew something was over those walls.

We knew what we were doing. It's not luck.

Do I miss the days of sushi and the Schubert? Do I resent the fact every single night at nine for how many more years you can find me holding her hand, whispering, waiting for her sleepy deep breaths?

The other night I left her for the very first time, after three months. A friend was to watch her while I went out, one simple cherished hour. I found her in the kitchen, singing away and scraping dishes (unassigned), and told her I was going swimming. She froze in the middle of the kitchen and wailed.

I slipped away and did my swim, sort of. In the middle of the second lap, I drifted to a stop. When I came home and opened the door, she jetted across the room into my arms. I hugged her as if it had been a light-year, as if we had been an ocean apart. As if both our orphanages sprang up at our feet. I squeezed her as if my life depended on it.

Doug Hood has recently published short stories in *Cimarron Review* and *Northeast Corridor* and takes Suki on medical trips back to China.

Shao Yin

Cathy Forrest
FCC-Toronto

Changsha, August 6, 1996. In the fifth-floor lobby of the Tian Xin Hotel, a baby was plunked into my arms. Her name was Shao Yin.

She'd just spent six hours jammed in a crowded jeep, bumping over bad roads in 40-degree-C heat—crying, the orphanage nannies told me, at top volume all the way. Now she lay limp and sweaty against my chest. And just when she must have thought her day couldn't get any worse, she raised her head to look at my face.

Brown hair, blue eyes, big nose. From her point of view, I was as ugly as an ape. She twisted away with a wail of such despair, my heart went out to her.

That's when I started to fall in love. Nine months later, I'm still falling. Her name now is Lyn, and she's the most interesting person I've ever met, observant, curious, and witty. At 17 months she doesn't have many words yet, but she has an opinion on everything and communicates it eloquently, just as she did in our first meeting.

I adopted Lyn as a single woman, but I didn't go to China alone. I took my best friend, Pam: mother of two teenagers, smart, practical, creative, and funny. She was a terrific ally, and believe me I needed one.

Lyn's orphanage used foster families to care for many of the babies. In our first few days together, Lyn missed her foster mother terribly. She grieved and raged for nearly a week. Early on she got a cold as well. Poor child! She was miserable, snotty, and achy, and she cried all night long. Every night I walked her up and down the hotel hall over my shoulder and, when I got too tired, in the cheap umbrella stroller I'd brought from Canada. Only constant movement could quiet her.

Breakthroughs: On day four, someone picked her up and she looked to me—to me!—to check if it was OK. On night four, as I walked the floor with her, patting her back, she began to pat my back, crooning in imitation of my crooning to her. On day five, she smiled. Hallelujah! She started to sleep for a few hours at night. And by the second week, we could see how bright, how intact this child really was. She was thin and anemic but feisty. Her foster family must have been wonderful—she'd clearly had lots of loving attention and stimulation.

At eight months she sat up very well, straight-backed and elegant, like a dancer. She could pull a whole box of tissues out, one by one, with glee, and with a developmentally on-schedule pincer grip. She played peek-a-boo games, she enjoyed rattles and other small toys. She babbled; she watched and imitated everything.

And she was HUNGRY! By this time, we were in Beijing, waiting for Lyn's Canadian immigration papers. Check out the breakfast buffet at the Yuyang Hotel: congee, milk, fruit, buns, scrambled eggs, fried noodles— she ate everything in astonishing quantities for a 13-pound person. We arrived back in Toronto on the 17th of August. On the 18th, Pam went home to her own family in Muskoka. And there I was, for the first time, alone in my house with Lyn.

Of course I'd already thought a lot about how to manage single motherhood, thought and read and talked to single mothers I knew, researched and planned and collected all manner of good advice. Still, in that first full day at home with her, the obvious hit me hard: you can't leave her alone for one minute.

If she's awake, you stay awake. If she needs anything, it's your responsibility to take care of it, your responsibility alone. Since that day I've learned a thing or two. Like, you can't do single motherhood on your own. Ask for help. Never turn down an offer of help. And be flexible. If you want everything to be perfect, you have to do it all yourself—and you don't have the time!

My friend Pam was a true partner on the trip to China. We both took care of Lyn, we brainstormed solutions to problems, we spelled each other off during the inevitable bouts of (adult) diarrhea. When it was necessary to really annoy the baby (e.g., squirting saline up her nose so she could breathe), Pam took on the job, sparing me the wrath of the outraged victim. We laughed more in those two weeks, I think, than in the previous 18 years of our friendship. Together we watched an amazing little person unfold; together we learned the basics of what this child needs from her caregiver.

And now Lyn has a whole other special family. Pam, her husband, and two kids live a two-and-a-half-hour drive away, but we visit back and forth often. They're somewhere between friends and family now—so important for a little girl who doesn't have much extended family through my blood. There's my 83-year-old father. He and Lyn are tight. She squeals with delight every time she sees him. And while they play together, I get time to read the paper, or fold the laundry, or talk on the telephone for 15 minutes without Lyn demanding my attention.

I took seven months' leave from work to be with Lyn. Now I'm back at work, and Lyn has a wonderful home-daycare provider. Ana Maria and her husband are from Bolivia. They have five children aged ten and up and they all adore Lyn. Their home is full of music, warmth, and good food smells. Lyn is very happy there.

In November, I found a woman from Sichuan to rent a room in my house. She works off most of her rent in baby-sitting evenings and weekends, plus some light housework. She gets to improve her English and live really cheap. Lyn gets to hear Mandarin every day. I give up my spare room/office and, let's face it, some privacy, but in return I can take a long shower or nip out to the corner store whenever Jane is home—the kind of thing you take for granted in a two-parent family. I can even have the occasional evening out. And it costs me nothing in cash terms—very important on one not very opulent income.

But the biggest benefit goes to Lyn. She understands Mandarin as well as she understands English and already speaks a few words in each language. Lyn now at 17 months is an active, joyful, babbling toddler. She loves a gang of people around, she loves to sing and dance, she's affectionate and bursting with baby-type jokes ("shoe on the head" is a current favorite). She's working hard on life skills like using a fork and removing her socks as fast as I can put them on. Her hobbies include stair-climbing and cupboard-emptying.

When I see how she's thriving, I think I must be doing a good enough job of this motherhood thing—so far, at least. OK, so I'm tired. I'm 45 years old, I work full-time, and take care of a little dynamo. Who wouldn't be tired? More important, I'm happier than I've ever been in my life. For every difficulty I've experienced these past nine months, I've never regretted for one minute my decision to take this fabulous little person into my home and my heart. And she's adopted me for her mother every bit as passionately as I've bonded to her, my child.

As far as I can tell, she's even gotten used to my looks. When she can talk a little better, I'm sure she'll let me know.

Cathy Forrest resides in Toronto, Ontario.

And Baby Makes Three

A Single Mom's Decision to Adopt a Second Time

Carrie Krueger
FCC–Northwest

My mom tells me that when I was little I would say that when I grew up, I wanted to have a house with 100 different rooms, and a baby from every single country in the world. I was very taken with the whole "It's a Small World" thing. I collected dolls from around the world and always knew some day I would adopt. I also figured I would get married. I was about half right.

College came and went with no sign of Mr. Right. Career, travel, friendship, and adventure took me through my twenties. Thirty hit, and the knight in shining armor still hadn't ridden up. I told my parents I was serious about wanting to adopt. My father asked me to take a year and work on finding a mate. I tried! But at the same time, I started researching adoption agencies and programs. China opened up, and suddenly it all became clear. I was one of the lucky early pioneers in the program, traveling to Hangzhou in July 1992 to break new ground and bring home my daughter, Claire.

At that point people pretty much figured my family was complete. But I knew in my heart it was not. As elated as I was with my daughter, as exhausted and overwhelmed as I was juggling work and family as a single mom, I knew I wanted another child. I felt at least three irresistible pulls:

1. I didn't want an only child. I wanted her to have a sibling growing up and later in life.

2. I wanted to help another child, to offer a family and love to another child in need.

3. I didn't want to be so completely focused, infatuated, obsessed with one individual. I knew it wasn't healthy for her or for me.

So I pushed forward and in February 1995 I welcomed my son Cameron home from Vietnam. (Getting a boy has been really fun, but I can't say wanting a child of the opposite sex was a reason for wanting two. I would have been thrilled with two girls as well.)

What's it like to be outnumbered by one's children, alone in the house with a toddler and a preschooler? Exhausting, overwhelming, and a whole lot of fun. While the first period of time with a new infant was not for the faint-hearted, things really are getting easier and more enjoyable all the time.

Many adoptive parents relate to the feeling that they were "meant" to have this child, that they got exactly the child that was supposed to be theirs. I feel that times two, plus I feel my two kids were "meant" to be siblings. They're a love match. It's beautiful, moving, and emotional to see them together and know that they will have one another for the rest of their lives.

The drawbacks? Time to myself has gone from none to nonexistent. Between work and home, I have ceased to exist as an individual. I've let myself go, do not exercise or even cut my hair. I have *no* free time. But these are the crunch years. I really believe things will get easier (and those of you with older kids, please don't tell me it doesn't get easier!). Besides having no time, I have no money. In a two-parent household, you have the option of two incomes, or one income and free child care provided by the stay-at-home parent. I have one income and pay full-time child care for two kids. It's killing me. Again, I think things will get easier. Lack of time and money sometimes leaves me feeling lonely (but never alone, of course). It would be nice to be sharing the ups and downs of all this with someone else. Anyone out there got a nice single brother who loves kids?

Some of the second-child issues are amplified in a single-parent household. For example, it's very difficult for me to carve out time to be alone with either child. And certainly those long nights of crying baby and cranky toddler are worse when there is only one parent to try to get everyone settled. Bedtimes are tough because kids of different ages need different routines. When I was rocking my eight-month-old, it was tremendously difficult for my three-year-old to stay away from us and let him fall asleep. I'm sure plenty of couples face these same dilemmas when one partner or the other is out of town, working late, or otherwise unavailable. Still, the pay-off comes when the two of them laugh hysterically over a private joke, comfort one another when grumpy mom yells, or run off to make "pancakes" in the sandbox. It's worth every ounce of effort for those moments!

Meanwhile, I have to say that in general, I've gotten far *less* support for my second adoption than for my first. I think it is often true that people are less excited about a second child than a first. But for me I got a message along the lines of, "I could understand you really wanted a child and supported you. But two? Now you're going too far." When I express feelings of being overwhelmed by this experience, I feel some people are thinking, "What did you expect when you took on *two?*" or "You asked for it." It's true, one child is a *lot* easier, more manageable, more contained that two. But that just means parents, especially single parents, need even more support when they take on a second.

The adjustment to two? It takes a good solid year. With one, I felt such bliss that the late-night feedings were a joy and an honor. With two I felt despair, even depression after months of sleep deprivation. I felt like I would finally get one of them happy or settled and the other one would wig out over something. It was rare that the whole household was happy at one time. But those days are starting to seem like a long time ago. Now we're mostly happy most of the time. The kids are busy together, running in the sprinkler, finger painting, or putting on a show for me. Everyone is sleeping better. Each child is becoming more capable and independent, and every day I'm even more happy that I decided to adopt a second child.

Can I hold the line at two? Everyone keeps asking me that. I don't know for sure. But I do know that we're all pretty happy right now. I've got no money for another adoption and I don't want another *baby*. But I could imagine a day when a third child, older than a baby but younger than the two I already have, would enter our lives. You never know…

My parting advice to anyone, single or married, thinking about two: It's hard, it's a lot of work, and I'm *so* glad I did it. I can't imagine life without my pair.

Carrie Krueger lives in the state of Washington with her four- and two-year-olds. She edits an online parent information magazine: http://family.starwave.com.

Top Ten Survival Tips for Single Moms and Other Busy Parents

Carrie Krueger
FCC–Northwest

1. Have lots of back-up plans. Figure out in advance what you might do if you're sick, your care provider is sick, one child is in the hospital, the car breaks down, etc. It's a good feeling to have plans.

2. Seek a variety of supportive friends. Married friends with a stay-at-home spouse can bail you out on weekdays. Single friends with kids know what you're going through. Single friends without kids are great for hikes (they can carry gear!). The point is, you need friends in all categories. Even a neighborhood grandma-type is helpful.

3. Pay for as much help as your can afford. If you can afford a cleaning person for your house, do it. If you can afford someone to manage your bills, take in your dry cleaning, walk your dog, whatever, do it. Preteens will often do a lot for little money.

4. Let lots of things slide. When I'm driving to pick up my kids at day care, I say to myself, "Nothing matters tonight as much as nurturing these kids. That's my focus." If you just lavish love and attention on them, get them fed and into bed, you've succeeded! Everything else can wait.

5. Cook dinner after dinner. No joke. Sunday night, make two dinners and put one in a casserole dish. Monday night, microwave it, and you're eating five minutes after you get home. After dinner when kids are more calm (and tummies are full), cook up the next night's meal and save it. I even set the table the night before because that first period of time at home after work is *so* hard, having dinner all set is fabulous.

6. Get organized. Set up systems for everything. Bills, laundry, recycling. Simplify it, set up a system, and stick to it. It helps so much to organize the essentials. (I teach a whole course in this, so I won't say more.)

7. Simplify morning and nighttime routines. Before going to bed, I lay out my clothes and the kids' clothes for the next day. I even untie their shoes so they're ready. I put dry cereal in cups with lids (easier to hold than bowls) and pour milk into cups with lids. In the morning, I hand them their cereal and milk and put on a video while I shower, dress, make my coffee (mandatory!). I dress them while they continue to eat and stare at the screen. They walk to the car carrying their two cups and continue to munch while we drive to day care. Simple, eh? I have a similar simple routine at night. It begins with me stating emphatically: "As soon as you're in your PJs with clothes in the hamper and teeth brushed, we can read books." I then sit down and begin reading their books to myself, inviting them to join me when they're ready. It works.

8. Trade off with other parents. Take their kids and have a "party" one Saturday night; hand your kids off to them the next. You're going to hear over and over again that you need time to yourself. It's very tough to do, but one night every few weeks will do you a world of good.

9. Lower your standards. Amazing discoveries: Bed sheets do not have to be laundered every week. Fast food isn't all that bad for kids. Children don't need baths every day, or even every other day.

10. Courage! You're not the first person to do this, and many others have done it without having a choice or having near the resources most of us have. Whenever I get to feeling overwhelmed, I focus on how fast these years go by, the difference I am making in young lives, the difference they are making in mine.

Carrie Krueger originally wrote this list as a sidebar to "And Baby Makes Three."

On Motherhood, or,
You Can't Always Get
What You Want

Eliza Thomas

FCC–New York

"Maybe we should take out all these potatoes and wrap them up in tin-foil!" I brightly suggest at the end of the day, at the end of my rope. My daughter disagrees; my daughter disagrees with almost anything I say these days. She is my defiant toddler, after all. "Look, Amelia, the moon is full tonight," I say, pointing to the unmistakable round orb in the deepening sky, the actual, the one and only full, bright moon. "Actually, it's not," replies Amelia automatically and firmly. "It's not full. Actually, that's not a moon."

At the moment she is tired and so am I. We are trying to adjust to our new schedules as I am working almost full-time now, and it is sometimes difficult. She's had a long, hard day of sandcastles and daycare, and I've had a long and frustrating day of boring office work. This is our only time together, it is precious, it is important, but all I really want is for her to go to bed. All I want is solitude and time to myself, things that are unattainable. It's midsummer, she's been staying up quite late. She can't sleep until it's dark.

Amelia is a careful, cautious soul and rarely throws a fit. She doesn't fling herself at walls or pound her fists upon the floor. She mostly simply fusses when she's tired. She tells me she wants noodles for supper, and I give her a plateful with a small pile of carrots and beans on the side. Yesterday she ate this dish with gusto and appreciation. Today, however, she stares at these same vegetables as if they were the very worst thing that had ever happened to her. She looks at me, broken-hearted, as if I'd broken her trust as well; she pushes her plate away with a wail of dismay. I catch it just before it falls to the floor, remove the offending items, and coax her to eat some noodles and then a plum. Dinner is over, such as it is.

She sees a cup and immediately she wants some juice, although not necessarily the flavor juice which tumbles unbidden from its precarious perch in the refrigerator. I clean up the spill and pour her some from what is left. She dithers, then declares she wants it in a different cup, the sippy cup with the lost lid. I explain again how the lid disappeared long ago, how the lid is gone forever; I bring out several workable alternatives, all of which are unacceptable to her. Instead she now informs me that she actually (her word du jour) wants a different flavor juice, one which we don't have. Moreover she wants it in a bottle with the kind of nipple that I know to be no longer manufactured. It's not quite dark enough to start the going-to-bed routines. I cast about for distractions.

I see a large bag of potatoes I'd forgotten that I'd bought; desperately I drag it out. The potatoes are sprouting of course, and have become a strange and rather scary life-form, with long pale tendrils coiling around each other; they're much too weird to eat. I disentangle them anyway, brush them off as best I can, find the aluminum foil, and carry the whole lot outside. At first Amelia says she doesn't want to help, but soon enough she's changed her mind again, and so we sit side by side at the picnic table in the front yard and set to work. She is two years and a few months old; I am 48. We come from opposite ends of the earth. We are family.

We hand each other pieces of foil and pass each other overgrown potatoes, and together we wrap them all up, one by one. Together we pile them all in a heap in the middle of the table, one on top of another, together we build from them a tall, shimmery pyramid that gleams and glitters in the moonlight now streaming through the trees. We balance the last silver potato on the very top, and together we marvel at our accomplishment, at its great beauty, at each other, and at our great happiness. Then we put the wrapped potatoes back into the bag.

Eliza and Amelia Thomas live in Randolph Center, Vermont. Eliza's book of essays, *The Road Home,* was published by Algonquin in 1997.

Perspectives

The more blurred and multifaceted our perceptions of China
become, the closer we may be to that most elusive thing:
the truth.

Jonathan Spence

China's Sunflower Children

*In China, Parents Who Have
Adopted Orphans Organize to
Give Their Children a Better Life*

He Ping
Translated by Shixian Sheng
FCC/New England

Last weekend, a group of adoptive parents gathered together in Taijiazai Restaurant in Beijing for a regular meeting to exchange ideas and experiences in child care. These parents are from different walks of life. What brings them together is their common concern about how to provide the orphans they adopted a better life. In order to make these orphans feel the same familial love and receive the same attention from the community as other children in conventional families, these adoptive parents formed this "Sunflower Group," which was started by Chang Lixin, an unmarried single mother of an orphan girl. By naming it Sunflower, these parents hope that there will be a shining smile on each face of their children.

Years ago, Chang Lixin, who is 30 years old, went on a tour to the minority region of Yunnan province. There, she happened to meet a little girl whose parents died soon after she was born. Chang Lixin took pity on the unfortunate child, so she took her home. She named the girl Sani so as to remind her of her Hani ethnic origin. Chang treats Sani like her own daughter and devotes motherly love to her.

But Chang's life has been greatly changed. She remains single. "No man dares to marry me," she says. "Is there any man who does not care to have a child of his own? I have got my Sani. She is and will be my only child." Chang's friends and family could not understand her. They could not figure out why she would sacrifice her opportunity of a happy marriage for an orphan. She does make a great sacrifice, but she says, "It is fate that brings this child to me....Though sometimes I worry, I never regret my choice. We should try our best to make these orphans happy, not lonely, not depressed, nor aggressive to others, and not revengeful to society."

An Yuan and his wife are both technicians. Their daughter Baobao is three years old. This orphan girl came into their life soon after they got married. They decided not to make their own child, and just to take Baobao as their own daughter. For this they received pressure from all around, especially from An Yuan's parents, since he is their only son. In Chinese tradition, leaving no male offspring is considered one of the three failures of filial piety. They were especially upset that he was adopting a girl.

An Yuan and his wife did not give in. "The conventional society looks down upon women. We modern youth should resist and reject this social injustice. We will take good care of her and be responsible for her until she goes to college."

Liu Xiurong is a bank clerk. Her own daughter is 18 years old. Six years ago, she adopted a newborn girl who, at that time, weighed less than two kilograms and was expected to die. Liu put the little one to her chest so as to warm her, took her to the emergency room in a hospital, and spent 800 yuan to save her life. Liu's husband was so supportive that he donated his blood for the girl. The little girl survived. Now, though Liu feels tired sometimes, she would not give up the girl under any conditions. This girl has become a member of the family. Lui's family is just one of many that share the difficulty of our nation.

Each Sunflower family has a moving story of this kind. Some of the adoptive parents are old, some are young, some have retired from work, some wait for employment. All are just ordinary people.

After a time, the members of the Sunflower group realized that they are much stronger if they work as a community to deal with problems. They have organized a series of activities to build up ties with each other. They advocate noble social morality, denounce the evil conventional practice, and attack the backward ideology. In addition, they are constructing a factory to produce a kind of noodle that will have the Sunflower as its trademark. Sales of this noodle will help the parents support their adopted children spiritually as well as materially.

Many "outsiders" have been drawn to the Sunflower circle. They show their support in different ways. Some poets wrote poems to praise the great love represented by the Sunflower families. Some biological parents encourage their kids to make friends with these adopted children; some donate clothes. Taijiazai Restaurant has been offering itself as a place to hold regular meetings. "If everyone has some love to offer, all the good deeds could be done with more ease," says Zai Jiumei, the general manager of the restaurant. "We offer our help for the kids' sake, and for teaching our employees that so long as they can offer a hand, never pull it back."

This article first appeared in the *People's Daily*, overseas edition, January 17, 1997. The translator, Shixian Sheng, is a visiting scholar in women's studies at Harvard University.

The Revival of Infant
Abandonment in China

Kay Johnson
FCC–New York

Examining infant abandonment in China is not easy. Statistics are predictably few. Understandably, top birth-planning officials are not eager to publicize the extent to which little girls have suffered from their policies. But even if the government were committed to gathering such statistics, it would be extremely difficult to do so throughout the vast countryside. Even in the U.S, figures on infant abandonment are estimates at best. In China, the records are of poor quality and have been given only limited circulation; some are kept secret.

The decision several years ago to permit international adoptions of Chinese foundlings signaled some willingness to allow the problem to be glimpsed outside China. And within China, at a time when Beijing is strapped for funds and urging provincial authorities to raise money on their own, there have been frequent public solicitations for aid, while local newspapers and magazines have published stories about abandoned children and the orphanages.

This article focuses on Hunan (1994 population: 65 million), where some unusually candid information was published in the late 1980s and early 1990s. According to a Hunan provincial history published in 1988, infant abandonment was common before 1949—and it involved almost entirely girls. In Hunan, as in many other parts of China, girls occupy a marginal place in the patrilineal family system that puts them at far greater risk of abandonment than boys.

According to that history, infant abandonment and infanticide became so widespread that the acts were criminalized at the end of the seventeenth century. At the same time, a network of foundling homes was established. By 1849, there were 68 county-run foundling homes in Hunan. In 1934, a provincial official told a national meeting of charity organizations that the largest of these institutions, located in present-day Changsha, had "saved the lives of several hundreds of thousands" of baby girls in its 220-year history. These homes existed until the late 1930s, when the entire network collapsed in the wake of the Japanese invasion.

After the establishment of the People's Republic of China in 1949, abandonment and infanticide declined, except in the famine years of 1960–62. But with the implementation of restrictive birth planning in the late 1970s, the problem reappeared. According to the 1988 provincial history, the problem was most notable in remote mountain areas. There, where peasants were still influenced by "remnant feudal thoughts" of valuing males and disparaging females and wanting male heirs to continue the ancestral line, they abandoned or even sometimes killed their infant daughters, claimed the report.

Abandonment grew worse in the late 1980s. Until then the one-child policy had been somewhat relaxed for most rural areas, allowing couples whose first child was a girl to have a second child. But by 1987, officials in Hunan began to increase pressure on local cadres to comply with the policy. Those who failed to meet their birth-planning targets became ineligible for promotions or bonuses, and their units were disqualified from becoming "advanced units" in agricultural production, a status that usually entails additional privileges. As a result, the number of birth control operations (IUD insertions, sterilizations, abortions) increased after 1986, an indication to provincial authorities that birth planning was improving. Unfortunately, this "improvement" brought with it a wave of abandonment.

In 1991, the Hunan provincial government launched a special investigation into the problem of abandonment in Hunan, the report of which was also published in China's Civil Affairs. According to the 1991 investigation, alongside the increasing problems of private adoption and of "secretly giving children to others to raise" as a means of getting around birth-planning restrictions, abandonment increased greatly in the late 1980s. Over 16,000 abandoned children were brought to Civil Affairs departments in the province between 1986 and 1990. The vast majority of these children were said to have come from rural areas. Some 92 percent of these children were girls, and most were very young, sometimes only a few days old.

In 1990, the last year covered by the investigation, the numbers of abandoned children in Hunan were much higher than in the preceding years. As an example, the investigative report cites Hengyang City, where the number of abandoned children found in 1988 was 233, in 1989 it was

352, and in 1990 it was 854. This was the trend around the province. It also reflects the trend found in neighboring Hubei during the same time period. The 1991 investigative report makes the connection between abandonment and birth-planning campaigns explicit: When birth planning is "grasped tightly," there are more foundlings; when the campaigns wane, the numbers decline sharply. It observes that it is even possible to take the province's welfare centers as barometers of birth-planning work in particular areas. For example, in November 1990, when Shaoyang district vigorously began to develop a new birth-planning campaign, the municipal government received as many as 16 foundlings in a single day. Some of the increased abandonment was also attributed to the "chaotic" sexual mores of the so-called floating population, especially village youth who go to work temporarily in the city and end up producing unwanted children out of wedlock. But most of the increase was related to birth planning.

While linking abandonment to birth-planning policies, the report blames the problem on the "feudal attitudes" of peasants who cling to the tradition of "raising a son to secure one's old age" and "to continue the ancestral line." But such beliefs are not without reason: Social security needs must loom large in the countryside, where the vast majority of peasants have no guaranteed old-age security. And, like it or not, daughters are expected to marry away and help care for their husband's parents. With births now severely limited, the "traditional" desire for sons has for some become a near obsession, placing some daughters, especially second-born daughters without brothers, in jeopardy.

Under the rural Hunan one son–two child policy, any family whose first child is a daughter is entitled to a "second child permission certificate." According to the 1991 report, this leads some parents to try an unlimited number of times to produce a son. When the second (or third, or fourth) child turns out to be a daughter instead of the wanted son, many end up as foundlings. Others may be taken elsewhere to be raised surreptitiously by adoptive parents, and a few may even be victims of outright infanticide. Local cadres abet this behavior by not inquiring into the outcome of particular pregnancies and births, merely requiring that the couple end up with the authorized number of children. When asked, peasants may claim that the pregnancy ended in miscarriage or stillbirth or that a young child suddenly became ill and died, and cadres make no further inquiries. Turning a blind eye to abandonment, it seems, is a cadre strategy for coping with desperate villagers.

The report blames local cadres for directly participating in "throwing away" children by gathering up locally abandoned infants and secretly transporting them outside their jurisdiction. Cadres are also criticized for turning their backs when residents engage in "traveling abandonment"— getting on trains and buses to transport a child to distant railway stations or other public places to abandon her. Presumably, cadres do not want foundlings to be found nearby, because this would indicate that local birth planning has not been sufficiently monitored, nor do they want the burden of caring for foundlings out of their own meager funds.

Local cadres argue among themselves about who is responsible for foundlings, but at most levels the responsibility falls to the civil affairs bureaucracy that runs the government welfare centers (*fuliyuan*). Yet civil affairs departments, reputed to be the poorest of all the bureaucratic arms of the state, were ill-prepared to handle the sudden increase of foundlings in Hunan, according to the 1991 report. Most welfare centers were said to be rundown and poorly equipped, with few if any medical supplies. In the entire province, there were only some 50 welfare centers, a mere 10 of which were said to be equipped to house infants, fewer than in 1849. Many areas used up their natural-disaster relief funds to pay for the care of foundlings, which no doubt encouraged cadres to transport foundlings to other areas.

Local cadres turned to domestic adoption as one possible solution to foundling care, but the report complained that too many prospective parents were discouraged by the bureaucratic hurdles posed by public security, birth-planning committees, and civil affairs departments. In fact, many of these hurdles are deliberate, created by the government to stop illegal or informal adoptions, thus preventing adoption as a means of removing daughters from the household so parents can try for a son. Hence, adoption regulations require that, unless a child is an orphan (i.e., both parents are dead, in which case friends or relatives may adopt without restrictions), the adoptive couple be childless, infertile, and above 35 years of age. In 1992, these restrictions were codified into a national adoption law. If a couple with a biologic child is discovered by birth-planning officials to have adopted a child, whether from a state welfare center or through some other channel, they can be fined as if the child were an over-quota birth; in some cases, the adopted child may be taken away.

After 1993, public attention to the problem of "orphans" and disabled institutionalized children increased in China, and the existence of a sizable population of foundlings was occasionally acknowledged in an increasingly diverse popular media. This change seems to have been spearheaded by the reform-minded Vice Minister of Civil Affairs Yan Mingfu and was endorsed in early 1994 by Jiang Zemin (himself adopted as a young child) and other top leaders. Since then, efforts have been made to attract charitable donations from Hong Kong and Taiwan to help fund orphanages, and institutions in several major cities have reported a significant increase in community support and involvement, including in some cases the provision of sorely needed free medical services from local hospitals. People have been asked to donate money, to do volunteer work, to invite children living in welfare centers to celebrate holidays in their homes, and to adopt eligible orphans and disabled children. In the past year, the Chinese government has begun to invite international development agencies and nonprofit organizations to fund the refurbishing of child welfare institutes in what is clearly now an open policy decision to improve orphanage conditions. Still, these efforts have not signaled a formal easing of the restrictions on adopting healthy foundlings, and the government media often insist that only orphans and disabled children live in the orphanages.

The opening of international adoptions in the past few years has also given several of the major orphanages, such as those in Changsha, Hangzhou, Hefei, Nanjing, and Wuhan, a new source of funds. While fees are relatively low by international standards, orphanages, or the local civil affairs welfare departments that run them, collect the lion's share, and these add substantially to their budget. Thus, these orphanages have been able to improve their care significantly. Some effort is being made in Beijing to spread these adoptions around a bit, but it is unclear whether poorer welfare centers outside major cities have benefited much from these developments.

While these efforts will help improve the conditions of care in some places, there is a great deal to be done. Mortality rates in the welfare centers that house these foundlings are rarely revealed, even in limited-circulation reports that are otherwise quite candid, such as the Hunan documents discussed here. But it is known from scattered government statistics published in limited-circulation publications in the early 1990s and from other sources that infant mortality rates reached 40 percent in some of the major state-run orphanages and may have been much higher in more remote, more poorly equipped, or more poorly managed welfare centers.

Not nearly enough is known to assess how much of this excessive mortality rate results from orphanage conditions. A sensationalized, hastily researched TV documentary on Chinese orphanages that aired in Britain in 1995 charged that high mortality rates resulted primarily from negligent care, including uncaring management. Human Rights Watch/Asia, in a report issued in January 1996, went further, alleging with little direct evidence that there was a deliberate national policy to maintain or increase high death rates in order to keep the orphanage population from growing as abandonment increased. While the poor conditions within welfare centers certainly play a role, and abusive or negligent staff may sometimes exacerbate the situation further, even a well-equipped and devoted staff would face a daunting task. Even brief investigation indicates that a significant percentage of children brought to welfare centers are in extremely poor condition when they arrive, owing to exposure, dehydration, malnutrition, and sometimes congenital disabilities, making them difficult to save, given the means of an average Chinese medical facility. Institutionalized care of infants inevitably contributes further to the difficulty, as has been shown in a variety of different cultural and historical settings. When the institutions are also poor, the situation is obviously worse.

Most solutions to the problem of abandonment involve either punishing parents more severely or enforcing birth planning more strictly. A worker at one welfare center in Hunan reported that the numbers of abandoned children started to decrease in the summer of 1992 for the first time in many years. She believed the reason was that birth-planning efforts in that area had been extremely strict for several years. Large numbers of women had been sterilized, and there were therefore fewer who could produce "over-quota" children. Also, she thought that people were no longer able to get away with giving birth, abandoning the child if a girl, and giving birth again, because authorities were monitoring births very carefully. Her reasoning represents the general thinking of the authorities about how to deal with the problem—more surveillance and more thorough birth planning, forcing unwilling parents to raise their daughters and forgo the chance to have a son. Yet it is difficult to imagine ratcheting up the birth-planning efforts even further. These are precisely the campaigns that produced the waves of abandonment. It is also hard to imagine fully motivating courts and local cadres to participate in a massive crackdown on parents when these forces have proven so weak in the past. Until fundamental issues such as social security are addressed more adequately, or birth-planning efforts become more flexible, abandonment is likely to continue, even if the rate can be brought down. Under such circumstances, the most one can realistically hope for is improving the conditions of the foundlings by providing better care and more rapid adoption.

Modifying domestic adoption regulations (which are even more restrictive than birth-planning regulations) could quickly increase the ability of civil affairs departments to find new parents for foundlings. Even in the absence of changes in the regulations, better coordination of domestic adoption through a national referral network (similar to the one managed by the China Center for Adoption Affairs, which handles foreign adoptions), might help a great deal, especially if accompanied by subsidies to help adoptive parents manage the logistics of adoption from welfare centers. These kinds of measures would reduce crowding in welfare centers and help lower the high mortality rates that obtain when young children are kept in institutions, especially when they are underfunded. Substituting foster care for institutional care, as some orphanages already do, has been shown universally to reduce infant mortality and morbidity. Of course, significantly increased funding for welfare centers as well as foster care needs to be sought.

For the most part, we can only speculate about the emotions of the parents who feel they must abandon their baby girls to try to have a son. Sometimes an abandoned child has a note tucked into her clothes. One found on a toddler abandoned in an area hit by a high-pressure birth-planning campaign in early 1991 excoriated the government's policy for pressuring them into giving up their daughter, whom they hoped to return to recover some day. A recent one from Hunan read:

> This baby girl was born on xxx, 1992, at 5:30 A.M. and is now 100 days old....She is in good health and has never suffered any illness. Owing to the current political situation and heavy pressures that are too difficult to explain, we, who were her parents for these first days, cannot continue taking care of her. We can only hope that in this world there is a kind-hearted person who will care for her. Thank you. In regret and shame, your father and mother.

Kay Johnson, professor of Asian studies at Hampshire College and mother of Jesse (age 12) and LiLi (Wuhan, 1991), is one of the few American scholars to write openly about the devastating consequences of China's population policy on baby girls. She wrote this article in October 1996. Interested readers may wish to read three of her scholarly articles for more details: "Chinese Orphanages: Saving China's Abandoned Girls," *Australian Journal of Chinese Affairs,* no. 30 (July 1993); "The Politics of Infant Abandonment in China, with Special Reference to Hunan," *Population and Development Review* 22, no. 1 (March 1996); and "Adoption and Abandonment in China," *Population and Development Review* 24 (September 1998).

As we go to press, China has proposed new domestic adoption regulations that would permit Chinese citizens age 30 and over to adopt a healthy foundling even if they already have a child. We are hopeful that this change, if implemented, will help reduce overcrowding and lower mortality rates in China's orphanages.

Building a Bridge

Huang Banghan, with Joe Kelly
FCC—New York

Today, more and more Chinese know about their country's international adoption program. Yet there is little understanding about why Americans want to adopt Chinese children or what the children's lives are like in the U.S. That may be about to change.

Working with Kay Johnson, who is Professor of Asian Studies at Hampshire College and mother of LiLi, adopted in 1991 in Wuhan, two university professors from Anhui province spent several months in the United States interviewing parents and learning firsthand about the lives of the over 7,000 children adopted from China in the past several years. The two professors, Huang Banghan and Wang Liyao, arrived in the U.S. in October 1996 and were stationed at Hampshire College while making forays to meet and interview families throughout the Northeast. They spent Christmas in New York conducting over 20 interviews with FCC families in Westchester, Manhattan, and Brooklyn and taking part in numerous holiday activities. In March they headed south to visit families in Washington, D.C., North Carolina, Atlanta, and Florida.

Their goal: return to China and ultimately publish their findings both in scholarly social science journals and in popular Chinese magazines that address issues of family and society. They also plan to organize a conference to discuss the work. The Ford Foundation has provided some funding for this study; FCC-NY also contributed a grant.

Increased understanding, they hope, will contribute to a stronger foundation of popular support for the program. While the size and pace of the program ultimately depends on decisions of the government, they believe that popular attitudes contribute to how such decisions are made.

When I left for the U.S., my relatives, friends, and the directors and staff of several children's welfare institutes in Anhui all said the same thing: "You must go visit the adoptive families personally to see how the girls adopted by Americans are living now." I understood that all of them were concerned about the adoptees' fate with some suspicions. "I will, I must," I told them. "That is the main purpose for my visit. I will speak the truth."

I visited 50 families in New England and New York City accompanied by Professor Kay Johnson of Hampshire College and Professor Wang Liyao from the Anhui Academy of Social Sciences in China. The preliminary results suggest that all of the adoptees from China are living happily and growing up well. They are smart, beautiful, smiling, talented, healthy, and strong—just as their parents so enthusiastically described them. The parents of the adoptees also seemed extremely happy. They told us that the Chinese girls make their lives richer and new, make their families seem whole and complete. They are proud of them. They consider these children to be their "first daughters." These girls are the center of their lives, the fulfillment of their hope and dreams of a happy family.

Of course, it is still too early to draw firm conclusions about these girls' lives. We need some more samples from other areas like the Midwest, the South, and the West to compare with our initial findings in the Northeast. Finally we'll get a comprehensive report to your families with children from China and to the public, both in China and the U.S. Several parents wrote letters on the Internet saying their daughters were linked to them by a "red thread," as if fated to become their true daughter. Almost 8,000 of the adoptees are twining a strong rope linking China on one end and America on the other. But I think that is not enough. We need a wide, solid, and permanent bridge, a special bridge for emotional and cultural communication.

As we know, there are huge differences between the two societies and cultures—different values, different norms, different symbols, different customs. No doubt, it will take us a long time and much energy to know each other, to understand each other, to learn from each other. Because of geography, history, and politics, there's little understanding between people in China and America. People in China often ask me why those *laowai* (meaning foreigners) come here to adopt their children? Why don't they give birth themselves? Why don't they adopt in America? Is it possible that they bring these girls abroad to be guinea pigs in experimental drug testing, like the Japanese did in their war of aggression in China during World War II? Is it possible that they will raise these girls for servants or arranged marriages or even prostitutes? Do these *laowai* without children know how to take care of the babies? These suspicions showed that many Chinese people just don't understand why Americans adopt children from China.

But it's not just the Chinese. Many American adoptive parents admitted they knew little about China and Chinese culture, even though they struggled to learn something—by reading newspapers and books, watching TV, movies, and videos, hearing information from friends and neighbors. To be sure, it's not an easy culture to fully understand. We have 5,000 years of history; our culture is abundant, rich, and complex. It varies among different places and groups within China. And it is changing. Frankly, it is hard even for a Chinese scholar to fully comprehend all aspects of this complicated subject, let alone an American facing a fast-changing modern Chinese society.

So I think we do need to create a bridge between our two worlds. Many adoptive families have begun to build: they have hired Chinese babysitters, even family Chinese teachers. They have their reunion groups and organizations like FCC. They send their daughters to participate in all kinds of Chinese cultural activities. Even they themselves are learning Chinese. When we interviewed these parents, they all said that it is extremely important for their daughters to learn Chinese culture. "Why?" I asked. Their answer: "They are American, but they are Chinese too."

At last, I understood: They want their daughters to know where they come from, who they are, what adoption is about, how they are both American and Chinese. Their motivation is clear. They believe the more they teach their daughters about their culture and where they came from the easier it will be for them to define themselves as they grow older. That is why so many parents keep and play the videos recording the experiences of the adoptions in China, why they painstakingly make albums or books telling the story of the kids, why they spend so much time, money, and energy to let the kids learn Chinese culture. Their real purpose for these activities, it seems, is to foster their daughters' healthy identity.

I used to argue with some British social workers in China who worried that cross-racial, cross-cultural, intercountry adoptions will create serious problems that the adoptees and the adoptive parents cannot overcome. I disagree. I think international adoptions are not only legal but also reasonable; they are beneficial for the children and for the parents. I believe as long as we work to build this bridge, this great "experiment"—in diversity of culture, in a special kind of family—will meet with great success in the present and in the future.

Huang Banghan is associate dean of the College of Letters and Science at Anhui Agricultural University. Joe Kelly is president of FCC–New York.

Chinese Scholars Study FCC Families

Steve Huettel

FCC–Tampa Bay

Some of their questions were ones we'd answered dozens of times—for social workers and friends at home, for government officials in China: Why did you decide to adopt? Why not a baby from the United States? Why from China and not Latin America or Eastern Europe?

Others flew in like a bird through an open window, flapping around in our heads as we puzzled over how to deal with them: Who wears the pants in the family? Don't you feel like you're wasting your education by staying home with the baby? What did you think about "The Dying Rooms" documentary on Chinese orphanages?

The interrogators in our homes were two Chinese scholars visiting Florida as part of a study, funded by the Ford Foundation, on children's abandonment and adoption in China. As more people in China become aware of the nation's international adoption program, they want to know why Americans and other Westerners want to adopt Chinese children and what the children's lives are like in the United States.

Huang Banghan and Wang Liyao focused their study on China's Anhui province. Both live and work in Anhui, the province where the most adoptions to Americans now come from. They are working here with Kay Johnson, a professor at Hampshire College in Massachusetts who has done extensive research on abandoned children in China. The two professors flew to the States last fall. They've interviewed adoptive parents in New England, New York, the Washington, D.C., area, and the Southeast. FCC–New York paid their plane fare down to Florida. They were hosted by and interviewed parents of seven children in Tampa in late March.

Let's face it. Bringing total strangers into your home is awkward under any circumstances. Add the language and cultural differences, and it's downright adventuresome.

They arrived at our house in the early evening, lugging old suitcases and clothes in plastic grocery-store bags. We chit-chatted for a couple hours over a take-out Italian dinner. Then they brought out a clunky, 1960s-style cassette tape recorder.

Their first questions about our decision to adopt—why and why from China—were pretty predictable. They were interested in potential cultural conflicts. Did your family have any trouble accepting a Chinese child? Did you experience any discrimination or expect your child would? They also pressed us and other parents on how much Chinese culture we'd teach our children. Would we make sure they'd learn the language? If we had to choose, would American or Chinese culture be more important?

A lot of their questions focused on home life. They asked mothers who worked why they did and wouldn't they rather be home. Moms who stayed home were asked if they'd lost their independence or were wasting a college education. Some of the questions made parents squirm a bit. Who's the boss at home? Who controls the money? If he wanted to give money to his family and you didn't, who would win?

The professors in return filled in some gaps in our knowledge. It's not true that Chinese don't as a rule adopt children outside their family, they said. They don't go through traditional government channels. But especially in smaller towns, everyone knows which childless couples want children. Babies are often abandoned on their doorsteps and adopted without paperwork.

How are adoptive parents from America matched with their children? Not at a government agency in Beijing, the professors said, but at the orphanage. The process they observed was simple: a worker took two piles of documents, one for children, one for parents. The papers on the top of each pile were matched together.

So far, Wang and Huang have been deeply impressed by the parents they interviewed in the Northeast, Kay Johnson told FCC–New York. "It is quite overwhelming to actually *hear* one parent after another declaring how special their child is to them, how wonderfully well she is doing, how they never have been so happy, often accentuated with tears and palpable emotion," she wrote.

The professors will work in the United States through the summer of 1997, making a final trip to talk with parents on the West Coast. Their work won't be published in English, they said, but we're hoping to get some version through Johnson. And we could see them again. The professors said they intend to conduct a follow-up study and interview the same parents again in five years.

Steve Huettel, a reporter at the *Tampa Tribune,* edits the newsletter of FCC–Tampa Bay.

Chinese American Perspectives on U.S. Adoptions from China

Tom McGuffey
FCC-Chicago

Following our decision to adopt a child from China, my wife and I wondered what Chinese Americans thought about intercountry adoption. In my business I have several Chinese clients, co-workers, and employees; it was easy and natural to talk with them about their perspective on Americans adopting Chinese orphans. The conversations I had with several people resulted in many interesting insights, comparisons, and shared thoughts.

Each of the people I spoke with was supportive of our desire to adopt a child from China. However, none was familiar with the adoption process. That lead to the first common line of discussion. Everyone I interviewed expressed that we should be very cautious of the parties assisting in the adoption process. When I shared with them that the Chinese government primarily works with accepted and recognized adoption agencies and that adoptive parents rarely deal with private parties in China, they were relieved. Some of the people I spoke with were aware of stories of illicit transactions involving young children.

The second common thread was concern about the Chinese government. There was a belief that we should expect delays, changing rules, and changing procedures, typical of any interaction with the government. We have already heard the advice of other adoptive parents: pack a healthy dose of patience before traveling.

Another shared perspective was that adoptive parents would have their own choice of children. Most envisioned parents entering an orphanage, reviewing the children, and making a selection. When told about the referral process, several of my contacts were quite surprised. Feng Weng, a co-worker, counseled me to insist on having the right to review the children. Through more conversation, Feng mentioned that mainland Chinese do have the privilege of choosing a child after such a review. Since most adoption procedures worldwide are "blind" matches, the expectation of a review and selection seems to be an exception.

Paul Wu, a computer programmer in Omaha, was much more attuned to the adoption situation. He was raised in a rural area of China; he explained that in the country there exists a greater necessity, not just a preference, to have sons. It is the son that will financially support his parents when they can no longer work. City people working in industry, government, and education have retirement benefits that do not tie them so closely to their son for support. Paul Wu was very sympathetic to the plight of children that could not be raised by their birth families. He stated that the decision to leave a child is difficult and illegal; many rural communities show their support by kindly looking the other way or offering assistance to the birth mothers.

Roger Hui, a computer consultant in Indianapolis, was very enthusiastic in his support of our adoption plans. I asked him to share what other Chinese might think. Roger said that in China there is a strong picture of the United States as a paradise; his relatives would think that any child raised in the States would be very fortunate.

Yisun Chang, a technical manager in Chicago, expressed a unique thought. Yisun felt that Americans would be more tolerant and accepting of Chinese girls than boys. The picture of a demure, pretty Chinese girl would be more comfortable to the general public than an aggressive boy.

My survey was done informally among colleagues and co-workers. Each of the people I interviewed was college educated; for the most part, each came from comfortable family situations in China. Certainly there could exist a wider range of perspectives than I was able to uncover. However, through these conversations I did gain insight into how some Chinese Americans viewed our plans for a family—and how they might view our daughter when we bring her home.

When this article was published in summer 1995, Tom McGuffey and his wife were waiting for their daughter's referral.

Nien Cheng
Intrigued by Adoptions
from China

Mike Feazel

FCC–Capital Area

Children adopted from China probably came from rural areas even if they were in urban orphanages, according to Nien Cheng, the author of *Life and Death in Shanghai.* Speaking to FCC–Capital Area on November 15, 1997, Mme. Cheng explained that rural families are more likely to pressure mothers of daughters to give them up because there's more need for the "social security" of sons in rural areas than in urban factories, where more government benefits are available to the aged. "The life of a couple with a son is like the difference between heaven and earth from a couple with a daughter," Mme. Cheng said. Although she quit making speeches two years ago at age 80, Mme. Cheng agreed to speak to FCC because she was intrigued about U.S. adoptions of Chinese children.

It probably took a great deal of pressure to cause a mother to give up her daughter, Mme. Cheng said, because "it's very hard to give up your child. For the Chinese to lose a child is a terrible thing." Despite the one-child policy, she said, the Chinese population continues to grow "quite badly."

Females' lives in the U.S. will be very different from that of Chinese females, Mme. Cheng said. Traditionally, females were so subordinate that most didn't even have their own names. It was "very unusual" for females to go to school, and those who did had "no hope of getting a job." At least theoretically, women achieved more equality under Communism, but there still were few women in "the upper echelons" of the government or party, Mme. Cheng said.

Recent loosening of government control has been a mixed blessing, Mme. Cheng said. Before, women were more protected by the government, but the move to private enterprise has been "a step back for the status of women" because the private sector tends to prefer men for jobs.

In contrast with the prevailing view of experts on international adoption, Mme. Cheng advised against extensive exposure to Chinese culture for adopted children, saying, "You have to bring them up as Americans. That way they won't be torn between cultures." Reflecting the more strict upbringing of traditional Chinese culture, Mme. Cheng also said all American children are "generally spoiled."

Mike Feazel edits the newsletter for FCC–Capital Area.

Culture, Language, Identity

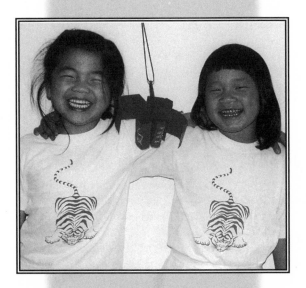

Culture does not reside in the genes. It resides in experience.

David Henry Huang

What is it like to be cut off from a past, to be born as if there
is no past? What obligation do your parents bear to expose
you to the ways of the old country?

Eric Liu

Chinese School

Cheong Chow
FCC/New England

Growing up Chinese American was not easy, but it wasn't particularly hard either. Then again, that's growing up in general, I suppose.

I was born in Hong Kong and came to this country at age three. I'm not absolutely sure when my identity congealed in my consciousness. I suppose it was kindergarten when I began to suspect I was a Chinese kid instead of just any old kid.

I remember thinking to myself in Cantonese: "Hey! They're not calling the horsey by the right name." I had a hard time trying to tell the blond-haired kid that he should share the plastic horsey with others.

The identity thing didn't quite make itself felt, though, until I was old enough to go to Chinese school. For me, Chinese school was a pain. My family was then living in a housing project in the South Cove area adjacent to both Chinatown and South Boston. My daily routine consisted of going to second grade at the Abraham Lincoln School in the morning and Chinese classes at the Kwong Gow School in Chinatown in the afternoon.

There were two things that made Chinese school tough for me and my brother. One was the unholy coincidence that the pickup spot for the school van was located in front of the house of the neighborhood bullies. (The twin Yee brothers did a thriving trade in "protection." I think they've since become cops.) The other was afternoon Hanna Barbera cartoons. We felt deprived as Americans because we had to go to Chinese school while other kids were enjoying Magilla Gorilla and Snagglepuss.

I don't think the act of learning was so hard. We already spoke fluent Cantonese, and calligraphy is actually a lot of fun for younger children who, I think, find it easy to associate a pictogram with a meaning or object. But the atmosphere was different back then. There were a lot of incentives not to learn. Magilla Gorilla was only one of them.

In the seventies, it just wasn't all that fashionable to be Chinese, especially immigrant Chinese. The *jook-sing*s, or American-born Cantonese, would beat us up for having that fresh-off-the-boat look. There was no cool Chinese person on TV other than Kane of "Kung Fu" (and Kane looked funny for a Chinese and spoke funnier.) People would say "egg foo yong" or "egg roll" to us as a matter of course, which made me feel bad even though I liked egg rolls. All our dads were restaurant cooks, and all our moms were seamstresses, which is kind of depressing to a kid who wanted to grow up and be like GI Joe or Speed Racer (which is a futile dream since it is well known that Chinese people can't drive.)

And there was always someone to make fun of us when we did speak Chinese in public. You know, the familiar "ching chong" routine. As an Asian comedian once said, "You should never do the 'ching chong' to an Oriental because it really confuses him."

On top of everything, you could throw in busing. My brothers and I were shipped as tender grade-schoolers to Charlestown in police-escorted yellow containers. They told us busing was for our own good.

Anyway, all this had an effect on our studies at Chinese school. We took to reading comic books in class, copying other people on exams (which didn't work because sitting in the back of the class, we were copying off of kids who were copying off of other kids, and somewhere along the line all the right answers got screwed up), and daydreaming.

It all came to a head when both my brother and I were kicked out of Chinese school in the winter of '76. I came home with a note written in Chinese stating that I had lived up to my Chinese school nickname of *sek-tow*, "rock-head." My dad was very upset at this. A slightly neurotic electrician and spray-painter who became a restaurant cook (what else?) in America, he got so mad that he decided to punish me with whatever he had on hand at the time. I believe I was the only Chinese child ever to be beaten on the behind with a Christmas tree. I was glad it wasn't the wok.

I really excelled at regular school after being kicked out of Kwong Gow. I got into advanced classes in the fourth, fifth, and sixth grades. Under a great teacher at the Clarence Edwards School in Charlestown, I was prepared for and entered Boston Latin School. I blazed my way through honor classes in that exam school before running into the stone walls of teenage malaise and "chick" problems during my junior and senior years.

It could have been the bite of the Christmas tree that drove me to academic success after being thrown out of Chinese school. But I think it could have been the easing of pressure that happened when Chinese school was no longer a factor in my young life. Actually, my schooling at Kwong Gow had lasted two years, during which I learned to write my name and a few other words in Chinese, such as *one, two, three, mountain, person, mother,* and *horsey.* But as the years have gone by, I've regretted never having learned how to read and write Chinese. Although I can speak my native Cantonese fluently, I wish I'd made more of an effort back then to learn Chinese characters.

This really struck me as I was going through a phase of intense interest in the history and culture of my homeland during high school and college. I realized as a person of Chinese descent that I could only read about Chinese history from books written in English.

The world was different then, I suppose. But sometimes I want to turn back the clock for a moment and go back to a day at Kwong Gow when I was giving Dick Wong a hard time.

"How come you actually do well in these classes?" I yelled at him. "It's making me and my brother look bad."

Dick yelled back: "Because I want to know some Chinese when I grow up."

Dick was blond and blue-eyed. He, incredibly, was the only full-blooded Anglo child I ever knew who was adopted by Chinese parents. I thought he was nuts for actually liking Chinese school. Now, I'm pretty sure he wasn't.

Cheong Chow grew up in Boston's Chinatown, a first-generation Chinese American born to parents in the restaurant trade. He is a reporter for the *Boston Globe.*

The Importance of Cultural Education

Jane Brown, M.S.W.
San Francisco Bay Area FCC

One of the questions that adoptive parents of internationally adopted children ask most frequently is whether or not it is essential to teach adopted children about their culture of origin. If it is important, how much is enough, at what age do you begin, what type of information is important for kids to learn, and how do you get started?

Although adoptions from China are a recent phenomenon, adoptions from other Asian countries have been taking place for decades, and there are tens of thousands of adoptees who came from Japan, Korea, Vietnam, and India to grow up in the United States. Adoption professionals and adoptive parents have had an opportunity to learn from those adoptees who were placed many years ago and are now raising children of their own. Those adoptees have been wonderful teachers! Here's what we have learned from them:

Although all children have the same basic developmental needs in the physical, social, and mental spheres, our internationally adopted children have extra needs in the arena of emotional development. That means that we have some extra parenting tasks, folks! Our children will, as they grow to adolescence and then to adulthood, need to explain first to *themselves* and then to their peers and to strangers who they are and how they came to be who they are. If their adoptive parents are not Chinese, they will need to understand, accept, and explain their racial identity. They will need to explain why they are not growing up with the parents they were born to. They will need to explain why they could not grow up in China. They will need to feel pride in the land of their birth and in their personal history in order to feel pride in themselves and to give these explanations to others. Thus, teaching them about their cultural origins is a very, very important parenting task.

In my work as an adoption social worker, I had the joy of working with many adoptees of all ages. One day, a little girl offered me an uncensored glimpse into the world of her thoughts and understanding. Our conversation went something like this:

"Jane, I never want to go to Korea, nope."

"Gosh, Karen, I'm surprised to hear you say that. Why don't you want to visit there?"

Karen responded by saying, "Mommy showed me pictures of pretty things there, but they are bad people. They give away all their little children. They don't like children in Korea, nope."

Last year, Karen's parents wrote to tell me of Karen's expedition to Korea as part of a "homeland" tour conducted by the Holt Adoption Agency of New Jersey. It was their sensitivity to Karen's emotional needs—her questions, her fears, the push-pull of I wish I could know more/I'm afraid of what I'd find out—combined with their excitement and commitment to learning all about the wonderful land from which their precious child had come that helped Karen get past her negative feelings and develop curiosity and then pride in the land of her birth. She had a wonderful trip and hopes some day to go again when she has children of her own so that they can learn about their heritage. Karen now understands that it was Korea's great love for and commitment to children that enabled its government to make foreign adoption possible.

What can you do now? As parents of young children, gather information and resources. This is a good time to purchase books, dolls, video tapes, pictures, etc., to share with your children. Educate the people around you. If they think of China only as a country that does not care for its children, they will very likely impart that belief to their children, who will discuss this with your child, possibly in the form of a taunt. Examine your own knowledge and openness toward all types of people and the cultures they originated from. Children, especially children who've joined their families through adoption, seem to have in-born radar about the prejudices held by those around them. When their parents display an active interest in and acceptance of *all* differences among people, children thrive. Prejudice, of any kind, in the family leads kids to the conclusion that they are not quite good enough—even when their parent vehemently protests. Displaying active interest in *only* your child's culture of origin usually produces the same result. Your child needs to know that you are open and interested in differences among people.

Become active in adoptive family support groups, and plan to make this a lifetime commitment. These groups can be a lifeline for both parents and children. They send the message to our children that being adopted is something special, something to take pride in. They network to gather information and ideas about adoptive parenting, adoption agencies, culture, and all sorts of things. They can move mountains when it comes to changing negative perceptions about adoption and adoptive families in schools, government, the workplace, foreign governments, and society in general. For children, they provide a peer network. While this may be of limited value while children are very young, it can be increasingly important as they grow older. They help families impart cultural information to children, and the children take in the information in a different kind of way from when they are isolated in individual families.

My older adopted children are now 26, 24, 21, and 18 years of age. We were fortunate to have lived in an area where there were many adoptive family groups. My children developed many friendships with other adoptees and their parents. We faithfully attended all of the group functions for many years. During the middle childhood years, my children, along with their peers, resisted attending those group activities. Only because my husband and I persisted did our children stay in contact with other adoptive families. During their teen years, they were even more reluctant to display any interest in their culture of origin, adoption, or their personal histories. Subtle clues led us to understand that they had many thoughts, feelings, questions, and opinions about these issues, but if there was discussion, it was because my husband and I initiated it.

Now that they are in college and beyond, we are reaping the rewards of our efforts in having taught them to appreciate their cultural heritage. They are, for the first time, interested in investigating the language, customs, and history of their country of origin on their own. They are not afraid to associate with Asian Americans and talk with them about what it was like to grow up in an Asian family in the U.S. and compare that with their own, transracial, upbringing. They tell us about the "bananas" and "twinkies"—the students who are yellow on the outside and white on the inside, who are afraid to look too closely in the mirror, not sure how they fit into the society around them and uncomfortable with their own identity.

Two of them have married. Our daughter, who is Amerasian (half Korean, half Caucasian American) married a man who is Korean. Our oldest son recently married a young woman who is half Thai. As adults, they have finally been able to tell us what it meant to them to grow up with knowledge about and encouragement to understand and accept their cultural origins. They have each renewed interest in and contact with their original group of friends from the adoptive family groups.

Finally, I will leave this thought with you, as you consider whether teaching about culture is important. If your child is to grow up emotionally healthy, she must be able to love herself. If she is to love herself, she must be able to respect her birth parents, for it is they who gave her her genetic endowment. For her to grow up and not feel shame about why those birth parents relinquished her, she must learn about the historical and cultural forces that shaped their decision and behavior.

Finally, if she is to understand and accept why China has a one-child policy, she must learn that there is a balance of good and bad, beautiful and ugly, joy and sorrow, ancient ways and new, in the land of her birth. The opportunity to learn about the richness, diversity, beauty, and longevity of China's culture will ultimately be a key to understanding, accepting, and celebrating the wonder of herself.

Jane Brown, a member of FCC-Arizona and the mother of eight children (four from Korea, three born to the family, and the youngest adopted from China), worked for more than 20 years as a social worker for two international adoption agencies. She is on the Advisory Board of San Francisco Bay Area FCC and is a regular contributor to the SF-FCC newsletter.

Lily Learns Mandarin

Is It Really Necessary That
My Daughter Learn Chinese?
A Mother Explains Why
She Changed Her Mind

Julie Michaels

FCC/New England

I have always considered myself some place in the middle when I thought about the issue of Chinese culture in my daughter's life. Lily is six years old, part of the first wave of China adoptees to come to the U.S. Like many who went to China, I returned with great enthusiasm for the country and its history.

In 1993 a Malaysian friend helped us organize our first Chinese New Year party. Ever since, we have had rats or oxen or roosters hanging somewhere in our house. We've read books about China, looked for it on the map, talked about it when it was on the front page of the newspaper. We've done our share of dim sum, art exhibits, and culture classes. But when the discussion turned toward teaching our kids Chinese, I always reacted skeptically.

Was learning the language really necessary? I had bought the books and tapes, tried teaching myself some basics, kept up my *nihao*s and *xiexie*s, but deep down, I wasn't convinced. My daughter, after all, was no longer Chinese. She would grow up Asian American. Why expend all this time and money on a language she would have little opportunity to use?

That was then. Now, six weeks into Lily's Mandarin lessons, I can't believe I ever hesitated. What brought about my change of heart? Several things. For one, we moved.

From the cultural melting pot that is Brighton, we relocated to western Massachusetts. Where once Lily attended school with other Asians, she is now the only one in her class. In Boston, we had Asian neighbors, a whole circle of FCC friends, even a Korean nanny who lived with use for eight months. Out here, we are far more isolated from that kind of everyday interaction.

Also, Lily has grown older. What she didn't notice at age three, she has begun to see clearly at age six. She looks different from her classmates. And inevitably, she came home one day to say that she felt embarrassed when a child in her class said her eyes were different. We talked about it, about being Chinese, about being adopted. I asked her if she wanted to bring her adoption book to school, if she wanted to talk about it at show and tell. Yes, she'd like to, she replied. Would I come and help her? Of course.

Not long before this school incident, I had begun to alter my reading list. During Lily's early years, my passion for China had led me to read Chinese history, folk tales, or memoirs like *Wild Swans* and *Red Azalea*. I even reread Pearl S. Buck's *The Good Earth*. But after I attended a talk hosted by an Asian American study group at the University of Massachusetts, I switched my focus.

I still recall one Asian student's comment. "If you're going to raise your daughters in this country," she said, "you'd better learn as much about Angel Island as you do about the Song dynasty." And so I started to read about the history of the Chinese in America, starting with *Unbound Feet: A Social History of Chinese Women in San Francisco*, by Judy Yung. The racism, discrimination, and sheer ignorance the Chinese experienced in this country was staggering to me. Though my daughter is growing up in more enlightened times, I began to understand that the greater her own pride was in her Chinese heritage, the better armed she would be for the inevitable slights and misunderstandings.

And finally, there are my own childhood regrets. I am the first-generation daughter of a Yugoslav father. Growing up in New York in the 1950s in a largely Jewish community and surrounded by my mother's Italian American family, my brother and I were not quick to embrace our paternal heritage. Aside from the odd saint's day, we were not much interested in being Yugoslav. And we certainly had no desire to learn the language. Now, 40 years later, I regret that I was so dismissive. Every time I hear Serbo-Croatian spoken, my heart gives a little tug. And I am sorry, deeply sorry, that I cannot turn and join the conversation.

So now my daughter studies Mandarin. Each week, after tumbling, she sits down with Zoe and Sam Laiz and learns her Chinese symbols and numbers. Zoe and Sam's mother, Jana, is a China scholar; their father, Joe, is Filipino American. Although Joe is the one in the family with the Chinese genes, Jana—a nice Jewish girl from New York City—is the one who knows the language. When I asked her to teach Lily, she decided it was time that her own kids, ages four and seven, also learn Chinese.

And no one is more delighted with these classes than Lily! She loves her lessons, loves the Laiz kids, and loves teaching her parents what she's learned. Last week, she taught her best friend Charlotte to count to 10 in Chinese. Charlotte was thrilled. Now, instead of being different, Lily sees herself as special. And for one hour each week, the Chinese side of her is celebrated. That she is joined by two other children with Asian features is an added plus.

Will Lily stick with the program? Will she turn around two years from now and say, "I don't want to study Chinese"? Perhaps. But for now the foundation is being laid. I am giving my daughter the tools with which she will build her identity. While the language may fade, the self-esteem will remain. And my daughter will march proudly into her life.

Julie Michaels is the editor of *China Connection,* the newsletter of FCC/New England. A former editor at the *Boston Globe,* she is the mother of Lily Rachel, adopted from Wuhan in 1992.

How Much Chinese Is Too Much Chinese?

Carrie Krueger
FCC-Northwest

They are questions we all have to grapple with: How much exposure to Chinese culture should our kids have? Do we do it at the expense of their American education? Do we do it as a family, or is it something the kids do on their own?

Sending my five-year-old daughter off to Chinese immersion school this summer raised eyebrows among family and friends, including some who have adopted kids from China. After all, these kids are American now. Some feared the program would be confusing, overly intense, or excessive. For what it's worth, here is my thinking on the subject:

I think we owe our kids a solid footing in their native culture, language, and history. Many studies of adult adoptees from places like Korea show that this kind of grounding is beneficial throughout life. My preference is to do as much of this as possible as a family, although this is complicated slightly by the fact that I have a son from Vietnam. This summer program is obviously not something I could join in on, so I sent her on her own. Just as we owe our kids exposure to their culture, I think it's also desirable to expose them in the context of the genuine Chinese community, whenever that's possible. Classes set up specifically for Chinese adoptees can be great, but it's also wonderful to be part of the real Chinese community, interacting with adults and kids who have nothing to do with adoption. I recognize that by doing this, I put myself in the position of being the minority, and I think that is a positive.

I thought it was awesome that my daughter learned math and character recognition in Chinese before English, and I can't imagine it will have any negative impact on her American education. In our school system, teachers don't expect kids to read until first grade. If she can do it in Chinese before then, why not? I did stress to the teacher that I didn't expect her to be doing homework and passing tests. She's only five. But if this stuff can come naturally and be fun for her, what is the harm?

My daughter is very excited about the fact that she is a Chinese American. She loves knowing more about the language and music of China. For her, this situation wasn't confusing; it was a way for her to learn more about something she's extremely interested in. The full-time aspect of it might seem excessive, but it was perfect for us because it solved any transportation difficulties (I work full-time) and also allowed her to learn a lot more than she would have in a less intensive program. She also squeezed in swimming lessons, a week-long sports camp, a five-year reunion with our China group, a trip to Disneyland, and a whole lot of other all-American activities this summer.

Was it stressful and confusing? She fell apart a few times during the first week, but I think a lot of that was exhaustion from giving up naps! I went into this prepared to quit at any point. I paid week by week, and I built in a break for a sports camp in the middle. She never wanted to quit, never exhibited any signs of stress, never seemed confused, anxious, or reluctant to jump back in each morning.

This kind of experience wouldn't be right for every kid, and it's certainly not a mandatory right of passage for adoptees. But for this kid, it was a really positive experience. Of course I also realize that this kind of school probably isn't available in most parts of the country. Where it is available, there may be some significant cultural barriers to overcome in integrating your adopted child into the non-adopted Chinese community. Where it isn't available, parents can still seek out other, less intensive opportunities for this kind of education or even form their own classes where necessary.

Whether we do a lot or a little of it, I believe it's vital for us to keep our children's native culture alive in our families. It's a tie back to their beginnings and a way of honoring the people and the place that gave us these gifts, these children, we call our own.

Claire Krueger was adopted in 1992 from Hangzhou. She lives in Washington State with her mom, Carrie, and her little brother, Cameron, who was born in 1994 in Da Nang, Vietnam.

Chinese Language Instruction for Children

Preparing for the Long March

John Bowen
Families with Children Adopted from China (British Columbia)

Most FCAC parents, I'm sure, have thought about making it possible at some point for their children to learn a Chinese language. While it is possible to find Chinese language instruction in most cities and towns in Canada, the variety of learning options, one would think, would be nowhere greater than in Vancouver.

In this city, we have the luxury of being able to plan a strategy for our children to learn Chinese, with the knowledge that options will always be available. The oldest FCAC children in BC are going on for eight years old. My daughter, Melissa, is now six and a half years old (yes, really!). A number of parents have already started their children on the road to learning a Chinese language. As one who is considering doing the same, I propose to raise some questions and points which have arisen in my conversations with other FCAC parents and from my own thoughts and experience.

Should Our Children Learn a Chinese Language?

This is not an idle question. If parents and kids embark on a course toward eventual fluency in a Chinese language, they should have a good sense of why the objective is worth the inevitable sacrifices. There is little question that for many kids, studying Chinese, year after year, when other activities look more attractive and more relevant, is going to require staying power.

A respectable argument can be made for investing the time and resources required to learn Chinese into extra math, French, a sport, or a creative pursuit. Our kids are Canadians, and in Canada, the return on investment in such endeavors is immediate and tangible. They lead to better grade averages at school and better jobs afterwards. And to the extent

248

that we want our children to learn "rounding out" skills and acquire "finishing flourishes," piano lessons, art history, or the like might do the job.

"But our children are also Chinese," you might say in horrified reaction to this grossly functional view. "Our kids were born in China. They will always be Chinese, and they need to acquire the ability to reconnect with their culture." So goes the argument. And this is more or less the reason most parents give for enrolling their kids in Chinese lessons. With some reservations, this is also my reason for taking Melissa to Mandarin lessons. I want Melissa to grow up self-confident about every aspect of her identity and proud of her Chineseness, however she chooses to characterize it.

My reservations have to do with the recognition that the reason is mine and not Melissa's and that, to some extent, it is self-serving. I want Melissa to give me a passing grade as a parent when she is grown up and she reflects on her childhood. I want to escape the charge that many parents have earned—of not validating and respecting the culture of origin of their adopted children. In addition, I want to keep my promise to the Chinese officials who helped me adopt Melissa—to make it possible for her to learn Chinese.

From a negotiation course I took years ago, I remember the instructor saying that one's children are the toughest negotiators one encounters in life. This is because children study their parents with great diligence and intensity. They know you better than they know anything. Knowing this, I try to anticipate Melissa's arguments against my choices made on her behalf. I am preparing myself for the following objections to my desire for her to study Chinese. Melissa might say:

> Why should I be singled out for this punishment? You encourage me to assess others as individuals. You want me to see no barriers in the way of my aspirations. Yet you want me to become a hyphenated Canadian. Jimmy Chan in my class speaks no Chinese, nor do his parents. There are lots of kids in my class whose parents came from Germany, Ukraine, Holland, and other countries. They don't have to go language classes. There are lots of other things and perhaps other languages I would prefer to learn than Chinese. If you are making me learn Chinese because you adopted me in China, that is your hang-up.

Of course, there is no predicting how our kids will react to our decision to have them learn Chinese. And doubtless, there will be many different reactions. The foregoing is conjecture and hyperbole. It is imagined only to indicate that good intentions of parents should never be assumed to be appreciated later. Remember, adoptive parents of earlier generations thought that denial of children's natural heritage and complete assimilation of children were in their best interests. Such a view today is heresy.

When the time comes, I hope to be ready to defend my choice to embark Melissa on a course toward learning Mandarin. I hope she will agree with me, but am prepared for the possibility that she will not. I will not rely on the ethnic- and sentiment-based arguments for my case. They are too open to ideological attack. Instead, I will use functional concrete for my battlements.

"Life is about choices. The more scope you have to make choices, the better off you will be," I will tell Melissa.

> My job as a parent will be successful, in large measure, to the extent that I make it possible for you to make choices from a wide range of options and make them well.
>
> China will be a major force in world affairs in the next century, and Chinese (Mandarin), already the most spoken language in the world, will be a useful instrument for accessing opportunities in all aspects of your adult life. And if I were the father of Jimmy Chan or the kids in your class of German, Ukrainian, or any other ancestry, I would encourage them to learn Mandarin.

Melissa's school will offer her the choice of learning Mandarin, Spanish, or Japanese after Grade 5 (she must choose one of the three, and French is compulsory) as part of the regular curriculum. If Melissa hears me out and still decides to learn Spanish or Japanese instead of Mandarin, I will support her in her decision.

Mandarin or Cantonese or...

There are many languages spoken in China, and our children come from many different parts of China. Traditionally, the most commonly spoken Chinese language in British Columbia—and indeed, most of North America—is Cantonese, in its numerous variants. And perhaps half or more of the children adopted by BC families in China come from Guangdong province, where Cantonese is spoken. Cantonese then, seems like an obvious choice for some, especially for Cantonese-speaking parents who want their children to communicate with extended family members.

For many of us, however, Mandarin may be an easier choice. Cantonese is not an easy language to learn without constant exposure to it. For one thing, it has an indeterminate number of tones (no one seems to agree on exactly how many), compared with a definite four or five for Mandarin (depending on whether you count "neutral" as a tone). For another, it is less standardized than Mandarin. And finally, it is likely to lose ground to Mandarin, with Hong Kong's takeover by China and the increasing proportion of Mandarin-speaking immigrants to Canada from Taiwan and China.

For people wanting their children to learn Cantonese, there is ample opportunity. Classes are offered by school boards, cultural centers, and other organizations all over the Lower Mainland and the rest of British

Columbia. In Vancouver at least, it is doubtless possible to find instruction in other Chinese languages as well.

What Is the Best Means to Having My Child Learn a Chinese Language?

For those parents who speak a Chinese language, or are learning one, the best approach to teaching it is at hand. Kids who hear a language spoken at home are going to have an advantage over those who do not. And those who learn it along with their parents will likely be more motivated to learn it than those whose parents are not learning the language.

But for old dogs like me, we will need to rely on the do as I ask, rather than as I do approach. (That is why I am refining a host of counter-arguments in anticipation of pointed questions).

Some parents have started children learning Chinese as early as three years old by hiring tutors. One West Vancouver parent who did this found her daughter very responsive and quick to learn at first, but considered it necessary to give her a break after a few months. The most common strategy adopted by local FCAC parents is to enroll their children in one of the many evening or Saturday Chinese language courses offered by school boards, continuing education institutions, cultural centers, recreation centers, or private companies. Most are very good and relatively inexpensive. I am aware of parents who have children enrolled in courses in Vancouver, Richmond, Burnaby, and North Vancouver. Melissa and two of her FCAC friends are enrolled at Lions Gate Mandarin School. All parents I have spoken to agree that the caliber of instruction there is excellent. No matter where you live, I am sure you will find similar offerings nearby.

In addition to weekly, evening, or weekend courses, there are continuous courses and camps offered. The Chinese Cultural Centers in Chinatown, Vancouver, and in Richmond both offer language and culture courses and camps in the summer. The Vancouver school board offers a similar array of courses. Melissa and some of her friends will be attending a privately organized Chinese Culture and Language Camp at a school in Vancouver this summer.

For the totally committed, there is now the option of Chinese immersion. A public school in Vancouver offers Mandarin immersion. It is very popular, and perhaps there will be other Chinese immersion schools opening soon.

John Bowen edits *Friends of the Family,* the newsletter of Families with Children Adopted from China (British Columbia).

The Unexpected Benefits of Language Lessons

Julia Fleming
Mosaic (UK)

My husband and I adopted a five-year-old from China 19 months ago. Prior to her arrival, we hired a delightful young woman named Shu Ling to come into our home, twice a week, to talk to Hazel in Chinese and at least keep some of her Chinese comprehension alive. We knew Hazel would never be bilingual. What we wanted to do was give her a foundation. We thought that with the Chinese she already had, if someone came in and kept her basic Chinese going, if she ever wanted to really learn, she would have a tremendous head start.

We wanted to do this because we had talked to several adult transracial adoptees who were struggling with identity. Two of the women—both adopted as infants from Hong Kong—were vehemently opposed to transracial adoption. So many studies show that a small percentage of transracial adoptees feel "disconnected" in later life—both from their adoptive community and from their ethnic community. Granted, the majority of adoptees are happy and well-adjusted; we just wanted to load the odds in our girls' favor—to keep them from becoming one the "unhappy" statistics. One of the things we determined was that the ability to speak Chinese would have made the women we met an awful lot happier (along with a whole lot of other things, but both really rued not being able to communicate in Chinese).

Finding a teacher where we live was difficult, and we only managed after advertising in the local university newspapers and putting flyers up in all the Chinese grocery shops and restaurants in our area. Shu Ling saw one of the flyers in a grocery shop. She travels to us by train, and we pay her train fare as well as her fee for teaching Hazel.

Like so many others, we initially thought that this set-up was not going to work out and that we would discontinue the sessions. First of all, Hazel was extremely institutionalized—she had fewer than 50 words of spoken Chinese at age five. She could understand basic commands in two dialects, but her receptive vocabulary was tiny. For instance, she had been told in her institute, "Eat this!" But she was never told, "This is a bowl. Do you want a spoon? This is called a spoon." She could not understand the names of even the most basic items. She was two to three and a half years delayed in all areas.

We felt that asking her to learn Chinese and English and learn to live in a family while she was also learning the concepts of colors, time, shapes, road safety rules, etc., etc., and everything she needed to take on board for her new life was just way too much to ask. We also didn't think it was fair to ask Shu Ling to cope with Hazel's behavioral problems. We also really doubted Hazel's ability to get anything out of the sessions. After three sessions, we told Shu Ling we didn't need her anymore.

The next week, Hazel announced in pidgin English that she wasn't Chinese and didn't like Chinese people. I know a lot of people have written about their children's desire to "fit in" and be "American" or "English" or "Swedish," whatever. But we felt with Hazel it went deeper. We felt that, because of her abusive past, she was equating "Chinese" with "bad."

There was no way we were going to let that happen. We looked at it this way: If and when Hazel was able to leave home (19 months down the line, there appears little doubt that she will be able to live independently one day), she would be judged on her face. No one would know she had white parents. She would be treated as if she were Chinese—and of course, she is ethnically Chinese. It would do her self-esteem tremendous harm if we allowed this situation to continue.

At a racial awareness seminar put on by our adoption support group, a transracially adopted adult said something that has stuck with me: "You must parent the emerging adult—not the delightful child you have now. Your child may spend three times as much time living away from you as with you. Please take care of that adult."

It was with the adult Hazel in mind that we called Shu Ling back. For the past 18 months, she has come into our home for at least four hours a week. Hazel initially fought it. She refused to speak Chinese, refused to smile at Shu Ling, refused to acknowledge her own Chinese looks. We persevered for many months.

But having Shu Ling has been remarkable for Hazel. She saw first-hand that she could be vile and dreadful to Shu Ling—and this young woman responded with kindness and love. You could almost see the cogs turning in Hazel's head—hey, not all Chinese people are bad!

Shu Ling and I were able to mount a double-pronged attack on Hazel's enormous areas of deficiency. One month we'd decide to attack colors or time or shapes or family. Hazel would hear all about these concepts in a language that she knew a bit of and a new language. Once we conquered these things, we went on to numbers, pencil control, etc. Always in tandem, always with the same goal—helping Hazel.

Hazel has transformed her opinion of herself with regards to her Chinese identity. She looks forward to Shu Ling coming. She seeks out Asian faces in crowds, sidles up to them to see if they are speaking Chinese—if they are, she introduces herself in Chinese. She wants to grow her hair long "just like Shu Ling." She asks Shu Ling about Chinese cooking, newspapers, writing, parties, clothes, singing, videos.

She has managed to acquire a balanced view of what "Chinese" is—it is not only what happened to her in China.

She now goes (with our other Chinese daughter) to a Chinese family twice a month (without us) for lunch. Before her "breakthrough" with Shu Ling, she would have nothing to do with this family.

Three days ago she came home and said that one of her classmates said Hazel's nose was "ugly" because it was flat. I asked Hazel how hearing that made her feel. She said, "Well Shu Ling and Yi (the mother of the Chinese family she visits) are really beautiful. Rose is stupid." I know her response would have been different without her language tuition.

Of course, her Chinese is not very good at all. But she is building a foundation. She can understand basic conversations. But most of all, she has gained positive, strong role models.

So, if you are thinking of language tuition, I would say that it can be an extremely positive experience. For our family, the benefits have been enormous, and we have never regretted our commitment. We have never believed that Hazel's English has suffered because of her Chinese lessons.

Julia Fleming, the editor of *Mosaic,* is a co-founder of One World Orphanage Trust, a UK charitable organization that benefits orphanages in China. "Sometimes we are able to support small projects that are unable to fund-raise freely in the West—primarily because they work in sensitive areas in China (both geographically and politically)," Fleming explained. "Our most recent project is the repair of 80 cleft-affected children in Yunnan. We fund Chinese doctors—all of whom do a good job—and it is a much less expensive way to work than sending in foreign experts.... In the past four years, we have done several projects like this; sometimes medical treatment is needed for only one child. We also give money for capital expenditure, fostering, and education."

Chinese Culture in the Home

A Caregiver's Perspective

Rongrong Shen
FCC-Toronto

I came to Canada with my twelve-year-old son in August 1993. At that time my husband was already working in Mississauga. In China I had worked my way up from computer programmer to director of a department. However, because of my poor English, I could not find a job in my field in Canada. I was tormented and lost the equilibrium in my heart. But I could not go back to China because by husband and my child were here. I am a person who does not like to attempt something and accomplish nothing. After thinking about it, I decided to do something and make some money at the same time.

One day, I read an ad in a Chinese newspaper. A family (FCC-Toronto members Paul and Barb Singleton) was looking for someone who could speak Mandarin and English to look after their two adopted Chinese daughters in their home. I was very interested in trying the work. I thought it would help me to learn English with an English-speaking family, and I also have special emotions for Chinese children. I worried that my English was not good enough for the interview, even though I believed I could do the work well. After the interview, to my surprise, I was hired.

I started work in September 1994. My responsibilities were to keep the children safe and happy, teach them Mandarin, and cook Chinese food for lunch. At that time, Paul and Barb's son Jamie was four and their adopted Chinese daughters Samiee and Emma were two and a half and almost two. Although Samiee had only been adopted for a few months, she had already forgotten Mandarin and would not speak any words. Emma was too young to speak.

When I stayed with the children, I spoke to them in Mandarin. If they could not understand, I spoke again in English. The children were young and wanted to learn many new things. Whatever we saw, I always spoke to them in Mandarin—they learned a lot and were not bored with a new language. Now the children can understand and speak some Mandarin. In order to help the children learn Chinese, Barb asked me to write down some Chinese words and sentences in their English and pinyin equivalents on a piece of paper. She put the paper on the wall of her kitchen so that she could read and practice every day. Also, she often tried to talk to her children in Mandarin and to have them take more initiative. Since children have a better memory than adults and learn every day, Emma and Samiee were usually Barb's teachers. In this way, Barb encouraged and helped her children to learn Mandarin with more interest.

After the children were three years old, I started to teach them to read Chinese word cards that Barb had purchased, with Chinese, English, and pinyin equivalents on them. At first I just taught the children to speak the Chinese name with the picture, because at that time the children were too young to read. To maintain their interest, I used many different teaching methods. The main method is learning while playing and having fun, sometimes with a material incentive! I taught them about six new cards every day because they could not remember more. Before we started learning new words, we always reviewed the learned words to ensure that the children remembered what they had learned.

Teaching occurred throughout their play activities. We drew pictures, played games, folded paper, colored pictures, and did handwork, all the while speaking in Mandarin. Even some words or sentences that they did not know before, they could understand.

To coordinate learning Chinese, Barb bought some posters of Chinese words when she went to China. Usually I taught the children first, then I asked them to be the teachers and to "teach" me in Mandarin. If they forgot how to say it, I reminded them. The children liked to be teachers very much. In this way, it also made the process more interesting for them.

I often taught the children to sing Chinese children's songs. Barb also bought many Chinese children's movies, karaoke videos, and song cassettes. The children often listened to or watched these tapes. Samiee and Emma love to sing and dance. I liked to sing while dancing in order to teach them. The children loved it and were able to remember the words of a song. Now Samiee and Emma can sing many Chinese songs.

After the children understood some Mandarin, I started to compose some ballads for them. Before I taught them, I always drew a picture first that had an association with the ballad and let the children color it in. Then I taught them the ballad, which the children found very interesting and could understand very well. After a few times, the children could recite the ballad, and now they can recite many Chinese ballads. Sometimes I borrowed some Chinese children's books from the library. Barb also bought many Chinese learning books. With these books, the children not only learned many Chinese words, but also many sentences. When they saw some Chinese words that they knew, they always pointed them out to me. In this way, the children could understand Mandarin and express their requirements and thinking.

After the girls were four, I started to teach the children to write some simple Chinese words. For the fun of learning, I asked them to write in different color pens and to make the process seem like drawing a picture. After they finished their writing, I gave them a sticker as a reward. Usually people think that writing Chinese words is very difficult, but I used a non-traditional association method to teach the children. I taught them from one simple word to many other words, from the shallower to the deeper, from the easier to the more advanced. In just a few minutes they could remember words and also write on their own. Jamie enjoyed writing very much, often using Chinese words to make sentences. Not only can he write his Chinese name, but he can also write many other sentences in Chinese.

In short, I feel that, in order to have children learn Mandarin in an English-speaking environment, you should:

1. Let your children learn Mandarin as early as possible. Children do not feel difficulty in learning and accepting a new language.

2. Use various methods to make learning fun. Children should be taught Mandarin while playing. Making them interested in learning and "feeling" Mandarin should not be difficult. After they understand some Mandarin, then there can be more traditional "teaching."

3. Help, encourage, and support your children's efforts. If the parents make an effort to learn Chinese from their children, the children have a sense of teaching that further encourages their initiative to learn Mandarin.

4. Use various kinds of Chinese materials to keep children hearing Mandarin and creating an environment for them to learn and speak Mandarin.

Rongrong Shen has started Rongrong's Post-Adoption Service, dedicated to helping families who have adopted Chinese children to instill Chinese culture and keep Chinese traditions.

Seven Ways to Celebrate the Lunar New Year

Ruth Laseski and Susan Caughman
FCC–New York

1. Start a new tradition by having a big family dinner on Chinese New Year evening (preferably all wearing new clothes). Red lanterns, red clothes, bowls of oranges, and fish are imperative. Chinatown shops sell calligraphy scrolls (*chunlian*), lanterns, and good luck symbols to decorate the house. Play Chinese music. Lots of families make dumplings together and all the children are given *hongbao* (red envelopes containing "lucky money"). Holiday seeds and nuts in a "tray of togetherness" are available at most Chinese groceries. For dessert, serve *niangao,* traditional Chinese New Year's cake. Here in New York, one group of three or four neighboring FCC families began celebrating Chinese New Year together this way last year and plan to continue each year.

2. At your child's school, for snacks, offer oranges and fortune cookies for children able to eat them safely, almond cookies, or cookies from your Chinatown bakery in the shape of the new year's animal. For special touches, use paper placemats featuring the Chinese zodiac (many Chinese restaurants will give you free placements from their stock or sell them for five or ten cents each) or red and white plastic soup bowls decorated with Chinese characters that are typically used at less expensive Chinese restaurants (the bowls typically cost less than $1).

3. Flowering plants are an important part of the New Year or Spring Festival in China. So, as gifts for teachers, baby-sitters, or relatives, make small pots of blooming narcissus. Buy paper white narcissus bulbs (about 80 cents each) at your local nursery or florist. Six or seven weeks before you want blooms, plant three bulbs in a five-

inch-diameter clear plastic pot filled with pea-gravel and place the pot in a sunny, warm window, keeping well watered. The blooms have a characteristic sweet smell and can last a week.

4. Send Chinese New Year cards (available at the Asia Society or in Chinatown bookstores) to family friends and to your child's orphanage in China expressing good wishes in both English and Chinese. Stamp your letters and cards with the Chinese New Year U.S. postage stamps that will arrive at your local post office about a month before the holiday.

5. For story time, at home or school, choose a picture book focusing on Chinese New Year. In *Lion Dancer: Ernie Wan's Chinese New Year,* by Kate Waters and Madeline Slovenz-Low (New York: Scholastic, 1990), a boy in New York's Chinatown prepares for his first role, under the light-blinking head, in a lion dance. In *Chinese New Year's Dragon,* by Rachel Sing (New York: Half Moon Books/Simon & Schuster, 1992), a girl's narrative with color sketches gives a simple overview of major New Year traditions. A touching new book, *Sam and the Lucky Money,* by Karen Chinn (New York: Lee & Low Books, 1995), available from AACP (Asian-American Books, 800-874-2242), tells the story of a boy who goes shopping in Chinatown to spend the lucky money he received for New Year but is disappointed when it's not enough to buy anything he wants.

6. For an art project for some preschoolers or primary school children, pick up a Chinese-language newspaper and let your little ones go to town reproducing Chinese characters—a great opportunity to build eye-hand coordination, artistry, and awareness of writing systems other than the Western one. For other simple Chinese crafts for young children, order the booklets *Paper Lanterns* and *Chinese Cultural Activities* (includes a dragon and a New Year's parade) from ARTS, Inc., 32 Market Street, New York, NY 10002. (ARTS, Inc., is a community arts organization on the Lower East Side of Manhattan. They also offer a wonderful tape of Chinese folk songs for children. Thanks to Kate Gill for this.)

7. Invite a Chinese neighbor, friend, or visitor to visit your home or preschool. These guests might be as eager to learn about American New Year customs as we are to learn about their traditions. If you don't have a ready guest, talk to a counselor of international students at your local university; many Chinese students or visiting professors or their spouses might welcome the opportunity to visit.

In New York, call the China Institute and ask Laura Tien to match you with a Chinese student.

More Ideas from FCC Members

Jeannette Chu of Merrifield, Virginia, advises:

> Generally speaking, gifts are not exchanged at Chinese New Year except within the immediate family. It is traditional for family members to have new clothes and for children to receive "lucky money" (often fairly nominal, i.e., a dollar or two) in red envelopes. If you really want to ring in the New Year properly, you would pay all your debts, clean your house, leave a small dish of honey for the Kitchen God (so that he will say nice things about your family in his annual report to Heaven), and take your children to visit their grandparents, particularly on the maternal side.

Susan Lore of Saratoga Springs, New York, suggests preschool activities:

> I have been asked by Katie's nursery school teacher to share Chinese New Year, so I plan to bring the kites we bought in China, a sample of Chinese clothing (a silk outfit purchased at the White Swan Hotel), red envelopes (*hongbao*) with a coin in it for each child in the class, a book on the New Year featuring a dragon, and oranges and almond cookies for the snack. We'll ask the children to wear red that day and play Chinese music in the classroom. For a craft activity, we plan to make dragon masks from red paper plates: cut out the eyes; add a face, eyebrows, and mouth; staple or glue streamers of crepe paper or long strands of colored paper or ribbon for hair. Dye an old sheet green or red. Everyone can then be a part of the big dragon parade too.

References and Further Reading

The following books are available from China Books & Periodicals (415-282-2994):

> *Fun with Chinese Festivals,* by Tan Huay Peng (Union City, Calif.: Heian Int'l, 1991).
>
> *Mooncakes and Hungry Ghosts: Festivals in China,* by Carol Stepanchuk and Charles Wong (San Francisco: China Books, 1991).
>
> *Red Eggs and Dragon Boats: Celebrating Chinese Festivals,* by Carol Stepanchuk (Berkeley, Calif.: Pacific View Press, 1994).

Ruth Laseski and Susan Caughman like to hang out in the Chinatowns of Houston and New York City, respectively.

First Chinese New Year

Karen Braucher

FCC—Oregon and SW Washington

Bundled like the richest Manchurian girl,
you were held up by your father to see
the dragon dancing through red firecracker
paper and snow in Boston's Chinatown.
High on Peking duck, whole crispy fish,
shivering, dodging sparks, I went *click, click,*
a silly woman really, silly with happiness
and wanting to save fragments for you,

wanting to remember our breath rose
in the frigid air like we were the dragons,
not the men in grimacing masks jazzing
the street with neon, grabbing money
hung from the restaurant foyers.
Bathed in the finest ginseng soap,
wrapped in red silk, you laughed
through the banquet's sweets and sours,
Lapsang Souchong tea, while boys outside
didn't lose fingers setting off kabooms.

Born in the Year of the Monkey,
all fire and rascal, you will receive
so many official scraps, hotel receipts,
snapshots, Chinese paper cutouts,
flurries of crisp confetti. But this day
could go to gray haze—I forgot
to put film in the camera—like your
first nine months and nine days.

Were you found in Hunan heat,
cavernous train station, drab department store,

were you torn from your first mother's arms,
or did she hide, cradling you, trying
to leave her baby somewhere auspicious—
there's no detail, no hue. Betty Li Bai,
the faded orphanage clothes you wore
when you first were handed to me
are wrapped in tissue. Blue Chinese pantaloons
with a drawstring, a shirt with a cartoon cat,
I'd take them with me if the house were on fire,
bottom drawer, left-hand side, of your dresser.

From *Heaven's Net,* a collection of poetry by Karen Braucher (Bacchae Press, 1997). Copyright 1997 Karen Braucher. Reprinted with permission of the author.

Race Matters

A Korean-born girl named Bridget O'Leary is still Asian to the world-at-large, and that facet of her identity needs to be affirmed and nurtured. White parents cannot draw on personal experience to help with that. Instead, we have to recognize that our child belongs to a group from which we ourselves are excluded.

Cheri Register

Why Are You Kissing That Child?

Martha Groves
FCC–Los Angeles

"Why are you kissing that child?" The Los Angeles police officer, dispatched to investigate a stolen car parked in front of my house, barked the question as I stood holding and smooching my three-year-old daughter, whom I adopted as a toddler in China in 1994.

Stunned by his implication—that I had no business kissing her—I could only answer feebly: "Because she's my daughter." His disbelieving eyes peered first at her dark skin and almond-shaped eyes, then at my blonde hair and pale face. Then he said: "The father must be—what?—Japanese?" Luckily, about that moment, my daughter defused the tension by burbling "Mommy, Mommy, Mommy."

Chalk up another episode in the life of one of Los Angeles' growing ranks of transracial families. This one tops my collection of strange or insensitive or downright ignorant comments from strangers. But there are plenty of others.

There was the Macy's sales associate who said sweetly: "You must be the baby-sitter." And the Chinese-born furniture store sales clerk who remarked: "Is the father Chinese?" ("Yes," I replied, "and so is the biological mother.") And the countless others who have wondered: "Is she yours?" "Where did she come from?" "How much did she cost?" "Does she speak with a Chinese accent?" (This last even after I had explained that I adopted Nora before she could do anything but babble.)

For more than two and a half years, Nora Tai-Xiu and I have experienced our share of probing eyes and questions. Adoption experts call them "grocery-store scenes," in which parents or other family members are approached in the children's presence and asked about their origins. This amazes me somewhat, given the boom in nontraditional or interracial families both in San Francisco, where I lived when she and I became a family, and in Los Angeles, where we are now.

Until lately, my standard response has been to recap the high points of how Nora and I got together. I've felt obliged to do this in part because, as often as not, the person who asks is seeking information about overseas adoption, and I love proselytizing. Plus, as my friends know, I still get a huge kick out of telling our story (over and over and...).

It pleases me to think that I might be helping someone else start down a path that has led me to such overwhelming joy—and, in fact, my experience has encouraged many friends and acquaintances to pursue transracial adoptions, many of them in China.

But with my daughter approaching her fourth birthday and suddenly becoming much more aware of the physical differences between us, I've been rethinking my wide-open, "What would you like to know?" approach with strangers. As the experts see it, it's not really my story to tell. It's Nora's. Therefore, the decision of whether to share details should rest with her alone.

For a time, I considered this a harsh stance. After all, I figure, most strangers who comment are merely curious. But adoption experts—many of whom themselves have adopted children from other races—view the questions as an intrusive and not-so-subtle form of racism. However well meant a remark—"My, what beautiful almond eyes she has!"—it still serves to highlight the differences and undermine a child's sense of belonging to the family.

"Answering such questions in any depth at all tells the child that he needs to be explained or justified," said Holly van Gulden, a nationally recognized adoption speaker and counselor and co-author of *Real Parents, Real Children*. Choosing not to answer, she added, helps teach your child how to protect her personal boundaries. And instilling some reserve in nonwhite children, Van Gulden and others say, can help prepare them to deal with the more overt forms of racism and name-calling that they will inevitably encounter as they go to school and get out into the real world.

Last Christmas, Nora and I had a tree-trimming party. Of the children there, two were girls from China, one was a boy of Vietnamese and Korean heritage whose mother is Caucasian and whose father is Japanese American, one was an adopted Caucasian boy whose blondness contrasted sharply with the appearance of his dark-haired parents, and the other was a girl whose single mother visited a sperm bank. Other neighbors—an Italian American woman, her African American husband, and their biological daughter—could not be there. I hadn't planned for my guest list to look like the United Nations; it just turned out that way.

And it often does these days in Los Angeles and other cities big and small. I guess I wonder when nontraditional and mixed-race families will become so commonplace that people will begin to assume that Nora is my daughter.

As I wrestle with these issues, I'm still finding it difficult to follow the advice of many other adoptive parents and consultants. Linda Bothun, a Washington, D.C., teacher and lecturer who promotes positive attitudes about adoption in the media, agrees with others that an ideal way to handle nosy questions is to turn things around. If someone asks, "Where did you get her?" respond with: "Why do you ask?" That helps restore the balance of power, rather than leave the adoptive family in the spotlight. I've not used that yet, but it's nice to have it in my repertoire. The details are, after all, "none of their business," Bothun noted.

Maybe it's not their business, but I happen to think that these new ways of forming families eventually will be the business of us all. For now, when people ask incredulously, "Is she your daughter?" I just smile and say emphatically and proudly: "Yes!"

Finding the Right Words

JoGene Kapell

FCC-Northwest

When I was still in the midst of the infertility nightmare, I read an article about the adoptive parents of two children from India. They were quoted as saying, "We can't imagine any children but these in our lives, and we feel extremely fortunate."

In my misery, my reaction at the time was, "Yeah, right." Now I know exactly what they meant.

My daughter Lily, now two years old, was adopted in Nanjing, China, in December 1992. She was almost four months old when she was put in our arms. She snuggled and smiled and seemed to say, "What took you so long to get here?" I am unapologetically insane about her. She is the brightest, most joyful and beautiful child on Earth. No, really, she is! And she is unequivocally OURS. My love for her is the walk-in-front-of-a-bus, give-my-right-arm kind of love. You know, the love a parent feels for a child.

This is not to say that adoption doesn't create its own issues. We know that our daughter bridges two cultures. We honor Lily's biological heritage. The whole family is studying Chinese, and Lily is picking up words in both languages very quickly. I'm very aware that as she grows, she will have to deal with some issues that her nonadopted friends won't have. But one of the issues we face right now is how to deal with the occasional remark that betrays a kind of insensitivity or ignorance on the part of people who may otherwise be pleasant enough.

A smart and empathetic friend was visiting recently. A loud noise scared Lily, and when she jumped into my arms and clung, my friend remarked with evident surprise: "My, she's really attached to you."

"I'm her mother, of course she's attached to me," is what I should have said. But I was so taken aback, I didn't say anything.

An aunt of mine (normally a bright and sweet woman) asked us if we had paid sales tax for Lily. She thought this was amusing. I was speechless. She had no clue that she had said something offensive.

We were shopping. A complete stranger asked, "Are you her mother?"
"Yes."

"No, really, I mean did you make her? Did she come out of you?"

This one was so totally obnoxious I was unable to respond. It's clear to me that, for the most part, people not directly touched by adoption just don't get it. I try to remind myself that before Lily, I didn't get it either.

Most of the disturbing comments that we've received have been made not out of malice or racism, but out of a different world view of adoption. I have to keep in mind that most people view adoption as somehow different or second best to raising a biological child. People seem to have the erroneous belief that because she is adopted, she doesn't really belong to us. This view is a kind of "reality shift" that catches me unawares and inhibits my pithy comeback (not particularly lacking in other circumstances). By the time I get over my surprise, it's often too late to respond.

I want to get better at the pithy comeback, something that stays positive, yet also transmits the message that an adoptive relationship is every bit as authentic as a biological one. My accustomed New York "**** you!" response is not behavior I want to model for my daughter. As Lily grows and understands more and more, I want to learn to model a clean and effective response to people, a response that comes from a stance of balance and power, one she can use successfully in her own life.

Not all comments I receive are negative. Some people are able to make wonderful acknowledgments, like the lady who said, "Oh my, what a beautiful baby. What country is she from?"

Sometimes people who are truly interested in adoption will stop us to ask about the process. Even so, I'm still aware that even kind comments may feel intrusive to Lily as she grows older. Cheri Register's writing (especially her book, *Are Those Kids Yours?*) has helped me a great deal. She explores this issue with clarity and grace. But reading isn't quite enough. I'd also like to work with other adoptive parents to role play responses to difficult or intrusive comments. Are any other families interested? If you are, please write me at jokapell@hotmail.com. If you send your own list of difficult questions or comments, how you responded to them or how you *wished* you had responded to them, I'll compile your responses for another newsletter article.

JoGene Kapell is a former New Yorker who has transplanted happily to the Pacific Northwest.

Valuing Difference in a Multiracial Family

Kirstin Nelson

San Francisco Bay Area FCC

I have been trying to think about how my parents raised me and what their parental philosophies were, and I think with them it came down to one thing: "sameness." I have three older brothers that are white, and my two younger brothers and I are mixed-race adoptees. My parents seemed to take the approach that it was essential to treat us all the same—as in, they loved us all the same, they treated us all the same, and we were the same as everyone else in our town and neighborhood. It was one big "sameness" fest! And this is pretty much true of my entire growing-up experience.

During the time I was growing up I didn't stop to think about this at all. But definitely as I got older I realized that we weren't all the same, and my needs, especially emotional needs, were very different from others in my family—as were (I think) the needs of my two younger brothers. We really didn't talk much about racial issues in my house, and when we did it was usually in the abstract—things in the news, books, TV, etc. It wasn't that my parents discouraged us from coming to them to talk about things, but I realize now, as an adult, I never wanted to stop being the "same" (or pretending to be the same) as everyone else, and so I didn't want to confront many of the issues that surrounded my life.

One of the biggest things I have struggled with as an adult is coming to terms with the fact that I am not the same as everyone else and my family is not the same and I don't have the same needs as everyone else. I think over time I began to believe that being different is bad. Now I relish my differences, but it has taken much soul searching (and many hours of therapy!) to reach this point.

I think the most important thing you can teach and share with your children is that they are different (not only because of race but by being adopted) and your family is different but that the difference is good and unique and special. Being different from others allows all of us to have rich experiences that other families will never have. Being different means being lucky and blessed.

I know that many parents believed this was the best way to deal with the many issues that inevitably came up. And I think many adoptive parents fall into this same trap of trying to stress that their kids are the same as everyone else's—at least parents of adoptees in my age group. Perhaps it has changed now, and many of you may deal with things very differently.

I think one important thing for me to stress is that although I disagree with a lot of the things my parents did (or didn't do) when I was growing up, I am very close to them—especially my mother. She is my very best friend, and it truly is amazing how much alike we are. People often even comment on how much we look alike. We both always have a good laugh at that one.

One last thing I wanted to mention, and I am sure you all have heard of this title before, is the book *The Gift Children*, by J. Douglas Bates. This is a fabulous book, and it is an extremely accurate portrayal of a multiracial family. There are many parts of the book that exactly mirror my growing up and many of my feelings and emotions. If you haven't read it, I highly recommend it. Both Mr. Douglas and his wife are very honest and realistic about their triumphs and mistakes.

At age 29, Kirstin Nelson has a teaching degree and a masters in library science and is currently enrolled in law school. She is black ("actually mixed race, but I consider myself black") and has five brothers—three white, one black, and one Native American. Her parents, both white, adopted her when she was six months old. She has located and corresponded with her birth mother and, she says, "my parents have been completely supportive of this and actually encouraged me to find her."

The Korean Adoption Experience

A Look into Our Future?

Patricia Gorman
FCC/New England

As I settled in with my second adopted daughter from China, many unanswered questions repeated themselves in my mind: How can I help my daughters become happy here? How can I help them to appreciate being both American and Chinese? How will our family change through the experience of adoption?

In the absence of research on the experience of China adoptions, I turned to studies of Korean adoptees, who number in the tens of thousands and have been arriving in the United States for over 30 years. As I reviewed studies of this cohort, I searched for what they could tell me about being a Caucasian parent of an Asian girl, and being an Asian girl growing up in a dominantly Caucasian world.

To my disappointment, the empirical research around this group is scattered, fragmentary, and narrowly defined. There is only one major longitudinal study. However, reading many separate studies, some dating back 20 years, suggested some partial answers, and even more questions, for the intercountry adoptive parent.

The studies show how the social context of adoption has changed. Society now attributes a different meaning to adoption, particularly to families created through intercountry adoption. Consider the difference between the description of a family with an adopted Korean child versus a more contemporary description of the same family as one that has become multicultural and multiracial through adoption. Older studies of the Korean cohort focus on the adaptation of the child to the American family. Smoothness of adaptation equals success. A positive outcome was the child's identification as an American, not as a Korean. No one ever asked how well the family adapted to its new identity as one with a diverse membership and diverse cultural connections.

There are also some important differences between the Korean group and our recently arrived Chinese children. For example, many adoptions of Korean children were for "humanitarian reasons" into families who already had biological children; many Korean children were escorted to the United States, allowing adoption to occur without any contact with the child's homeland or culture; and many Korean children were abandoned and adopted at older ages than our Chinese cohort.

Adoption literature reflects the culture in which the study takes place. Since our culture elevates biological connections and casts shadows on adoptive parenting, I expected to find that reflected in the studies I read. For example, the psychological literature about adoption persistently shows the assumption of the overriding importance of infancy bonding. This idea immediately puts many intercountry adoptive families at a disadvantage. In addition, most psychologically oriented studies focus on the problems of adoptive families. Many studies are based on clinical populations of families who have approached mental health professionals for help with their adoptive children. Those studies always find that the adoptive children are having troubles primarily because they are adopted children. This idea is quite controversial, since most of these studies do not differentiate between children adopted early in life and those adopted later in life after multiple placements.

For most adoptive parents, the important information is that these studies on intercountry adoptees paint an optimistic picture. The general impression from reading the studies of specifically Korean adoptions is that of good outcome based on positive indicators such as educational achievement, good relationships with families and peers, and a general feeling of positive self-worth and confidence enjoyed by the adoptees. Most adoptees adapted well to American society, both kids adopted in infancy and over six years of age, with about 10 percent showing serious adaptation problems.

The vast majority of Korean adoptees showed positive self-esteem and a good sense of integration into their nuclear and extended family. Most intercountry adoptive parents said they would definitely "do it again" if given the choice.

Identity formation has always been a major concern in intercountry adoption. Intercountry-adopted children have a more complicated identity formation task due to the stigma of belonging to a different ethnicity than their parents. Some studies suggest that children who are ethnically different from their parents end up identifying with both the ethnicity of their parents and that of the people like them. The intercountry adoptee's identity formation task is similar to the nonadopted mixed-race child who has parents from different racial and ethnic backgrounds.

The question of connection with cultural heritage and racial identity was considered in all the studies. The commonly held position is that "pride in cultural identity is essential to reducing the crisis of adolescent identity and resolving role conflict." Longitudinal studies also described parents eagerly providing cross-cultural experiences for children until adolescence. At that point, the children's interests seem to naturally wane as they become involved in teenage pursuits that require "fitting in" to their mostly Caucasian peer group. A group of Korean adult adoptees cautioned parents to be sensitive during this period. They advised parents to be responsive to their children's reactions to cultural activities native to the child. Interactions with Asian Americans may be awkward for children of this age, as the thoroughly American behavior of the adoptee may perplex and disappoint the Asian American. Other studies emphasized that such factors as self-esteem are more important than cultural identity for successful adoption results.

One frequent question from parents of transracial adoptees is how their children's different physical appearance from their parents will affect them. They worry that their children will endure comments or slurs directed at them based on their physical appearance. A study of Korean, Latino, and other Asian intercountry adopted preadolescents found two-thirds of this group were not bothered by looking different from their parents. The children mentioned that they felt most aware of their differences when attending large gatherings of extended family members. About a third of the children recalled problems during the preceding three years of other children calling them names and making fun of them because of their racial backgrounds.

The consistently positive outcome from intercountry adoptions surprises some researchers, though probably none of the adoptive parents. Why does intercountry adoption work as well as it does? Some researchers' explanations build on David Kirk's belief that adoption works best when there is openness about the adoption and acceptance of the difference between parenting biological and adopted children. The researchers suggest that parents of ethnically different children approach the inherent difficulties of adoption in a more open and accepting fashion. Some even suggest that intercountry adoptive parents have a qualitatively different approach to parenting which supports the identity development of their adopted children.

Most studies of adoptive families focus on the effects of what is missing. The studies highlight the lack of the "biological connection," the single cultural identity, and the knowable past and predictable future. I want to read not just how intercountry adoptees adjusted, but also how the families became different as they developed a multicultural, multiracial identity. Researchers have the opportunity to investigate in depth why intercountry adoption works as well as it does. They could then consider what positive outcomes imply about the resilience of children, the definition of family, and the role of parents. Intercountry adoption research would benefit by considering the adopted child's heritage a gift that expands the family's sense of what is valuable and possible in their own lives and culture.

Patricia Gorman is a sociologist who lives in Amherst, Massachusetts. She and her husband, Rick Tessler, have two daughters adopted from Hefei, Hannah and Zoe.

The Changing Outlook on Transracial Adoption

Susan Tompkins

FCC—Oregon and SW Washington

Twenty years ago, adoption professionals were just beginning to see the tip of the iceberg concerning transracial adoption issues. At that time, African American children adopted by Caucasian families in the 1960s were starting to go through adolescence and early adulthood, and they were being studied. The findings were disturbing.

Many of the African American teens had good self-esteem but lacked a racial identity and skills for coping with racism. As a black child in a white family, they were often protected from racism; those families who did not foster same-race contact found that they had raised "white children in black skins." While growing up, this did not pose a problem, but once the children began separating emotionally and physically from their families, these issues became major problems. They didn't know how to act "black," so they didn't fit in with blacks. Once they separated from their family, they were often not accepted by whites either. Many were encountering severe adjustment problems in early adulthood.

From studying these children came the first ideas about the importance of same-race contact and developing a knowledge of racial history and culture for children adopted across racial lines. In 1978, when I took my first adoption education class before adopting my daughter from India, I was told that I should learn to cook Indian food and have Indian art on my walls. I was also advised that it would be a good idea to take my daughter to Indian cultural events.

I followed this advice and enjoyed it, but nobody told me that my daughter might not. She wanted to be a regular American kid and balked at any Indian event. She went along because she was really too young to resist. She did love Indian food and helped me cook it, but that was as far as it went. I never made any inroads into the Indian community as far as same-race contact. In school she made a few Indian friends and had some contact with other adopted Indian children. However, she made it clear that these relationships were not important to her. In having Indian magazines and Indian art in my home and in dragging her to Indian events, what did I accomplish? I believe I drove home the message that her birth culture is important to our family. Just as any parent tries to impart values to their children, I had emphasized the value of Indian culture.

Years later, what have we learned from experiences and research? Barbara Tremitiere, an expert on transracial adoption as a professional therapist and adoptive mother, says that even when white parents make every effort for same-race contact and cultural and historical knowledge for their children, these beloved children of color have the white world view, the white perspective. In short, they are white children in a skin of color.

This is sobering for parents working hard to give their transracially adopted children the best upbringing possible. However, even though I believe Barbara is correct, it doesn't mean that we can't do a good job in other ways—fostering self-esteem, racial identity, and coping skills for racism while teaching about the culture and history of their birth country.

Professional adoption literature all points to same-race contact as an excellent way for children to obtain racial identity and coping skills. However, same-race contact does not mean contact with other adopted children of the same race. This is good for support, both for children and for the parents, as they have a shared experience and are not alone. But these children need to know adults and older children of the same race who have established a racial identity from their same-race parents and who have developed skills for coping with racism. It is important to note that I have found that not all minority families have healthy ways of coping with racism (some deny it exists while others may fight it in destructive ways), so it is important to evaluate potential role models.

Barbara Tremitiere also pointed out that research is showing that genetics plays a larger role in individuals and races than people previously believed. She cited studies of Native American, Vietnamese, and Korean adopted children, many of whom have specific patterns in terms of adjustment and behavior. Barbara firmly believes that genetics are responsible for 75 percent of a child's make-up, while 25 percent is environmental. This is quite different from 20 years ago, when many parents felt that when their baby arrived they were starting with a "clean slate."

What have adoptive parents with older children learned from their experiences over the years? Many of us have seen a perfectionism in our children that doesn't come from their role models. Since often people do not get positive reinforcement for failure, these children may shy away from new experiences. If we accept that many adopted children have at the core of their being a sense of lowered self-esteem because someone chose to "give them away," then it's easy to see that they strive for external cues to reinforce constantly their sense of self. Recently, an adoption therapist at an international adoption conference suggested that families model failure—go out on ice skates and fall, make a fool of yourself, ski and fall in the snow, etc. This may or may not have an impact on your perfectionist child, but it's certainly worth a try.

This therapist also mentioned the importance of *claiming*, which is part of the bonding cycle. Claiming is the facet of bonding where the child and parent feel a sense of belonging to one another. The adopted child comes to feel that she is truly part of the family. Claiming gets accomplished through family rituals and through more seemingly insignificant events or actions. (Family rituals are habitual events that are in some way unique to a family. These range from the ordinary, such as dinner together each evening, to more elaborate holiday rituals, such as each person having their own Christmas ornament or toasting each family member at the holiday table.)

Telling your children that traits they exhibit are like their adoptive family helps them truly feel a part of the family (for instance, telling your child that they walk or talk like Mommy or Daddy). Adopted children may take an intense interest in family stories. My daughter can tell family history and descriptions of personalities that go back for generations. She has taken this family history on as her own and is intensely interested in it.

In addition, it is important to preserve what we can of their former lives. There are adoption experts who think it is very important not to change an adopted child's name if she or he is adopted over 18 months of age. Adopted children have lost so much that the loss of their name may cause them a further loss of identity. Often the impact does not surface till the teen years.

Ten or fifteen years from now, we will know much more about adjustment issues for our children adopted from China. Some of what has applied for adoptive children of other races and cultures will no doubt apply to our children, while they will probably have their own distinctive set of issues as well. For now, we continue to learn how to make our transracially adopted children emotionally healthy. We learn from professionals and from families who have gone before us as well as from our own experiences, and we will teach those who come after us.

Susan Tompkins is executive director of Journeys of the Heart, an adoption agency in Portland, Oregon. She is also the adoptive mother of children from China, India, and Romania.

The Elephant in the Living Room

Amy Klatzkin
San Francisco Bay Area FCC

On June 28, 1997, I attended an all-day seminar on transracial adoption put on each year by Pact, An Adoption Alliance. The audience represented the diversity of our community: Asian, black, Latino, white, gay, straight, single moms, single dads, parents who had adopted domestically or internationally through dozens of different agencies, parents with birth kids and adopted kids, even parents in transracial marriages raising mixed-race birth children. It wasn't a big crowd, but it covered all the bases.

In the opening session Liza Triggs, Shira Gail, and Julia Sudbury talked about growing up African or Asian with white parents. As Julia Sudbury put it, in the transracial family "racism is the elephant in the living room." White parents, not knowing how to handle racism because they lack direct experience, often try to navigate around it without really acknowledging or confronting it. But it takes up a lot of space.

Overachievement, Sudbury said, is typical of transracial adoptees, who inside often feel that if they aren't perfect they'll be "sent back." And they often also fear their community of origin because they don't feel they fit in. As adoptive parents we must find ways for our children to be part of the Chinese community while they are young, even if *we* feel awkward. We may not belong, but they do, and it's our job to nurture the ways they are different from us as well as the ways they are the same. Sudbury said it most succinctly: "If you don't have a sense of roots, you can't stand up straight."

Pact's founders, Gail Steinberg and Beth Hall, hammered home difficult truths and offered lots of practical advice. The hard stuff came first.

Only people of the dominant race can say race doesn't matter, claim Steinberg and Hall, both white parents of children adopted transracially. Attitude matters. Race matters. And "race is part of every conversation," even when it's deep in the background, because our racial identity informs our view of the world. Those of us who are white parents of Chinese children have to learn to see the world from a different perspective, because our kids will, sooner or later, and they will need our support. "The goal is not to teach our kids to be victims of racism or even survivors of racism," Hall explained, but to teach them to be enriched by *all* their experiences, the tough ones as well as the fulfilling ones. "The hardest experiences," Hall emphasized, "are also the greatest opportunities for growth."

Hearing that our children have been hurt by racist remarks or behavior can be hard on parents, and the first instinct may be to try to solve the problem. Recognizing that we can't solve racism can make parents feel helpless. Moreover, our old support network may not help. White friends raising same-race birth children can't understand the issues we have to deal with, and their advice is unlikely to be helpful. As Hall put it, "They have absolutely no life experience to bring to this occasion."

Things will happen to our kids, and they will hurt. So what do we do? The goal is not to try to rescue them—we can't—but to help them deal with it. And that means talking about racism *before* they are hurt by it. Model appropriate responses to racist comments or actions of any kind whenever they come up, even when your child is very young. And when your child experiences racism personally, acknowledge her pain and anger. Above all, externalize the message for your child: "Race and gender come with birth, which neither you nor anybody else chose or earned. But being a racist is a state of mind and a choice." Your child, Steinberg and Hall advise, "needs to believe in herself and not let anybody, of any color, limit or define her solely by race or undermine her acceptance and love inside herself for who she is."

Kids also need to learn that they are in charge of their own attitudes. Teasing, insults, nasty comments, or rejection are very painful, and you can't prevent people from hurting you in this way. But someone else's ignorance and meanness have nothing to do with who you are. And there is always *something* you can do—confront or withdraw, whisper (so they have to get quiet to hear you), ask what they mean (put the responsibility back on them), make a joke at their expense…then brainstorm later with parents and friends about what to say next time.

Transracially adopted kids are not alone in experiencing racism, but they may feel alone if they are not connected with their own ethnic community as well as yours. The danger is that your child could feel that she doesn't belong anywhere. As parents adopting transracially, we have to some extent chosen not to care if people look at us differently. But our children didn't make that choice. "Transracial families *are* more scrutinized," Hall said. "Our kids have so many opportunities *not* to fit in. We have to give them every opportunity we can *to* fit in." How? Steinberg offered the following tools:

Give your child the opportunity to develop real skill mastery in areas where she has talent.

Develop the 150 percent person: one person with two cultures plus the ability to navigate both.

Transmit positive cultural values from your child's birth heritage. She can help carry them forward.

Cultivate anti-bias thinking. Confronting and eliminating learned preconceptions about Asians is not enough. We need to pull *all* our biases out of the closet (e.g., how do we *really* feel about gays, blacks, Latinos, Jews, Muslims, Catholics…you get the idea). Our biases *will* create problems for our children.

Develop family rituals unique to your family. You are your child's parent; she will never doubt it. But you can help strengthen the sense of family by celebrating the things that make your family special.

Live in an area with as many people of your child's own race as possible. If you can't live in a largely Chinese neighborhood, go to one as part of your regular routine. Instead of shopping in the local supermarket, catching a movie down the street, or eating at the local Chinese restaurant filled largely with non-Chinese, make the effort to shop and seek entertainment in a community where your child is in the majority.

Make connections with Chinese American families, and learn respectful ways to interact. Put yourself on the line so your child can learn to fit in even if you don't.

Remember that true biculturalism isn't all serious. It's knowing how to have fun in both cultures too, inside and outside the family.

In closing, Steinberg urged us to continue the commitment. "You've taken on something very special in adopting transracially," she reminded us. "You owe your child your very best effort."

Amy Klatzkin edits the newsletter of San Francisco Bay Area FCC. For information on Pact's educational programs and a free issue of *Pact Press,* or to order *Pact's BookSource: A Reference Guide to Books on Adoption and Race for Adults and Children,* contact Pact, An Adoption Alliance, 3315 Sacramento St., Suite 239, San Francisco, CA 94118, USA, tel: (415) 221-6957, or visit their web site at www.pactadopt.org.

An American of Asian Ancestry Votes for the Majority Viewpoint

Wil Sugai
FCC-Colorado

As I grow up with our daughter, Leah, I learn things every day both about her and about myself. A few months ago in a flash of brilliance I realized that there was a reason why Sheryl constantly gets comments about Leah that I never seem to get.

My wife Sheryl is Caucasian, I am Asian, and Leah is Asian. Are you getting the picture? In the words of the teens of today—DAH! I did not realize that visually Leah and I fit together, where Leah and Sheryl did not. As obvious as it may seem, there are some underlying issues that speak to this realization on my part.

We receive the Texas Families with Children from China newsletter, and in one edition there were articles speaking to some of the issues around growing up Asian. It was interesting for me to read about experiences of growing up as an Asian child in an American society. The message, albeit subtle, is critical: "Asian Child" in an "American Society." I will return to this in a few paragraphs, but I ask you to keep those phrases in mind.

As our children grow and venture out on their own, they will be inundated with all the prejudicial stereotyping both negative and (perceived) positive. The manner in which we as parents react will ingrain in them the definitions of self-worth they bring to themselves.

As a member of some minority organizations, I have the opportunity to meet and get to know a diverse cross-section of humanity, many of whom have grown up in the numerical minority. There are also many that were reared in situations where they were part of the numerical majority. In talking with the people that were reared in situations where they were in the minority, there seems to be an underlying mindset of being a minority and not belonging (knowing your place). On the other hand, the people that were reared in situations where they were in the majority have the mindset of being in control, of being perceived as being a part of the society as an equal.

Messaging is important. The types of messages that are passed from parent to child are critical. Are we passing messages that our children should view themselves as a minority in a majority-controlled society, an "Asian Child" in an "American Society"? My hypothesis is that parents of the numerical majority send a more positive message to their children regardless of race or national origin. This is not to say that we should not prepare our children to deal with the issues of prejudice. We have a responsibility to do so. But in my opinion there is a line which we often cross. In wanting our kids to embrace their birth culture, understand their birth heritage, and respect their birth ancestry (all very important aspects of who they are), we neglect other aspects of their makeup. The facts are that (1) they are as much a part of the American fabric as anyone else, (2) there is an American culture and heritage, and most important (3) there is a new set of ancestry in their life to be respected, understood, and embraced. Are we sending our kids the right message? Only time will tell.

It is probably easy to see that I grew up in the numerical majority. For those of you who don't know me, I grew up in America. Where I hail from, the numerical majority are Americans of Asian ancestry. I grew up first American, then Asian, more specifically Japanese. "American of Asian ancestry" or "Asian American"—a subtle linguistic difference, a subtle message difference that says that I am part of the fabric, or an outsider striving to be.

I do need to correct something in the first paragraph. I am an American of Asian ancestry, and so is Leah. American first, then Asian. As I grow up with Leah perhaps I will learn in another flash of brilliance that I was all wrong, but then that is the beauty of always being in the process of growing up.

Wil Sugai lives in Wheatridge, Colorado, with his wife Sheryl Mosbarger and their daughter Leah.

Chinese or American?

David Jue Lam
San Francisco Bay Area FCC

The thing about being a Chinese American is you have no choice. You are born into the world already half-formed. Your facial features are like genes independently determining your life choices, ignoring your wishes altogether. It doesn't matter what kind of person you really are. Every day you get pressed further into the mold. You either go along with it or expend lots of energy breaking out. You can spend your whole life thus occupied.

You are Chinese American because you live in America and you *look* Chinese. It's a funny kind of paradox because you were born between two cultures, and you think that entitles you to choose, but you will be subtly and continually nudged toward Chinese culture even if you don't know the first thing about it. You keep getting lumped together with other people who look Chinese. It doesn't matter that your experience is nothing at all like that of other Chinese.

There are constant reminders for some of us that we are not "American." For example, I know that most Americans don't have picnics in cemeteries. For that matter, how many Americans bow exactly three times before their ancestors' graves at those cemeteries, then leave perfectly good food? How many Americans visit the cemetery as often as Chinese Americans do? How many American kids have names like Gaymond and Guymond? And in the same family! My favorite name is still Guido Gee. He grew up in the old Italian neighborhood of North Beach in San Francisco, but he was 100 percent Chinese American. And I still don't understand why I had to jump over a flaming pie pan at my father's wake.

One day in junior high school, everyone I knew came to school with new last names. Victor Chin became Victor Chun. Lester Quan became Lester Chin. Sam Yee became Sam Leong. That threw the teachers and administrators, most of whom were white, into complete confusion. It just so happened that the U.S. government had decided to offer amnesty to the Chinese who had come to America illegally, using false papers.

My father, like most Chinese who came to America in the 1920s and 1930s, when the Chinese Exclusion Laws were in effect, came under false pretenses. Whenever a Chinese immigrant returned to visit his home village, he would return to America claiming he had fathered a son who remained in the village. This created a slot for someone to get through. At the age of 13, my father had to take on a new name, a new family, and a new home village and then convince U.S. Immigration that he was that fictitious person. His father tried as well. Twice in fact, but failed each time. The second time he waited two years at Angel Island, only to be sent back.

So finally, decades after the end of Exclusion, these "paper sons" were allowed to turn themselves in and claim their real names. Turned out my father was not the only illegal alien. More than half of my class came in that morning with new names. It was oddly comforting, knowing that my family wasn't the only illegal one.

Those are the more amusing and interesting things that happen to the typical Chinese American. There are less amusing things, too. Like being called "Chink" and "Chinaman." Being told to go back to China. Being the object of whispers and stares on the bus. Growing up is a perilous time, but so is being grown up. I remember cringing with shame and embarrassment when the president of the company I worked for used the dreaded phrase "Chinese fire drill." I was even more mortified when a subordinate of mine used the same phrase. Or when I was told a racist Chinese joke by the clerks in Accounts Payable. I didn't know what to do. They meant well, I think. And the only thing worse than being the only Chinese American in a business meeting is to be one of *two* Chinese Americans. From that point on, you will be continually confused with, and compared to, the other. It doesn't matter that he was born and raised in Hong Kong, speaks with a Chinese accent, is 5'7" and wears glasses while I was born and raised in San Francisco, speak perfect English without an accent, am 7 inches taller, and wear contact lenses.

So you go through life standing outside the mainstream you so desperately want to join. You are constantly being pushed and pulled. Your parents try to make you genuine Chinese and white society wants you to be a cartoon Chinese. My advice is to keep your sense of humor.

David Jue Lam (Lam is the "paper" name and Jue his true surname), his son Zachary, ten, and daughter Lindsey, three, live in San Francisco. Lindsey was adopted from Guangdong province.

Going Back

You've just come from my old hometown.
You must have some news of home.
The day you left, was the plum tree
By my window in bloom yet?

Wang Wei (trans. Minfong Ho)

Return to China

Betty Brickson
FCC—Oregon and SW Washington

In March 1997 I had the rare and wonderful opportunity to return to China as a volunteer escort for an adoption trip. The opportunity came suddenly, and my response was equally sudden. I vowed to move heaven and earth to clear my calendar and find a way to be on that airplane.

I first saw China from a distance 20 years ago, passing through Hong Kong on my way to Taiwan to teach English. I remember peering with fascination at the Mainland from an observation platform in the New Territories, north of Kowloon. Soon after that China opened its doors to Westerners, but my first trip to China wasn't until late 1994, when my husband and I adopted our daughter, Rachael Min Yu. Rachael, who is now four years old, is from Jiangxi province in southeastern China. The group I was to accompany was bound for Maoming, in Guangdong province, and to Hefei, in Anhui province, to pick up five baby girls.

I was very excited about going, but also nervous. The thought of returning to China to watch the people, dodge bicycles, inhale the coal and exhaust-filled air, eat until I burst, and shop for those outrageously appliquéd children's clothes was too good to be true. But to be a witness to the amazing and life-altering transaction of adoption was my heart's real reason for going. My apprehension came from knowing all the unexpected problems that could arise—the children could have serious developmental problems; the new parents could be anxious, impatient, and uncomfortable so far from home. There could be problems with the travel arrangements, the paperwork, the authorities. I know a little Mandarin, but for anything more complicated than a shopping trip, my language skills are pretty worthless. Even though a Chinese guide would accompany us for most of the trip, I felt humbled by the responsibility of making sure that all five babies arrived home safely.

I also had some personal concerns. I wondered if I had the emotional strength for the trip. Like many of my friends who have one Chinese daughter, I have yearned for a *meimei* for my Rachael. In truth, a second child may be unrealistic and unaffordable for us, but the dream has persisted. So I feared I might collapse in tears every time I saw or held those babies, just as I have done at the airport when meeting friends as they arrive home with their new Chinese daughters. Making matters worse, my daughter knew the reason for my trip and he repeatedly asked me to bring back "her baby sister" who, she said, "was so lonely without her." This request always left me speechless and sad. What would I tell Rachael when I returned empty-handed?

I wasn't the only one worrying. For the rest of the group, mostly single women from throughout the United States who had been waiting well over a year for this trip, worrying had become second nature. As it turned out, all our worrying energy could have been used much more constructively. It was a very successful trip. Aside from a few colds and ear infections, the babies were beautiful and strong. To a person, the members of the group were good sports, good travelers, and good parents. Our travel connections, document processing, and all other official business went smoothly, and our accommodations far surpassed what I experienced in 1994. My modest language skills came in handy, and I was able to help the parents in ways I hadn't expected. The food, as always, was intoxicating. The memories I most cherish are these:

The night the babies came—the patient and respectful manner in which the parents received their daughters from the foster moms, and the difficulty the foster moms and orphanage workers had leaving that night.

The birthday party—complete with hats, streamers, noisemakers, balloons, cake, and candles—that the parents threw for all the Hefei babies because they had missed their daughters' first birthdays.

Getting to know the couples in an adoption group from Holland who had been waiting four long years to get their babies. Apparently Holland's immigration quotas are so low that it takes people more than three years to get their domestic clearance.

Our shopping trip to help clothe the orphans of the Hefei Welfare Orphanage—we nearly cleaned out the children's section of the department store.

Our boat ride down the Pearl River—nine adults and two babies on a rented double-decker ferry, rubbing our eyes and squinting at Guangzhou's riverfront landscape through the smoke-choked air.

The view from my balcony at the White Swan Hotel just after a rainstorm as steam rose off the tiled roofs of the pastel colonial buildings of Shamian Island.

As it turned out, I didn't weep at the sight of the babies or even plot to stow one away in my suitcase. Reason prevailed. After my first long walk through the park surrounding old Hefei, I realized how liberating it was to be unencumbered by an infant this time around. I walked at all hours and in all weather, and was richly rewarded. In the early mornings in the park I found old men hanging their caged birds in the trees, old women raising their swords in the synchronized motion of tai chi, and middle-aged couples waltzing to Western pop music in the pagodas dotting the lagoon. In the afternoons I found produce markets bursting with color, schoolgirls eager to practice their English, and, in Guangzhou, trinkets and treasures in the narrow, dark alleys of the antique market. At night, when I could walk without being noticed, I found lovers huddled in doorways.

Caught in the rain one night in Guangzhou, I ducked into the lobby of the Victory Hotel, where my adoption group had stayed in 1994. I sat down on the same curved bench where I had sat more than two years ago holding my precious, pink-cheeked nine-month-old daughter. And that's when I cried, because as it turned out, I didn't really ache for a second adoption trip. I ached for my first trip, to do it all over again, to relive every minute, to watch Rachael sleep in her seven layers of handmade clothing and hold her little warm body with the bewilderment of a new parent. Back then, in 1994, she was such a fresh bloom and so close to her Chinese roots. For just a moment I wanted to have her as she was then, as she was given to me.

And that, for me, was the lasting impression of the trip—that these adoption trips are a remarkable and singular moment in time. It's difficult to comprehend the magnitude of the experience when you're there, exhausted, mixing hot cereal in a cup, washing bibs in the sink or waiting, always waiting, for the next document to sign. It's later—when you look at your pictures for the fortieth time, when you pack away the little shoes your daughter has outgrown, when you watch her absorb and reflect American culture—that the significance sets in. That's when you know how special it was. Because even if you return to China as I did, your experience will never be the same.

Betty Brickson is a trained journalist who works in the environmental field. She lives in Portland, Oregon.

Shining Light into Dark Corners

Two Daughters Return to China

Val Free, M.A., M.F.C.C.
San Francisco Bay Area FCC

Recently I took my two daughters, both born in China, back to the places where they had lived before my husband and I adopted them. Li was almost five years old at the time of her adoption in 1992 and came from Guangdong province just outside of Guangzhou. Tian was two years old and came from Jiangxi province. Both of them came from conditions that were far less than ideal, less even than the conditions we now see in Chinese orphanages. For the most part, conditions are improving in the orphanages where adoptions to foreigners are allowed. Of course, there are still many orphanages throughout China that do not allow adoptions, where the babies are not cared for well, and where medical and emotional issues remain untreated. There are still so many babies and young children who are not adopted and brought into a new life with a family to love them. My daughters are among the lucky ones who survived the system and then found their family at last, for which we give thanks each day.

Returning to China was a difficult decision for my oldest daughter, Li, now ten and a half years old. She has been watching her young sister, Tian, age six, travel with me back and forth to China for about two years now. Since we founded an international adoption agency, our family talks about adoption a lot, and I often travel with the adopting families to China to assist with the adoption process. Two or three times each year since Tian was four we have traveled together on these trips, and she loves it. We travel well together, enjoying the adventure, loving the babies, and reconnecting with the man who assisted in our family's adoption of Tian. China now feels like familiar territory to both of us. Still, Tian had not been back to see her own orphanage or her foster mother and the others who took care of her before she was adopted.

289

As for Li, she had more memories of China, and many of them were not good. Since she had been there for so long she had more to miss, too, when she was adopted. Preferring more routine in her life than her little sister, Li likes staying at home and having "her things" around her. Traveling anywhere is a little more difficult for Li. Up until recently traveling to China was out of the question.

Both girls were offered the choice to go to China with me on this recent trip, where I accompanied families who were adopting their babies from Jiangxi province, Tian's birthplace. Since I knew the families would start their adoption journey there, and then finish up in Guangzhou close to where Li had come from, I decided it might be time to offer to take them both back to revisit their pasts. For Li, it would be an opportunity to heal some old hurts, and for Tian perhaps a time to hug her foster mom whom she loved dearly for the first two years of her life. They both decided to go.

About two weeks before we were to leave, I noticed different behavior around the house. Tian was getting excited, as she often does before a trip. She began to talk about the food in China, the hotels we would be staying in, the babies, and the families. Anticipation! However, for Li there was nervousness, getting into trouble at school, and some old behaviors that were present when she first came to us—sneaking, a few lies, and hypervigilance to things around her.

After about a week or so of this, my husband Dick and I finally pulled her aside and had a talk with her about whether or not she really wanted to go to China. She was able to express her intense nervousness at that time and said that she had changed her mind about going. We told her that she did not ever have to go back to China if she didn't want to, or that if she went this time she did not have to go back to her orphanage. No strings attached. Our love was there for her no matter what she decided to do about her roots in China. Following a hunch, the last thing I did before ending the talk that night was to tell her exactly what we would be doing in China each day, if she did decide to go. I told her about arriving in Hong Kong, staying in the hotel there, waking up the next morning, and then going on to Guangzhou and the orphanage city. I told her that she and her sister and I would be sharing a room and that we would have the same room each night for several nights in each city, where we could have our "home base" and where we could play games and watch TV. I let her know that even though we were traveling and that this was her first time back to China, we could have some routine and some comforts along the way.

Then of course there are the babies! Li is not normally interested in babies; she prefers toddlers that she can really play and interact with (like her sister). Still she was curious about the babies and interested in the adoption part of the trip after hearing a little more about it. She changed her mind again and decided to go. Clearly, her ambivalence was showing up in all kinds of ways, but she was able to feel much better after she so clearly chose to go that second time.

Soon we were done with preparations and travel meetings, and we and the rest of the group were ready to get on the airplane. The four movies en route helped to pass the time and were important distractions for both girls. When we arrived in China it was late and we were tired, but I could feel the energy building for both girls. We had a great first night and were rested and eager to start out the next day. We had breakfast with the group and then boarded the airplane that would eventually take us to the city where the babies were, Nanchang. The group was in high gear, we worked and laughed well together, and excitement mounted as we arrived in Nanchang and then waited for the time when the babies would be brought to us at the hotel there.

Nothing compares to the anxious excitement and wonder as adopting parents wait for their new baby to arrive. We all feel it for each of the families, and as the children were brought to the hotel everyone in the group was present to witness the miracle as the new families were brought together. My girls enjoyed this part tremendously. I saw so much in their eyes as they witnessed the families coming together—the magic of the moment, the wonder as the babies were first touched and held, the questions about where the babies came from and where they are going now in their lives. It's a lot to take in for such young children, especially children who had been on the other side of this process at one time!

After we were in Nanchang for a few days and the adoption work for the families was done, we went with our coordinator to visit Tian's foster mom and the orphanage where she had lived for the first two years of her life. She was very excited to see it all. A last-minute problem almost stopped the trip, and Tian cried so much the coordinator redoubled his efforts and managed to correct the problem and arrange the trip out to the orphanage once again.

After about an hour's drive, we arrived at the orphanage. It looked the same to me, surprisingly. I expected that in the intensity of that original visit when I went to meet my new daughter I would have missed a lot about the physical surroundings, but I was glad to find a familiarity in my mind about the place, the workers there, and of course Tian's foster mother. We spent a wonderful afternoon there with hugs all around and had a banquet given in our honor. This was the first time an adopted daughter from America had come back to see the orphanage, one that does a lot of adoptions in China. They were very excited to see Tian and her family and to know that the adopted children are doing so well. We visited, talked about our original visit there, and after promises to write back and forth we made the trip back to the hotel. What a successful reunion it was! Tian was beaming all day.

After our work was done in Nanchang we all flew to Guangzhou to finish the adoption work there. Things went smoothly, and when the time was right we arranged for a visit to Li's orphanage, about a half hour's drive from Guangzhou. Li was much more nervous in the car on the way to the orphanage than Tian had been, but she wanted to go and was also excited. We had prepared for the trip. Li had written a letter to the orphanage director, had several carefully chosen gifts to give her, and had brought photographs of our home and family life in America. We had also discussed questions that Li had for the orphanage director and the workers there, questions she had about how she had once lived, where she had eaten and played, and where she had once learned to sing and dance.

When we arrived the director was there to greet us, and so were several of the workers who had known Li. They were all smiles. Li could hardly wait to give the gifts, and there was much excitement as hugs were exchanged, gifts were given, and our coordinator helped with translations. All of the staff commented on how tall and beautiful Li had become. One thing she had worried about was how the women would greet her. Li takes her time to warm up to people and does not appreciate the loud, "in your face" style of the workers from Tian's orphanage. I had reassured her that in her orphanage home this would not be the case—the people there were more reserved. Thank goodness this turned out to be true! In fact, Li was the most outgoing of all. She was very present to the situation as we were given a tour and shown exactly where she once had lived and interacted with the other children and staff at the orphanage.

We were graciously offered the chance to see the original rooms where Li had lived, dispelling a lot of Li's memories of dark corners and long, empty hallways. The rooms were bright, and the echoes of laughing children were loud as we walked all over the grounds and into the various buildings that day. I have never seen Li able to be as present as she was that day. She did not wilt, she did not go inside herself, instead she took in everything and asked her questions with confidence. The visit for her was extremely important. Afterwards, on the way out of the orphanage back in the taxi, we agreed that we would never again think of her orphanage as dark and lonely. To her that day, it became a place full of light and laughter. These thoughts filled her heart. She had been given a real gift—part of her past had come back to her bathed in light and love instead of blackness and tears. She was obviously full and more complete for days afterward.

Since our return home, we have continued to talk about the events on this trip for both Tian and Li. I know that Li, in particular, is still processing what happened at the orphanage that day. More layers are coming out as she is able to verbalize about things. Some surprises: She is angry with herself for remembering the orphanage as a terrible place; she wonders about what it would have been like to stay there instead of being adopted. Some nice results of her trip there include a new and better impression of her birth country in general, new feelings of care for her orphanage director and the other workers there, and a firsthand look at families coming together through adoption. She now has a new interest in babies! She has discovered how playful they can be and loves to baby-sit. She can also share with her sister the experiences of being in their birth country together—a new and very special bond between them.

I will undoubtedly experience more of Li's layers as feelings about her adventures in China continue to be worked through and then expressed. In all I think it was a wonderful and exciting time for both Li and Tian, and a trip that they will each remember forever. What a gift to be able to go back in time, to revisit such an important place in their lives, and to discover how loved and cared for they were!

I hope that every adopting parent will consider making this trip with their child or children some day. It is not without its ups and downs, and as I say I think more will bubble to the surface in the months ahead, but I believe that it was definitely a positive thing for my daughters to have made this trip. For us, shedding light on the darkness of the past can do nothing but enhance their lives and complete a circle for all of us.

Val Free, M.A., M.F.C.C., is the executive director of Heartsent Adoptions, Inc., in Orinda, California, and the mother of three children adopted from Asia.

Going Back

A Father and Daughter Return to China

Doug Hood
FCC/New England

I was going back to China. It had been over two years since I adopted my daughter, Suki, there. I'm a physician's assistant, and the chance came to do volunteer work for a medical organization.

When invited, I told my supervisor I would gladly go if Suki, now six, could come along. It would be an ambitious trip. Thailand and five big cities scattered over China, ten flights total, eight Asian airports. We had to stay healthy, watch out for mosquitoes, use bottled water.

I found Chinese people in cities I never heard of to watch Suki while I worked. I threw in a leg that would get us back to her orphanage in Hangzhou. I even sent a letter to Mr. Li, the director. He left a message at a Shanghai number; he'd meet us.

Was Suki ready for this? One day getting ready for camp, I said, "Suki, do you want to go back to Hangzhou?"

"Yeah." She was tying her gimp and said, "You know you have to make this flat."

"How about Fuyang where your orphanage is?"

"Do I have to get a shot?"

"No. No shot."

"Yeah, I want to go."

"This won't bother you?"

She looked up. "Me? Why?" Good point. Nothing bothers her.

In Kunming she stayed with Wendy, whom she'd met in New Haven. In Shenyang she met Xiaotsun, sister of her girlfriend in Northampton. In Beijing, she followed us through the corridors of the Children's Hospital and made fast friends with a nine-year-old with chest tubes.

Finally, we arrived in Hangzhou.

Suki and I walked down the tarmac to the terminal. She was carrying the box of toys she'd picked out for the orphanage.

We met Mr. Li, who looked the same. He was plain with an average build and gray pants. A colorless man. We greeted him. Suki shook his hand. They asked her if she remembered him. She shook her head no.

One of the men, Jimbo, who spoke English, said they had made all arrangements. I told him we would stay only for the afternoon.

Suki sat on Mr. Li's lap. He looked awkward. Suki gave him the box of toys, which he put under the seat without looking at them. I was told he lived in Fuyang and has two boys that are older. Then as the van was going, he fell asleep.

We walked around West Lake. They bought Suki a red flexi-fish on a string. We found a restaurant that specialized in dumplings.

Outside we bought some peaches from a woman with a straw hat and no shoelaces. They felt she weighed them wrong, that her balance was tilted. They argued over pennies.

Once inside I had questions for Mr. Li. This was a rare chance to get answers. A chance I had thought about for two years.

"Can you ask Mr. Li if anyone else has come back to visit."

"He says one."

"Where was Suki found?"

"In Fuyang."

"Where? Train station?"

"He doesn't know."

"Who was the farmer that found her?"

"He doesn't know." I felt a conspiracy not to give any answers.

"Did she have a red tag left by her mother?"

"Don't know." He never asked Mr. Li.

I looked at Suki and said to myself, I'm trying.

They brought a bamboo steamer to our table. I took the meat out of Suki's dumpling and she ate the bread. Suki said, "Do you remember the man that moved his nose for money."

"What are you talking about?"

She wiggled her nose with her fingers. "Remember? And his ear went like this." She flapped her ear.

"Okay, yeah, I remember." It was on the Boulevard St. Michel in Paris. A mime was powdered to look like a statue. As the kids gathered at his feet, his nose or ear would barely wiggle.

I pulled out a photo I had taken in Suki's orphanage. There were four girls Suki's age. I asked, "Are these girls still there?"

One was Hishee, Suki's bed mate.

They studied it. Mr. Li said something and Jimbo translated. "He said all are adopted. One went to an American family, her." He pointed but not to Hishee, "and the others to Chinese."

I pointed to another photo. It was her caretaker, Zhou Chimin. One of the other men said, "She is gone."

"Where?"

"I don't know."

He offered to take us to the orphanage to visit, which surprised me since Americans weren't allowed to enter them since the "Dying Rooms" fiasco. I knew Suki's friends were gone. I saw no reason to go.

They brought out soup.

"Daddy, tell them not to drink it."

"Why?"

"It's lake water."

"How do you know?"

"Cause I saw someone at the lake dipping a dish. Daddy, tell them it's lake water."

"It's OK. It's a magic lake."

When we left I asked to go the Yellow Dragon Hotel. That was where Suki and I had spent our first week together. We got in the van and drove across town.

As we walked in I hoped someone would recognize us. We tried the desk, the gift shop. The girl in the shop had been there for ten years but didn't remember us. The elevator to the floors was broken, so we couldn't go to our room, number 310. Suki had almost no recall of the hotel, although she had been four at the time.

We saw the bar where she climbed over the plants. I pointed out the pool where she screamed at the water. The scales were still there in the gym. She was 96 centimeters then. Suki stood on it and measured 119 centimeters.

There was nothing more to do. No more to ask. It was time to go to Shanghai.

When we got to the train station, it felt suddenly like Morocco. It was chalk white, blistery hot, dusty. The poor were lying around with their roped-up bags, there were men on crutches with withered legs, and shrill sounds came from the speakers. They helped me get our tickets. We went into a waiting area. It was huge and not a seat was left. Everyone looked sweaty and ragged. All eyes were on us, the only non-Chinese there. I contemplated the idea of lugging four bags, leading Suki, and trying to find our train. I asked if they could find a man to help me for a few dollars.

Jimbo scanned the room for a "good man." Then he left, returned 20 minutes later, and said, "Follow me."

We met a man with a makeshift conductor's hat, green with two red circles. He led us through an alley, then around to the back of the station. We stood on the quay until the train arrived.

The woman conductor for our car, with a prim green dress and red sash, did not smile to take part in our special treatment but finally flicked a reluctant hand, allowing us to board. Suki and I put our bags by our seat on the top deck, first class. We returned to see the three men standing on the quay by the train's door. Jimbo said, "You need to come with me to get a ticket for her."

I motioned to Suki and Jimbo said, "No, leave her there."

I looked at the woman to see if she acknowledged. Would she watch Suki? She was stone-faced.

Jimbo said, "Leave her and come." I looked at Suki. She sensed our separation and was starting to cry.

I said, "No, I can't go. I'll say good-bye."

"Okay, You can pay them. But you get no seat for her."

"That's OK, I thank you for a nice day. Suki, say good-bye."

Suki still had tears in her eyes. She weakly waved her hand to the men. They said, "Good-bye, Suki."

Mr. Li waved. Perhaps he did not understand why Suki was crying. It appeared she was sad to see them go. I hoped Mr. Li thought so. I wanted him to think that she will miss him. I wanted him to feel a tug from one of his girls. But he doesn't know she doesn't cry that way.

Mr. Li has one more year left at Fuyang. Then, because he will be 60, according to Chinese law he must retire. He is what is left from Suki's early years. The only one who saw her from baby to toddler. The only link to all that she came from, the farmer, her house, her father, her mother. He has no way of explaining what gave her an inexplicable joy born out of a once insufferable life. Suki and I must now accept what we know, don't know, and aren't told. We have closed the door on that part of her life and are going home.

Doug Hood has recently published short stories in *Cimarron Review* and *Northeast Corridor* and takes Suki on medical trips back to China.

Ying Ying in China

An Adopted Child's First Trip Back

Amy Klatzkin
San Francisco Bay Area FCC

Despite the perils of traveling with a four-year-old, Terry and I decided to take our daughter, Ying Ying, back to China in October 1997 for the first time since she was a baby. We thought she was old enough to retain a few memories from the trip, and we wanted to make China a real place for her—a place where she could feel comfortable now and in the future. We didn't go to Changsha, where we'd adopted her, because we had heard that sometimes very young children have fears they can't express about returning to the place where they were adopted, and we didn't want her to worry that "going back to China" might mean leaving her there. So we plotted three weeks in three other cities where we have friends with young children. We planned to spend most of our time in Xi'an, where we had lived in the mid 1980s, learned to speak mediocre Chinese, and maintained friendships with people who would do their best to make Ying Ying feel at home.

Going sooner as well as later was important to us. China is changing so rapidly that by the time Ying Ying is old enough to "appreciate" a trip there, in the grownup sense of the word, it won't be anything like it was when she was born. I knew from Terry, who'd been back several times over the past four years, that the city of Xi'an and our friends' standard of living had transformed almost beyond recognition. Nothing in the U.S. has changed that much in my lifetime. I simply had to see it. And our friends were eager to see Ying Ying.

The worst part of traveling with a spirited four-year-old was that she behaved just as she would at home if we disrupted her routine, went somewhere she'd never been before, and introduced her to dozens of new people every day. As long as we could rustle up other kids for her to play with, especially older girls, she was happy. But other times she missed her teachers and preschool friends, got fed up with strangers, and, at one memorable lunch out with the head of the Shaanxi Provincial Women's Federation, threw herself on the floor and writhed for an hour. Fortunately Ying Ying has a double cowlick, which in China signifies a big temper, so when she acted out we'd shrug and say, "She's got two cowlicks," and everyone would make sympathetic noises and tell us we were lucky she didn't have three. We learned to keep part of each day the same (especially food: the first week she ate only *doufu*, the second week *jiaozi*, the third week chicken and rice), to revisit the people and places she liked best, and to find "big sisters" for her to play with. Beyond that, we just put up with the occasional outburst because it was worth it.

The best part was watching Ying Ying develop a real sense of herself as Chinese. "*I* was born in China," she'd announce to us. "When I'm big, I'll speak better Chinese than you do." (It already sounds better.) She loved everything she saw that looked really Chinese. Even though we live in a largely Chinese neighborhood in San Francisco, she's always had Mandarin at home, and she was in her second year at the bilingual Chinese American International School, there was something about being in China that made it all click. She delighted in every upturned tiled roof, demanded to have her picture taken next to every stone lion, and understood without translation that the word for foreigner didn't apply to her. Walking on the Great Wall—familiar territory from *Big Bird in China*— she spent hours searching for the Monkey King. ("Look, Mom! He's over there! He made my hat blow off! He made that leaf fly!") In Beijing she quickly mastered the art of flagging down a taxi and sat in the back seat reciting our hotel's location in Chinese: "Bamboo Garden Hotel," she'd mumble, imitating a Beijing accent, "near Old Drum Tower Avenue." When our taxi pulled into the right narrow back lane of old courtyard houses she'd shout, "We're home!"

The biggest surprise of the trip was how people on the street responded to us. Chinese friends living in the States had warned us we'd be quite a spectacle. After an embarrassing experience that summer with Canadian customs, I was more concerned that we carry copies of our Chinese adoption paperwork with us at all times in case someone in authority questioned our right to travel together. Less ominously, I expected to hear people wonder loudly, "Where are that girl's parents, and why is she going around with foreigners?" Since Ying Ying would understand these comments, we were prepared to stop whatever we were doing, squat down to her level, and talk about why people didn't recognize us as a family. But we never heard comments like that, and none of our precautions were necessary. After a few days we put the paperwork at the bottom of our suitcase and forgot about it.

The fact was, people hardly noticed us, even when we skipped down the sidewalk singing, "Doe, a deer, a female deer…" Apparently urban Chinese have had foreigners around for so long now that we aren't very interesting anymore no matter what we do.

The only crowd we drew was a group of American tourists at the terra cotta soldiers. Spotting Terry taking a picture of Ying Ying, they thought she was a local girl and asked to take her picture too. She obliged, lips sealed. I returned from getting soft drinks for our family and Chinese friends to find the lot of them surrounded by the smiling Americans, who'd given Ying Ying Hershey's Kisses and a Delta Airlines pin. They were the only ones the entire month who got it completely wrong—and my family and friends weren't telling.

When local people happened to notice us and do the double-take we see so often at home, the comment we heard over and over was an expression of simple surprise: "Their daughter looks just like a Chinese girl!" It was clear that most people saw us first as a family and only then wondered how two foreign adults could have such a normal-looking child.

I loved it that no one, not even children, asked whose child she was. I loved it that no one asked how much money the adoption cost (although it's not impolite in China to ask about money). And I loved it that by the end Ying Ying would tell perfect strangers, "I'm Chinese *and* I'm American," and that that was sufficient for the average curious onlooker. I felt that we were accepted as a "real" (if unusual) family more readily by urban Chinese than by most Americans.

Another thing I expected to hear but didn't was the conventional wisdom that people in China would never adopt "someone else's child." We did hear *fuqi* a lot, and I tried not to wince (at home we call "lucky" the "L-word"), but when we chose to talk about adoption with strangers, we found people curious but matter-of-fact about it. Friends uniformly accepted Kay Johnson's contention that many more abandoned girls are adopted by Chinese in China than by foreigners and that the orphanages might well be cleaned out of healthy infants if the law were changed to allow couples with a boy to adopt an abandoned girl. To say that attitudes are changing is a massive understatement in a country undergoing sweeping economic and social transformation.

One afternoon in Beijing, while Terry was in a meeting, Ying Ying and I headed for the children's playground near the Temple of Heaven. I had a long conversation about adoption with a mother of twin boys while our kids jumped on a trampoline, and then Ying Ying and I went off to get some slurpy Beijing yogurt to quench our thirst. Ying decided she didn't want to talk to the street vendors and asked me not to talk to them either. "Let's pretend we don't understand," she said and then babbled a little

Yingyingese, a nonsense language she uses to confound nosey strangers. I paid the yogurt vendor and smiled but didn't answer when she asked where we came from.

While Ying and I sat slurping our drinks, three vendors behind us tried to figure us out. One woman suggested that my husband must be an Asian man because my daughter certainly didn't look like me at all, and everyone knows Asian characteristics are stronger. Another demurred: "Look at her skin; it's so white. That comes from her mother. All the rest must be from her father." Ying Ying started to giggle. Grasping a teaching moment, I told her I guessed she probably looked a lot like her birth parents, and maybe they were also fair-skinned. "Yes, but Mommy, *they* don't know that," she said, referring to the women behind us. Then she cupped a hand to my ear and whispered, "Shhhhh. It's our secret." And she grinned.

Travel Tips for China with Kids

Our trip was not about going back to our daughter's orphanage or trying in any way to confront or resolve issues from her past. That's for another time, when she's older. For this first trip we wanted to bring China into her present and future, to make it a real place for her—a place where moms and dads and children live and play, work and relax, just like people do at home. The following list is what helped us meet that modest goal and enjoy ourselves (most of the time) along the way.

Prepare your child. For months beforehand we talked about squat toilets, unfamiliar smells, crowds, and the importance of hand washing (we carried "Wet Ones" everywhere, since most public bathrooms don't have soap). *Big Bird in China* got heavy use. We also pored over pictures from our adoption trip and picked up travel brochures with big color photos of places she'd be visiting. And to allay any possible fears that we might be taking her back for good, we never talked about going to China without also talking about all of us coming home again.

Prepare yourselves. If your family doesn't speak Chinese, talk about how it might feel to hear people say things about you that you don't understand. In our experience, we didn't get more attention in China than we do in San Francisco, and we never heard anything rude, but if you can't talk with people who are talking *about* you, it could be disconcerting. Make contingency plans for escaping unwanted attention.

Limit your itinerary, and stay where you'll be comfortable. Your child will take her cues from you. If you're comfortable, she can relax—and she can also express her worries knowing that you're in control. If you haven't traveled much in China, this probably isn't the trip to do *Asia on a Shoestring*. At the same time, a luxury tour of six cities in ten days could be a disaster for kids used to a routine. Pick a few places you really want to see and learn everything you can about them ahead of time so you know where you are when you get there.

Find playgrounds. If you haven't been to China for a few years, you'll be amazed at how much there is for little kids to do. Practically every park and historic site has a children's play area off to the side with inexpensive rides appealing to the under-ten set.

Find families with children. If you don't know anyone in China, this can be a challenge, but it could make the difference between a great trip and a nightmare. We didn't know any "big sisters" in Beijing, but a friend who is also a professor of anthropology introduced us via e-mail to the fifteen-year-old daughter of a colleague in the capital. Guan Guan came with us to the Summer Palace and the Beijing Zoo, and we spent a delightful evening at her parents' apartment. Ying Ying adored her. When Guan Guan was in school, we sought out families in playgrounds and marched right into kindergartens to take a look around, including the Ministry of Culture's kindergarten next door to our hotel. No one minded.

Travel light. If you really need it, you can buy it in China. A Chinese friend returning home last June for the first time since 1992 packed everything she thought her three-year-old son would need for six months, including a suitcase full of disposable diapers and cases of juice boxes. When we caught up with her in October in Xi'an, she flourished a Chinese-made juice box, available practically everywhere, and said, "Now I tell everyone, 'Don't bring anything. Just bring money.'"

Be a little adventurous. We didn't know how Ying Ying would take to a 20-hour train ride, but we knew she liked bunk beds, so we booked tickets from Xi'an to Beijing in hard sleeper, where they stack 'em three high in an open car. She loved it. She also got to see a lot of countryside, where the vast majority of people in China live.

But be careful crossing the street. As one Beijing taxi driver put it, "There are only two rules of the road in China: Drivers aren't afraid to die, and red lights don't mean anything."

Amy Klatzkin edits the newsletter of San Francisco Bay Area FCC. Ying Ying Fry is one of half a dozen FCC children attending the bilingual Chinese American International School in San Francisco.

Adoption,
the Lifelong
Journey

What is not there is just as important as what is there.

Deng Ming-dao

Dumpling's Questions

Jan Keane
Children Adopted from China (UK)

I.

Dumpling, age eight and a half, was in the bath recently when Dad came in to shave. "Dad, when you've finished would you mind going and getting my condom please?" Dad's neurons fired as he tried to work this out, causing a temporary loss of focus to the task at hand, and a resultant nick to his neck.

"Eeerk, you're bleeding," announced Dumpling with considerable contempt.

"Umm, right, where is the co-, um, where is it?" he asked.

"By my bed. Near the light I think."

Dad rummaged through the clutter on Dumpling's chest of drawers. He pushed aside several Roald Dahl books, a tube of pogs, three odd Barbie shoes, and a small pair of scissors. He peered underneath a discarded page of jottings, checked the base of the bedside lamp. Nothing. At least nothing resembling an object bearing a name that could be confused with a contraceptive device. Somewhat bewildered, Dad padded back to the bathroom.

"I can't find it," he declared.

"Oh, never mind. I must have left it somewhere else," said Dumpling, and went back to creating a foam sculpture out of her hair.

We never did find out what Dumpling was looking for that day. Like so many of Dumpling's utterances, we have filed it under "amusing anecdotes." Life, as someone said, is like that. Nothing involving the raising of a child is neat or complete. There are no a priori rules, or even principles, despite the outpourings of experts such as Stoppard and Leech, to apply to

the many dilemmas of parenting. Sensible parents know they are ill-prepared; sane parents feel totally inadequate to the task. We, as adoptive parents, are no different. We merely face an added problem, that's all. It's a
simple but monstrously profound problem though.

"Why didn't my mother want me?" That's the question we all dread.
And no matter how well prepared we think we are, no matter how welcome we have made our adopted children, no matter how much and how
achingly we love them, the dreaded question will be a complete show-
stopper.

Dumpling's first foray into the world of gut wallopers came when she
was a little over three; the time when her developing autonomy was grop-
ing to find its magnitude. Dumpling was refusing to accede to a "perfectly
reasonable" request and I began to make "controlled" threats. Very
quickly we became locked in a battle of wills—Dumpling shrieking, "No, I
don't have to!" and me assaulting her with the complex grammar of the if-
clause. Finally Dumpling came up with a master stroke. "Anyway, I don't
have to do what you say. You're not my mother."

Imagine something the size of Frank Bruno's fist being thrust into your
lower rib-cage by a force the strength of Bruno's shoulders. Emotional distress has a powerful physical dimension.

I AM your mother, you little sod. The woman who gave birth to you
never looked at you, never held you. I was the one who looked after you in
that Chinese hospital while you were treated for septicemia. I was the one
who punched the nurse and stopped the porters from spraying DDT
around your cot. I was the one who laid you on my stomach every night in
that ward, protecting you from the mutant cockroaches by swatting them
off my legs with a rolled-up newspaper. It was me, NOT HER, who fed you
every fifteen minutes for two days as your poor little body tried to recover
from its allergic reaction to antibiotics contra-indicated for babies. It was
ME, not her. And I was the one who, during the second week of your recu-
peration, realized that I loved you more intensely and more completely
than I thought possible, that I would give my life for you without question, that you were my epiphany.

Dumpling and I held each other tightly and cried for a while. The comfort and reassurances came easily, for I had no desire to weaken
Dumpling's sense of her own worth with tales of one mother's rejection
and another's martyrdom. But the words still ricocheted around my
brain. In one hugely important sense I am not Dumpling's mother.

Adoptive parents are almost as vulnerable as their adopted children when
it comes to the big issue. We can do, will do, everything for our children,

but we were not able to give them their existence. So we live our lives with ghosts in the wings.

Dumpling's procreators, referred to as her first or Chinese mum and dad, have always been part of our family history. They are spoken about often, but not gratuitously; in the same way you would refer to the antics and anecdotes of dead or absent relatives. They have faces, names, ages, and occupations, but have no day-to-day influence. At least, most of the time. When the ghosts make an entrance, we just fumble through as best we can, then go away and lick our own wounds.

When Dumpling was very small she wanted to hear the same story over and over again. She called it "the story of how you found me."

We wanted a Dumpling baby very much, we said, and we looked everywhere for her. We looked under bushes, in trees, in fox holes, and in cupboards. Everywhere. We asked all the animals in the wood if they had seen Dumpling. None of them had. We became very sad. Then one day we got a phone call from Uncle Wang in China. He told us that he had found Dumpling. We were very happy after that. Mummy flew to China straight away and held Dumpling and kissed her. Two weeks later, Daddy came to China. He phoned Mummy from the lobby of the hotel. Mummy went to the lift to meet him. She had Dumpling in her arms, and handed her to Daddy, saying, "Here's your daughter." Daddy cried.

It was easy to give Dumpling a sense of her past for a number of years, because none of her questions was potentially damaging to self-esteem. Young children want simple stories in which they have the principal role. Then, at about the age of seven, Dumpling's storybook view of the overlap of fact and fiction began to falter. She went through a stage of asking questions about her Chinese mother. Was she married now? Did she have another child? If she had another child, did that mean that she was no longer Dumpling's first mother? Was Dumpling an orphan like Annie Warbucks? Why did we adopt her and not a different baby? How many babies were there to choose from? We fielded all of these with cautious honesty, and the ghosts slowly returned to the wings.

Dumpling was almost eight when the dreaded question was uttered. Predictably, it made an entrance at the most unexpected moment. Tuck in, lights out, kiss kiss, and then, "Mummy, Daddy, why didn't my first mummy want me?"

We sat on the bed either side of her like a pair of android therapists. "Oh Dumpling! It wasn't you she didn't want. She was too young to look after a baby. Babies take a lot of time to care for properly. And they're little and fragile, and they cry a lot, and they pooh all the time. But, honestly, it wasn't you she didn't want. And we wanted you. We wanted you very much."

Dumpling was sobbing inconsolably. "Look, sweetheart, this is rather hard to understand, but now you are Dumpling, and you think of yourself as Dumpling, but when you were new-born you were just a screaming baby with a red spotty face. You weren't the bright, sweet, pretty girl we love more than anyone else in the world. Your Chinese mummy couldn't look after you. It's very difficult for unmarried women to bring up children in China."

"Then why did she get me in her tummy if she didn't want a baby?" Dumpling wailed.

"Well, she and your Chinese dad probably didn't mean to make a baby, but sometimes it happens by accident. People often make love because it feels nice, but…"

"Yuck, I don't want to hear about that!" Dumpling interrupted, and a little grin appeared. She looked at both of us and exploded into tears again. "I'm a nice little girl, I am. I'm only naughty sometimes and…, and…"

Dumpling cried for a long time. We held her, kissed her, told her how much we loved her. Eventually she grew quiet. Dad crept out of the room, and I patted her back until I thought she was asleep. As I made a move to the door, Dumpling mumbled, "Mum, what do you think my Chinese mummy would think of me if she saw me now?"

"She'd think you were beautiful and kind and clever."

"Mmm. What would you do if she said she wanted to take me back," Dumpling challenged.

The ghosts skulked back to the wings, soundly defeated. "That's easy," I said. "You're our daughter. No one else can have you. I'd tell her to bugger off, and if she didn't, I'd push her over a cliff!"

II.

A five-year-old friend of Dumpling's announced recently that she knew what "messy" was in French. Her parents were most relieved, sensing there might be an object lesson in view, for Miss Five was, without a doubt, of an untidy disposition.

"That's very appropriate," her mother replied pointedly. "So what is messy in French?"

"It means 'thank you,' Mummy. Messy, messy, messy!"

Dumpling was highly amused by this story. "Messy, messy, mercy, mercy, merci, merci. What did the mare see? It saw the sea," she chanted. Children of Dumpling's age revel in the oddities of language with puns and homophones making up the bulk of their innocent riddles. Dumpling loves a good tongue-twister too, and roars with laughter when her aging parents fail miserably in oral calisthenics. On top of all this Dumpling is something of an expert on the French language, having done a couple of modules with "Le Club Français," and an optional lunchtime activity on French at school last term where they ate tinned fogs' legs and snails, and learned to say "Yuck" with appropriate Gallic body language.

We have French to thank for the fact that Dumpling is also an expert on gender, an issue she treats with enormous contempt. Even at this early age she has decided she will never master the definite and indefinite articles of a Romance language. As for Chinese, well, her hopes were raised when told that the spoken words for "he" and "she" were exactly the same, but dashed when she found they were written differently. "It's not fair," she proclaimed. "All this masculine and feminine stuff…it's stupid!"

Stupid maybe, but these linguistic issues are very much the lighter side of gender.

About three months ago Dumpling was abruptly alerted to gender's dark side. It all started with India.

"Mum, is it true that women in India only want baby boys, and that they make their girl babies be born early when the baby is too little to live?"

Wow! Where did this information come from? Not from school, surely. Possibly from television, which goes to show the perils of unsupervised viewing.

"Yes, Dumpling, it is sort of true. Some families in some cultures prefer boys, so a woman might end her pregnancy early if she knew she was carrying a girl, and then try again for a boy. Not all people feel like that though. We don't, and most of the people we know don't either. We think girls are wonderful."

Dumpling was incensed. "But why? What's wrong with girls?"

"There's nothing wrong with girls, Dumpling. The world is a complicated place and…"

"So why?" Dumpling interrupted. "Why do some women in India kill their girl babies then? It's killing them really, isn't it? If you make them be born early when they can't live? It's killing really! And God said you shouldn't kill. All those poor girl babies!"

Oh dear. Dumpling was now fully wound up with pity for scores of dead girl babies. She sobbed while I tried to console her with adult wisdom, offering those cultural and economic explanations I no longer find convincing. As I held her, it seemed to me that Dumpling had a sounder, simpler, and more profound notion of human rights than most adults. It was also evident that she would soon make the connection with China and her own circumstances.

You have to be extremely determined and single-minded to adopt a baby, especially from overseas. You have to become a fanatic. If any one of our social workers had asked us to turn cartwheels, swear on the Bible, give up alcohol, learn Icelandic, chop off a finger, we'd have said, "Yes! Yes! Anything. Just give us a baby." As to the "what ifs" and "what will you say whens," I remember discussing at length our potential strategies for handling an adopted child's difficult questions. The strategies seemed sensible at the time; when we got three-week-old Dumpling, we forgot all about future difficulties and focused on the wonders of parenthood. Eight and a half years later we find ourselves in a "what will you say when" situation. Unfortunately the strategies offered with such confidence to social workers at a time when Dumpling was only an idea don't seem nearly adequate to the task.

How do you tell a child that she was abandoned at birth because of her gender? How much do you tell? How little? Do you tell her at all? Perhaps the best move is to invent a romantic story: budding prima ballerina of the Beijing Number One Ballet Company has an illegitimate daughter, but rather than wreck her promising career chooses to give the child up to a well-off foreign couple who can offer said child a better material life. You've got to say something, so what the hell do you say? Forget the theory spouted to social workers when trying to impress. This is real life now. We've opted pretty much for the truth around here so far. It's the brutal truth we cringe from.

The penny dropped more quickly than I anticipated. Dumpling asked a series of questions about her Chinese mother and father, showing more than her usual interest in details. The factual questions were easy; the psychological questions were not. Dumpling seemed particularly concerned about her Chinese parents' feelings for one another.

"But if she wasn't married and he wasn't married, and they loved each other, why didn't they get married?"

"I don't know for sure, darling. Perhaps they weren't sure they wanted to get married. Besides, they were very young."

"Oh," Dumpling mused, and after a few seconds asked, "How long did she look after me?"

"She didn't. The nurses at the hospital looked after you until Uncle Wang and his family took you to their house; then Daddy and I came along to care for you. The nurses said you were the most beautiful baby they had ever seen. Uncle Wang thought so too…"

My compensatory prattle irritated Dumpling. She wanted facts, not flattery. "I don't want to know about that. I want to know what she did when I was born."

Dumpling is a confident child but prone to reflection. At these moments the two-headed Mummy-Daddy tend to act in tandem, pacifying, explaining, and above all reassuring. Dumpling was not consoled by our sanitized explanation this time. Her voice was quiet and timid when she asked, "What would have happened if I'd been a boy?"

Consider this sad story. A young peasant girl travels illegally to Beijing to work as a domestic. She meets a handsome university student, becomes pregnant, doesn't have the pregnancy terminated, hopes against hope for a boy and therefore marriage. The baby, a girl, is left at the hospital, the university student returns to his family's home in the south of China, the peasant girl is sent back to the countryside.

Truth has many dimensions. Call us cowards if you like, but we shied away from this version of Dumpling's creation, and we certainly didn't have the heart to tell Dumpling of her Chinese mother's actions directly after delivery, of the one and only question she asked about the baby. Nor did we mention the refusal to see Dumpling on determining her gender. We didn't talk about what might have happened if Dumpling had been a boy; the probability of marriage and the raising of a fine *xiao huangdi* (literal meaning, "little yellow emperor," an expression used widely in China since the single-child policy to describe the status and behavior of only children; colloquial meaning, "spoiled indulged child.")

A day does not pass without us feeling immensely grateful to Dumpling's Chinese mother. She did not, as she could so easily have done without any scandal, have her pregnancy terminated. Even so we do not feel sorry for her. Loving Dumpling makes it impossible for us to empathize with that moment of abandonment, abandonment because of gender. If it's hard for us to see that action in a generous light, how much harder will it be for Dumpling? She will have to know one day. Hopefully instinct will tell us when Dumpling is secure enough to deal with the brutal truth.

The Other Mommy
in China

John Bowen
FCC–British Columbia

"There's a time when you have to explain to your children why they're born, and it's a marvelous thing if you know the reason by then." I found this admittedly obscure quote by Hazel Scott, the entertainer, by accident. It has poignancy for some issues at hand.

The other night my wife repeatedly coaxed, then finally instructed, our nearly seven-year-old daughter to get ready for bed. "You're mean," our daughter reacted. "I want my other mommy in China!"

"We can talk about that later," my wife replied, "but right now I am asking you to brush your teeth."

I was expecting this. I know other FCC kids of the same age who are showing similar curiosity about their birth and birth mothers. I was almost impatient for it to happen. The adoption fact came out early. We discussed it from time to time. And really, it has not been difficult at all.

The other mommy issue, though, is a bit tricky. It is only a membrane away from the probable abandonment issue. It is true that few if any of us know how and why our children came to be found and brought into orphanages.

It is possible, I suppose, that some infants were lost, confiscated, given up, or whatever. But most of us, I think, are under the impression that most of our children were foundlings, abandoned, probably because of the population control policy and the traditional need for a male child to care for parents in their old age and carry on the family line.

My wife had to leave town on business early the next morning. So at breakfast, I showed Melissa pictures of her supposed birthplace, Sanshui, and the orphanage and explained that there was little beyond that that we knew.

I explained that she was found and brought into the orphanage. She asked if anyone knew anything more. I said not as far as I could find out. But I promised to seek out as much as I could, if she wanted me to. I also explained that it was not uncommon in China for children to be found and brought to an orphanage. The country is crowded, and life there is more of a struggle than it is here. Melissa said she wanted to hear no more. It made her cry, she said. And I suspected that her mention of the other mommy the night before was not really an expression of curiosity. I probably jumped the gun, a bit. So I dropped the discussion. Frankly, I was relieved.

Melissa is not the sort to brood about things. She is enjoying her childhood in a way that makes me envious. Nevertheless, I know the question about "the other mother" will return. Of that, I am sure. I wish I could be as certain that we will deal with it every time in the best possible way for Melissa. My wisdom at this point goes no further than the following five antidotes:

1. Love her demonstrably, as we always have, to mitigate any possible future sense of loss or pain of rejection.

2. Let her know that she is free to discuss and stop discussing these issues any time she wants, with anyone she wants.

3. Make every effort to support and satisfy her curiosity, to the extent that it manifests itself.

4. Reassure her that the desire (if there is any) to explore her birth circumstances, irrespective of where it may lead, will not change her relationship with the family she owns and belongs in.

5. Maintain and cultivate friendships and associations with other adopted children from China.

Over the next few years I will read all I can find on the subject and will consult experts. As Melissa's teen years rush toward us, it may be reassuring to have anticipated at least one aspect of an age typically full of surprises for parents.

John Bowen, Melissa Lihua Bowen's dad, lives in West Vancouver, British Columbia, and is the newsletter editor for FCC-BC. He is also the author of the *Canadian Guide to International Adoption* (Self Counsel Press, 1992).

The Importance of Loving Your Child's Birth Mother

Susan Tompkins

FCC–Oregon and SW Washington

A decade ago, family therapists were fond of telling men that the best thing they could do for their children was to love their child's mother. Showing a loving, affectionate, and respectful relationship between mother and father was seen as an incredibly powerful tool in raising emotionally healthy children. It was good advice then, and it's good advice now. I would take this concept one step further for those of us with adopted children and say that one of the best things we can do for our children is to love their birth mother, and let our children know it.

Families involved in open adoptions have many opportunities to show that love by welcoming the birth mother into their lives. But for those of us with Chinese children, where we will never know the identity of their birth mother or the real circumstances of their abandonment, this process is more difficult. Still, we can recognize the women who bore our children, women with whom they share a genetic, cultural, and historical bond. By welcoming them into our hearts, we honor our children's past and help build their self-esteem.

I came to this understanding in part by working in the adoption field, but more so by seeing my eldest daughter go through a painful episode working through these issues. She came to us as an infant from India, and throughout her childhood we discussed her birth mother when telling her adoption story. We touched on the economic and cultural reasons that would lead a birth mother to abandon her child. As our daughter grew older, however, the adoption story was rarely told. We spoke of other adoption issues, and of racism, but our daughter's silence about her own past made me feel she didn't need to talk about it.

Then, at age 13, she had an emotional crisis. When she finally received counseling by an adoption specialist, I was shocked at the cause. Birth mother issues were at the core of her struggle, as well as other adoption and racial issues. She wanted to know why her birth mother had abandoned her, and whether she was still alive.

That was when I resumed talking about her birth mother. As the years passed I realized that we were accomplishing quite a lot through these discussions. We touched on my daughter's self-esteem, personal history, and what her life would have been like had she remained in her birth country. I spoke of how much I cared about her birth mother, how beautiful and smart she must be, how sad her life must be, and of course, what an incredible gift she gave us. And I realized that I have never felt so connected to my children as when we are talking about their birth mothers.

It was about that time that our family watched the movie *The Joy Luck Club*, with no forewarning of the story. Toward the end, my daughter sobbed uncontrollably as I held her, sobbing myself. "Can you talk about it?" I asked. She nodded no. I said, "You're thinking of your birth mother, aren't you?" She nodded yes, and we continued to cry. Later we were able to discuss how the birth mothers in the movie were trapped by circumstance and culture. We also talked of their pain. Now we watch the movie about once a year—we can't take it any more often.

I believe our Indian daughter has come to honor her birth mother, and herself, through these discussions. I further believe she has a more global view of our world and the role of women than do most teens. Recently, she was on an adopted-teen panel speaking to would-be adoptive parents. I smiled as she nonchalantly and confidently said she rarely thought about her birth mother, and that I was her "real" mom, the mom who raised her. I believe that she can speak confidently before all these people because she, as well as her family, loves and respects her birth mother. But I also know that she is not as cavalier as she seems and that we will be talking about her birth mother and abandonment for a long time to come.

I recommend that parents not wait for their children to bring up the subject of their birth mothers because they may not. Our children are curious about their birth mothers, but they may fear hurting us with their questions and curiosity. They also may feel conflicted about their birth mothers because they blame these women for giving them away.

Children vary as to when they're ready to talk about their birth mother. I began having these discussions with my son, whom we adopted from Romania at 10 months of age, on his fifth birthday. As I spoke of loving his birth mother, a broad smile broke out on his face, and I knew this was the right time. He asked her name, and I told him. This year, at age seven, his response was different. "Mom," he said, "she left me in that horrible hospital where there were mean people." (He's thinking more critically now.) I validated his feelings but went on to talk about the positive qualities he had that may have come from her and our family's gratitude. Again, the broad smile came to his face. Next year I'll add more cultural details to the story, which will help him grasp some of the reasons why children are abandoned in his birth country.

If the birth mother's identity is unknown, then you and your child can fantasize about her. You can ask your child, "If you could talk with her, what would you say?" or, "What do you think she might be doing right now? What do you think she looks like? What qualities do you have that might have come from your birth mother?" Collect stories to tell her that may reflect her birth mother's situation. For example, I recently heard about an adopting couple in China who had gone with their interpreter to see the place where their daughter had been abandoned. There they saw a Chinese mother and father walking down the street carrying a bundle. The mother followed behind in obvious emotional distress as the father put the bundle down. The witnesses walked across the street and found the baby. This story, while not your child's, illustrates the pain of many birth mothers as they are forced to abandon their children. It will make them feel good to know this "giving away" was not easy.

For older children, watching movies with an adoption theme, such as *The Joy Luck Club,* can be an excellent way to open up dialogue and emotion regarding birth mothers. *Welcome Home Roxie Carmichael* has been a tear-jerker in our home for many years. In this movie, the adopted child fantasizes about her birth mother, providing a perfect opening for further discussion. I would recommend it for children who are at least 12 years old. *Secrets and Lies* (appropriate for ages 15 and up) is another excellent movie that shows the first meeting and growing affection between a birth mother and her adult child. Watch these movies yourself first and then make your own judgment about when your child should see them.

Many families will come up with their own ways to celebrate their child's birth mothers, such as special prayers or ceremonies. Birthdays and Mother's Day are natural times to recognize her importance in our lives, as are special occasions. Several years ago, our family was at the Portland Airport to greet our newest member, a baby girl who had just arrived home from China. It was such a joyous event. As we approached our car and began putting the new baby in her car seat, our Indian daughter began to cry. She said to me, "If only our birth mothers knew how much we are loved." I held her and shed a few tears too. I agreed, "If only they knew."

Susan Tompkins is a licensed clinical social worker, executive director of Journeys of the Heart Adoption Services in Hillsboro, Oregon, and an FCC member. Three of her four children have come to her through international adoption.

Did Our Children's Birth Parents Love Them?

Jane Brown, M.S.W.
San Francisco Bay Area FCC

From my personal and professional experience in working with young adoptees, I believe that growing up adopted greatly complicates the task of figuring out one's identity and understanding one's history. Trying to figure out what birth parents are all about is a large piece of that. Learning about and understanding birth parents is a long and continuous process. Children can't take a few isolated instances of discussing things with parents and then put it all together.

Researchers have found, in fact, that adoptees seem to take over 12 years to really be able to conceptualize the whole picture of what it means to have been adopted. It takes even longer, into adulthood, to be able to understand adult problems that might contribute to birth parents' needing to make an adoption plan and then to identify with their own birth parents' possible set of problems.

Did the birth parents love their child?

Should we tell children that they did, if we don't know for sure? This is tricky, in my opinion.

What we say *does* have a great potential impact on our children's sense of identity and comfort with their past. They may come to worry a great deal about their genetic endowment, wondering, Were my birth parents good or bad people? (Young kids see this as very black and white.) Did they love and care about me and what would become of me? Were they such inadequate people that they couldn't raise their "own, real" child? (Remember, although we—birth parents and adoptive parents—may use accurate terminology, our children will pick up what their peers say and are quite likely to use those words, sometimes, instead of the accurate ones we give them. The terminology affects how they think, too, while they are processing all of this.)

Before I discuss my own thinking about what we, as parents, might consider in deciding whether or not to say that the birth parents were loving, I want to talk about how children take in and process what we say. I believe that regardless of *what* we say, our children are likely to get things mixed up and confused, and they will reflect back to us some of the information that either they didn't hear accurately or that got skewed as they tried to make sense of it. They will need lots and lots of repetition. They'll hear many things from peers and outsiders that will conflict with what we, their parents, tell them, and they will need to think about all of this and reach their own conclusions. Also, their ability to understand the more subtle aspects of adoption comes only with time and cognitive development.

Each time my husband and I would discuss some aspect of adoption or sexuality or racial identity or culture with our children, we found later that they understood only a portion of what we had said, confused other parts, and elaborated on others so that they were nothing like what we had intended (and these we needed to correct and then check out again). Still other parts had gone completely over their heads. Each of them had their own timetable of understanding and even willingness to discuss the issues at hand.

To my mind, honesty is critical to whether our children will continue to trust what we say about their history and most everything else that we discuss, so I refrain from telling my child that I absolutely *know* or even believe that a birth parent loved them if I don't actually know that. There are many reasons why birth parents relinquish, abandon, or make an adoption plan for the child they give birth to. In China, many do so because they believe they need to have a son, but prostitution also exists, and there are unwed birth mothers and people with other problems who make this decision too.

My guess is that the vast majority of birth mothers have a great deal of sadness in saying goodbye to the baby they bore and that many keep their child for a period of time to give them a better chance at life, but that this is not always so. We need to, perhaps, be careful about what we say and make sure that it *is* the truth.

We use lots of tentative words in our explanations about birth parents. We have, when specific history is unknown or unclear, given several possible explanations to our children, and I encourage other adoptive parents to consider doing the same. Statements like "My guess is…" or "I like to think that…" or "Although we don't know for sure…" are always a part of our explanations. We acknowledge that we don't really know, but then go on to make guesses, based on our children's need to identify positively with their birth parents and to feel as strongly as possible that they were cared for all along their route to us, even though the birth parents weren't able, for some reason, to be their forever parents—which is the *only* truth that we can be sure of.

Still, I believe that young children need to think that their birth parents made a caring decision, unless we know otherwise that this was not so (as in the case of rape, for example, where we know that the birth father was not even aware of the birth and probably would not have cared). One can say to a child that she had another set of parents who were not able to raise the child they gave birth to, and these are some of the reasons (describe them in a simple way) that birth parents sometimes make that decision. Then one might say that although the birth parents didn't get to love their baby/child like I/we do because love takes time to grow, that I/we believe that the birth parents *did* make a loving decision because they probably wanted their baby to have a good life with a family who could love them and keep them forever.

We can say that in the United States—where birth parents don't have to leave their babies in a place where people will find them, as they do in China, but instead can go to an adoption social worker and tell about their family without getting into trouble—we know that many birth parents care very much about what will happen to the baby, make sure that the baby will be well taken care of until he gets into a forever family, and sometimes write letters to the baby. They usually feel love for their baby and wish that they could give the baby a home, food, clothes, and the other things that he will need to grow, but they know that other parents will be able to do that and that they can't. We can say, with honesty, that birth parents in China usually hope that their child will be sent to a forever family.

Does this confuse a child? I can't see how it could *not* confuse a child. It is confusing and difficult for *us* to understand most of the time. If kids are confused, might they equate our love with the possibility that we could make a similar decision some day? Yes, I believe so, but I think that *all* adopted children worry about that to a certain extent during childhood and that we cannot prevent it. It is one of the things that makes growing up adopted a little more challenging. I don't believe it is possible to protect them from this worry any more than it is possible to protect them entirely from the worry that we will die during their childhood, or from grieving for their birth parents (learned grief), or from the challenge of coming to terms with their racial identity in a race-conscious society. The fact is that they *did* lose a set of parents and they *know* it.

Can children who don't talk about their birth parents come to equate love with rejection? Again, I believe the answer is yes. It is very important for us, as adoptive parents, to consciously and consistently discuss adoption issues with our children, whether they ask or not. Children who do not ask often feign disinterest or deny a need to know because they have decided that they are "bad" and that their parents may find out and give them away. Some feel enormous shame in their birth parents and in themselves because the birth parents "gave them away" or "abandoned them," and they really don't understand the adult problems that made this happen. They feel rejected, grieve for what was lost, lament that they can't get answers, and act out their feelings instead of expressing them and getting additional or corrected information that could help to dispel some of those feelings. They can get "stuck" instead of being able to live their lives happily and securely. They may behave as rejected, bad children, too. Often adoptive parents miss the clues.

Adoptees will have to build trust that the loss of a family will not happen again through our behaving in ways and saying things that can help them to know that we *are* forever families. They may have to test this out, periodically, throughout their lives, and so commitment is very important in adoptive families.

There is, in my opinion, a silver lining in the cloud for our children, and it is this: When children grow up knowing that their family has been formed through adoption and that along with the happiness of having joined a family who yearned and hoped and waited for them there is the sadness of having left one family behind first, they come to place great value on their forever family and feel a special degree of love that they know they might not otherwise have had. When we do our job of helping them to build security and trust, then just as we feel quite fortunate and blessed to have been joined with our own dear children, they too feel blessed and know that they are where they belong.

Jane Brown, who worked for 20 years as an adoption social worker, lives in Scottsdale, Arizona. The mother of eight children (five through adoption), she is a member of FCC-Arizona and on the Advisory Board of San Francisco Bay Area FCC.

Messages from Our Children's Birth Parents

Compiled by Susan Caughman
FCC–New York

One of the difficult aspects of adopting in China is the lack of information we have about our children's birth parents. Because it is illegal to place children for adoption in China, birth parents must be careful not to identify themselves as such.

How then will we explain to our children the loss and grief their birth parents must have experienced? How will our children understand the powerful forces which drove their birth parents to such desperate lengths?

Here are the texts of notes pinned to their baby's clothing by birth parents who probably speak for many others in similar straits.

From Wuhan, Hubei province:

> In our countryside the thought that man is more important than woman is very popular. I myself don't have the strength to say something against it and overthrow it. But I believe on this big world there must be some kind, good-hearted uncles or aunties who can rescue my little daughter. I would do anything for him or her on my next life if I have another life. Birth Mother

From Fuyang, Zhejiang province:

> To the adopter, please keep this note. In this life, in this world, I am not able to provide for you. I am giving you up so you can have a life. Good luck and be well.

From Hunan province:

> This baby girl was born on April 28, 1992, at 5:30 A.M. and is now 100 days old. She was born in a large hospital. She's in good health and has never suffered any illnesses. Owing to the current political situation and heavy pressures too difficult to explain, we who were her parents for these first days can-

not continue taking care of her. We can only hope that a kind-hearted person will take care of her. Thank you. In regret and shame, your mother and father.

From Fuyang, Zhejiang province:

She was born on May 24, 1992. Please help my daughter.

Susan Caughman co-edits the newsletter of FCC–New York. She asks adoptive families who received notes that accompanied their children to please share them by sending a copy or translation of the note to FCC-NY, 255 West 90th St., apt. 11C, New York, NY 10024, USA. Anonymity guaranteed.

Reflections on Mother's Day

Robyn Leo

FCC–Connecticut, Rhode Island, Central Massachusetts

For years, while waiting for children, I was so envious of all the moms out there who received handmade cards with lots of Xs and Os from their children on Mother's Day. I had lost my own Mom years ago, which only compounded the feeling of loss I had on this very special day. I seriously wondered if the day would ever come that I too would feel fulfilled— opening gifts, breakfast in bed…Those doubtful thoughts now seem like just a hazy memory from a lifetime ago.

Life is very different now. I have two wonderful girls my husband and I adopted from China. Parenting has been everything we hoped it would be. Those smiles, hugs, kisses, and handmade cards are what makes my world go around. Life has redefined itself while I turned a brief moment to look the other way. Gone are the expensive clothes, movies, shopping excursions, nights out with the "girls," flashy cars. The funny part is, I don't even think I miss any of it—or remember it. Our life is now filled with preschool, swimming, dance class, Chinese class, coloring, and many visits to the pediatrician's office. We work on art projects with macaroni, take field trips to see the ducks, and watch the Disney channel. PBS has given my life new meaning. A day without "Arthur" is a day without sunshine.

But aside from all this glory, every now and then I stop to think. I think not only of where I've come from but where the girls have come from. I think of China, its people and history. Each day that goes by, it gets harder for me to visualize my daughters as babies in their birth cities. The people, the faces, the buildings—sights, sounds, smells. I am afraid, as I do not want to forget even the smallest detail. I remind myself their life did not start the moment we met. There was another piece to their life, one which is so important, yet so vague with so little known. It is this part that I reflect on every now and then. Mother's Day, their birthdays, the day we united and became a family—they all have a bittersweet piece to them.

I think about our children's birth parents a lot. Do they resemble them? Are they alive and healthy? Are they aware their daughters went abroad to live a new life? Are they sorry they could not remain as a family? What thoughts do they have about the children they will never see again? At the stroke of midnight the day their child was born to them, what, if anything, are they feeling? It saddens me to think that we may never have answers to these questions. We can give our children just about anything in our world except this vital information.

Lately, I have done a lot of thinking on what we can do, however. I have begun to take little steps to recognize my children's birth parents and country. Taking some of the great children's books that were recently written on adoptions and China makes a good platform to begin a discussion. Asking questions about the photos is a good place to start. "Do you think you liked your orphanage? What do you think you did while you were there?" Taking the time to make a life book which includes your child's life before you came into it is also helpful. Pictures of the orphanage, what events were taking place in China when they were born, the weather, the economy, etc.

Lately my older daughter and I have taken the time to send "thanks" via balloon to those who loved and cared for her during her life there. She draws a picture, writes a short note, and we tie it to a helium balloon (I know, I know—the environment!) and watch it go off to a faraway land to deliver a very special message. It is a ritual we began together that directly touches this fragile area.

I have also found it helpful to share my sadness when my daughter experiences hers. Sugar coating never worked well for me; besides, kids are too smart. If she wants to cry and be sad, I have no trouble being sad with her—side by side, sharing those feelings. I, too, mourn for the relationship my daughters will never have with their birth families, but I hope that by talking about it and bringing it out in the open it will lessen their pain. I think about all those people who owned a piece in bringing our family together, and I am very thankful and will be forever indebted to them. On this Mother's Day and all of those to come, my thoughts drift to a faraway place, a place that my children were very much a part of and will always be.

Robyn Leo is chair of FCC–Connecticut, Rhode Island, Central Massachusetts. She lives with her family in Thompson, Connecticut.

What Can We Offer?

Missy Shen Ming
Upper Midwest FCC

On June 30, 1992, in Fuzhou, Fujian province, at the Fujian Children's Welfare Orphanage, I met my six-month-old daughter, Shen Hong Shan, who later became Mei-Mei Hong Shan. We were the sixty-second American couple to adopt a child from China. We were among the "pioneers" in China adoption. This is the third Families with Children from China organization with which I have been associated, having been a charter member in New York, the events chairperson in Chicago, and now a recent member of the Midwest chapter. Although we share a common bond through our China-born children, I feel the vast difference between us each time we all get together. Now, six years after adopting our daughter, few people ask us for information, advice, or suggestions. What can we offer to families adopting in China today? I think we can help by sharing what might be down the road for you and your family.

After the baby and toddler years, our children from China will develop, behave, and experience many of the same things as all children. But their perceptions will always be filtered by their having been transported to another culture and raised in a multiracial adoptive family. Society won't ignore these facts, your children can't ignore them, and we can't ignore them either. To ignore the differences is to deny a critical part of our children's identities—their connection to the people who gave them life.

Adoptive parents often find it difficult to remember that we were not and never will be the first ones in our child's life. The grief children can feel over the loss of their first family is profound, and they can begin to express feelings about this loss earlier than we might expect. When our young children begin to shed tears over being "homesick" for China or for their Chinese parents, the grief and sense of loss can be overwhelming for them and difficult for us as well.

You have probably been advised or have thought about how you will handle questions about adoption that inevitably come from family, friends, and total strangers. "How much did she/he cost?" "Do you know her/his 'real parents'?" Just when you have worked out suitable answers for yourself and rehearsed them until they sound natural, your child may begin to ask the really tough questions.

When my daughter was three and a half years old, we were traveling in the car one rainy day, when at a stop light I turned around to see how she was doing. She seemed focused on something outside the car window, so I asked her what she was thinking. I will never forget it as long as I live—she looked right at me unblinking and asked if I thought her Chinese parents ever think of her. I expected this question someday, but not when she was so little. How does one answer such a question?

Around age three to four and a half, don't be surprised if your little one, who used to love to hear her adoption story over and over again, suddenly doesn't want you to tell the story or details of her adoption to anyone. As adoptive parents, we love to share our adoption experiences with others— especially to waiting families. At some point, however, our children may experience this as an invasion of privacy. My three-year-old daughter gave me an incredibly painful lesson that I share with you now so that you will be more aware and not as insensitive as I was. We had invited a couple who were in the process of adopting from China to our home. They wanted to hear all about our experience, and we told them everything with great excitement. We showed the videotape and walked them through Mei-Mei's life book. When I went to the kitchen to bring out refreshments, Mei-Mei followed me. I hadn't noticed that she had become unusually quiet. When I asked her if she wanted milk or juice, she looked up at me with her lip trembling and said hoarsely that she was mad at me. Her words were, "This is my life. I don't want you to tell all about it." She and I cried as I knelt there on the kitchen floor that day. I learned my lesson. I apologized to her and made a vow never to do that again. Now, I ask her permission and respect her wishes about this.

Going to preschool, kindergarten, or grade school can present some nightmare situations for adoptive families. If the books, posters, and dolls at the school include only white people, either don't enroll your child in the school or donate items from a variety of ethnic backgrounds and speak to the principal about the need for diversity. "Family tree" projects can also be horrible for our children. If you know your child will be expected to create a "family tree," talk privately with the teacher about how the project can be sensitive to adoptive families and can reinforce the fact that families are built in a variety of ways. One possible suggestion is for the teacher to consider the "family houses" approach, showing the houses in which family members live rather than using the tree metaphor. Parents can also suggest that photos of Asian American friends, other children adopted from China, or famous Chinese Americans be used as "stand-in" relatives placed in the "root system" of the family tree. We have encountered the family tree issue as early as preschool.

Around three or four is also the time you may need to begin addressing racial prejudice against Asian Americans. Some believe parents should wait until their child is actually involved in a racist experience before the subject is discussed. Others believe children need to be prepared and armed ahead of time with ways to respond. Some African American friends of ours said they used the latter approach with their children. If you are Caucasian, you may want to form or make use of connections you already have with families of African, Asian, or Latino ancestry to help your child learn how to deal with racial prejudice. These families have first-hand experiences which can be more helpful than the second-hand knowledge of Caucasian parents.

I believe that pretending your child is somehow going to escape prejudice and racial bias is a big mistake. Likewise, pretending that as Caucasians we are not more privileged in our society is also a mistake. I was shocked when my four-year-old daughter came home from preschool one day saying a little boy had called her "flat-nosed." This was in preschool! We are teaching Mei-Mei to think on her feet and to choose from a variety of responses, depending on the situation. She can give an educational or informational answer to curious questions or comments. She can choose a humorous response, or she can choose to be flip when she wants to give a stinging retort to blatantly mean remarks. We have given her permission to be rude when the situation calls for it. We've already seen how this has been an empowering approach for her. Talking to our children before their peers are already experimenting with drugs and having discussions with them about how to be strong enough to say no has been shown to be important in drug prevention. I believe that being proactive in talking to our children about racial bias and how to deal with it is just as important.

I also believe that making friends with folks from other ethnic backgrounds is very important. Sometimes I hear adoptive parents say that they are actively involved in FCC to mix culturally. Being involved in FCC is terrific, but it isn't mixing culturally since 99 percent of the parents in FCC are Caucasian! Really mixing through involvement in an organization would mean getting involved in something like the Chinese American Association of Minnesota or the U.S.-China People's Friendship Association of Minnesota. Being around other families like our own—such as FCC—is very powerful for our children. It is also powerful for them to see us connecting with families whose parents are not only Caucasian. You may want to consider this issue when joining a church or becoming involved in community activities and organizations. You may even consider changing some of the organizations to which you belong in order to see the colors of diversity in the faces of those around you!

Birthdays for adoptive families can sometimes be filled with dichotomous feelings. We expect our children to be overjoyed at their birthday parties, but "birth" days may represent losses as well as gains for our adoptive children. Few nonadopted children have to explain why they don't look like their parents when friends meet their parents for the first time. These days our daughter seems really tired of having to explain her existence—something her friends who were born into their families never have to do.

Around four or five, you may see your child playing "orphan," "orphanage," or "adoption" with stuffed animals or dolls. The fantasy may be that the doll's parents were killed in a car accident or similar catastrophe. Don't panic! It's a good sign and provides great "teachable moments" about how families differ, and that the love and commitment to be there for each other is what matters most about families. During this stage in our home, we read the books *A Mother for Choco* and *Horace* over and over.

Adoption and orphanage fantasy play is also important as children begin to comprehend what adoption really means—that the people who conceived and gave birth to them are not parenting them. They reach for reasons to explain the separation from their first parents. For a time, adopted children often fantasize their birth parents' deaths, rather than facing the more complex issues of why these parents chose not to parent them. At some point, regardless of how well these issues are navigated, your child may get stuck. Seeking professional counseling from a therapist skilled in working with grief and loss issues in adoptive families is by no means an admission of defeat and can often be of immense help to your family. Cognitively your child may "get it" that there are happy and sad parts of their life story, but they may be unable to process this emotionally without help from someone outside the family. We "older" adoptive parents can help by suggesting therapists or counselors who are located in the area and are adept at working with adoptive families.

Just three more beliefs I will share with you about our children in middle childhood. Everyone in our family is part of an adoptive family. Our child from China is not the family project. She is not the only one who needs to be exposed to Chinese people and Chinese American culture. All our children—whether birthed or adopted—need to be a part of all the cultures represented in our family. My husband is Swedish and French, so last year our daughter wore the crown of candles for our Feast of Santa

Lucia celebration. Mei-Mei may have been the only Lucia with dark hair and almond-shaped eyes that night in Minnesota, but she was participating in the cultural heritage of her father, and she loved it! We celebrate Mardi Gras as part of the Cajun part of Mei-Mei's family. And as part of our Chinese New Year celebrations a couple of years ago, my husband and I added Chinese middle names to our own. We take Chinese language classes and practice t'ai chi to participate in the cultural heritage of our daughter's part of the family. Children in middle childhood are keenly aware of cultural rituals and celebrations, and they want everyone to participate.

Middle childhood is a time when children look to identify with their parents—both in how they are like and unlike us in their talents, skills, abilities, and interests. Our children who have been adopted from China also want to sort out how they are like and not like their Chinese parents. And we need to help them in this. I believe it is useful to speculate out loud about what interests and talents may have come from their Chinese mom or dad's side of the family—avoiding ethnic stereotyping, of course.

Finally, as little ones approach middle childhood, it is useful to practice "dropping pebbles" to encourage them to articulate what's going on inside. It is an art and takes some thought and planning, as well as excellent listening skills, but I have marveled at how beautifully it works with my daughter. Dropping pebbles involves statements rather than questions—giving children overt permission to think and feel about specific issues. "You know, some adopted children wonder what their birth parents are like" is an example of "pebble dropping." The child is not put on the spot or expected to answer. Then days or weeks later you'll be amazed when your child initiates a conversation related to the issue. I suggest reading the book *Real Parents, Real Children,* by Holly Van Gulden, for more about this idea. It's pretty frightening to do at first, but you get better with practice, and the rewards are enormous.

These are examples of what I think we have to offer waiting and newly adoptive parents. Welcome us to share in the joy of your newly formed or forming families, and tap into our experiences that may be predictive of similar experiences awaiting you and your families.

Missy Shen Ming, the author of *For Mei-Mei: A Love Story of Four Parents and Their Child,* is the pen name of Missy Bouchard, who resides in Maple Grove, Minnesota, and Longwood, Florida. She and her husband took on Chinese middle names, given to them by Chinese friends, after adopting their daughter from China.

Coming Full Circle

Adoption in Our Family

Winston Lee

FCC–British Columbia

In March 1997 my wife Donna and I traveled with Bonnie Wong and seven other families to adopt our daughter Meaghan. The preceding 13 months of paperwork, delays, and emotional ups and downs left little time to ponder how this adoption figured in our family scheme. The 12 days in China gave me a chance to think of my family, where it came from, where it is going, and how adoption in my family has come full circle. I also thought about whether there are any lessons from the past that can be applied to the present and future.

My great grandfather started our family in a new direction when he left China to come to Canada as cheap labor to build the Canadian Pacific Railroad in the 1880s. A few years later my grandfather joined him in Canada, but he left behind my grandmother and my three aunts. My grandmother, whom I affectionately refer to as Granny, is the central figure in how my family evolved. Because of cultural pressures to have a son, Granny had to adopt one. In 1938 China, there was no formalized or organized adoption process, so she acquired a son from a family that needed money to survive. Granny's new son was my father, James Lee. Dad was five years old at the time and very aware of who his birth mother was, so he did not accept Granny as his mother. He reluctantly accepted his role in the family, but his birth mother never escaped his thoughts. Unfortunately, this traumatic childhood experience would only haunt Dad years later, as an adult, when he developed schizophrenia.

Dad came to Canada in 1949 to live with my grandfather, but he went back to China in 1955 to marry my mother. While in China, he searched for his birth mother, but was unable to locate her because he had no place to start. Dad and Mom returned to Canada to stay and had Wally, my brother, in 1956 and me in 1961.

Dad's first diagnosis with schizophrenia was in 1966, after he voluntarily checked himself into Riverview Hospital. After months of treatment, it was under control, and he returned to mainstream society in the workforce. He suffered a relapse with this illness shortly after Granny came to Canada in 1968. Family pressures associated with Granny's arrival possibly contributed to this relapse, and, as a fallout, Dad refused to acknowledge Granny ever again.

This time Dad's schizophrenia was left untreated until 1975, nine months after Mom's death. The treatment was only able to stabilize the schizophrenia, but Dad was unable to function in the mainstream like he used to. He remained this way until his death in 1990 of a heart attack.

Our family came full circle with adoption when Donna and I pursued this avenue to have a family. Obviously, because of my Dad's experiences with adoption, I had many fears about it. I hope that for the future, we can draw from those experiences from Dad's past and not repeat any mistakes. There are certainly differences with Meaghan's experience as opposed to Dad's experience. First, Meaghan was abandoned at birth and has no recollection of her birth parents. Dad was basically abandoned at five years of age, knowing very well who his birth mother was. Because of that, Granny had a tough time dealing with Dad and could never be close to him. When Meaghan was handed to us at the Zhanjiang orphanage, Donna and I spent the first few hours just talking to her and cuddling with her. At the hotel in Zhanjiang, I held her and sang "Edelweiss" to her (it was the only song that I knew the words to at the time). It did not take long for us to bond with Meaghan. Now that we have been home with her for over a year, we continue to give Meaghan lots of hugs and kisses. Meaghan, in turn, has given us the love back twofold. Just the other day, Meaghan tried to sing the first couple of words to "Edelweiss" back to me.

Dad was not raised in a hugs and kisses environment because it was not our family's way to openly show love. Maybe that was why Dad often felt detached from the family even though Granny loved Dad very much. With Meaghan, we will continue to raise her in an open and loving environment with lots of family support. She is very close to her grandparents (Donna's parents) and to her great grandmother (Granny), who is 96 years old. Hopefully, by following this course, Meaghan will turn out to be a fine citizen. We cannot ask for anything more.

Winston Lee, his wife Donna, and daughter Meaghan live in Surrey, British Columbia. Winston's dad died in 1990. His last year was one of his happiest.

Connecting the Grounding Wire

Caroline F. Daniel

FCC-Colorado

In our family, being adopted is the norm, not the exception. Both of my brothers and I were adopted as infants here in the U.S., and my daughter Chloe was adopted in Hangzhou, Zhejiang province, in July 1995.

My brothers and I have each utilized the confidential intermediary system that has given rise to the reunification of adoptees and their birth parents. My older brother has successfully reunited with both of his birth parents, neither of whom I have met, and I have also successfully located my birth mother. But about six months ago my younger brother was finally reunited with his birth mother, Virginia, and I was reminded yet again about the complex emotions which are at the core of the adopted person's image of self.

I have given much thought to what I will tell Chloe about her birth parents and how I will try to help her accept the fact of her uncle's birth mother while she will probably never know hers, as I will probably never know mine. While my birth mother was located, she ultimately made the decision that there would be no contact between us.

As an adopted person I have felt not only great joy, but also great suffering from those decisions made regarding my life. Yet, through the help of a good counselor and terrific adoptive parents, I have found comfort and acceptance of my life as an adoptee. There are three lessons I have learned that have helped me to resolve many of the issues I had surrounding my adoption, and as Chloe grows older I will offer her the elements of these lessons that have blessed me with feelings of connection and grounding.

My parents never had a birth story to give to me, nor do I have a birth story to give Chloe. For many adoptees, this lack of narrative often leaves an open wound. It felt to me as though I had never really been born; that I had no real entrance into the world before the day of my adoption. Every bit of information I could garner was like a speck of gold; not a whole lot, but invaluable.

The other day my older brother received his original health report from the hospital where he was born. I watched him enviously as he devoured the information: his birth weight, the length of the delivery, the pediatrician's evaluation of his health. Some of this information we already knew, but to him it was like a motherlode.

While neither Chloe nor I will likely receive this type or amount of information, we must hold on to what we do have. For Chloe, the motherlode will most likely be our pictures of China, the clothing and gifts given to her by the orphanage, the videotape of her adoption ceremony in Hangzhou, the little red piece of paper that was found with her upon her abandonment, and ultimately her continuing relationships with the three girls from the adjoining crib who were adopted into families with whom we traveled.

I cannot stress enough the importance placed by many adopted people upon the details of their lives prior to placement with the adoptive parents. I highly recommend to future adoptive parents to glean and gather as much information and resources as they can while still in China. Ask the orphanage caregivers about notes, daily routines, anyone involved with the baby, the other children who shared her crib. And, if you can, establish a relationship with those orphanage workers who had a vested interest in our children for a period of time by sending photographs and letters.

Another connecting element I discovered and will share with Chloe is that we can also find solace, reality, and grounding in the universal experiences of all people. While we as parents of young Chinese children seek out the stories of that magnificent culture, I would argue that we must supplement them with concurrent stories from other cultures appropriate for children. "Lonpopo" must equivocate "Little Red Riding Hood," and our children will learn that all people occasionally fear the Big Bad Wolf.

Having understood that many life experiences are universal, including adoption, our children may be able to latch on to the human race and find a comfortable place within it for themselves. Our young daughters and sons may not recognize themselves in the faces of their mothers or fathers, but they may find themselves in the experiences they share with the rest of humanity.

Attending the multicultural heritage camps springing up around the nation is an excellent way to expose our children to other adoptees from

India, Korea, Guatemala, Russia, Romania, and a myriad other countries. Traveling is also a fine way to expose children to other cultures, even those within our own cities and states. I want Chloe to understand that in the past and on the globe is a face of familiarity for us all.

Another area that I found extremely helpful in establishing "connection" was my religious faith. In religion I have found a lineage whose core belief system was based on an established set of convictions. While the people of my church may not look the same, our tenets are the same and can be unifying, which is, of course, the familiarity for which so many adoptees are searching. Whether it be Christianity, Judaism, Buddhism, Islam, or any other faith, religion brings with it a story of origin. Regardless of how that origin is interpreted, it is still a heritage—a heritage that we may not have of our own biological origins, but which can stand in good stead. My story of origin includes Moses, an adoptee who rose to great power and whose leadership changed the history of mankind, a role model for all adoptees, all human beings.

For a long time I embraced the history of my adoptive family. I loved the time I spent with my parents finding the "dead relatives," as one cousin put it. But it still wasn't enough, it just didn't feel like it was mine, and so I sought out the biological history I desperately wanted. Unfortunately for all parties concerned, that history was never allowed to become mine either. I have found resolution in the fact that I am shaped not only by biology, but also by psychology and sociology. I have found my attachment not only as a member of a particular race, clan, or family, but as a member of humanity. Within our human family, I am as closely related to Chloe as I am on that adoption certificate in the safety deposit box.

I suggest to all adoptive parents that we continue to give our children their heritage as Chinese people, as well as a heritage as believers in something deep and profound, and a heritage as members of the ancient and encompassing human family. In the end, Chloe will simply grow up with the relationship between her uncle and his birth mother, and through it she will see how much he was loved by this woman all through his life, and not just as he turned 34 when they were reunited. Chloe will have an opportunity to learn, as I have, that there is a reason for our being here; our adoption stories are complicated, but we are *family* in the consummate sense of the word. I want to help my daughter develop that natural connection to the human grounding wire so that she can experience everything it has to offer throughout the current of her life.

Caroline F. Daniel, a college writing instructor and editor of the newsletter for FCC-Colorado, is the single mother of Chloe and of Robin, adopted December 4, 1997, in Hanoi, Vietnam.

The Candle Thing

A Ritual for Celebrating Adoption

Jenny Bailer

FCC–Greater Cincinnati

For the past few years, our family has been celebrating the anniversaries of the days that each of our children joined our family by using a ritual celebration ceremony that recognizes their heritage and origin in their birth families as well as affirms our relationship with them as an adoptive family. The basic idea for our candle ceremony came from an article written by Holly Van Gulden years ago in *Adoptive Families,* the magazine of Adoptive Families of America. We do it at our house this way:

Two years ago, when my oldest was eight, the two of us spent an afternoon making our Family Candle. We used crayons from our craft cabinet, sand from our sandbox (for the mold), and wax left over from when I was a kid, and made "groovy" candles reminiscent of the sixties. We ended up with a wonderful, lop-sided, dome-shaped, purple-hued candle that is kind of ugly, but is OURS!

We then went to the store, and Sara picked out a candle for her birth family. She took much time and care in making her selection, handling and smelling each and every candle. She settled on a small, round, sweet smelling, rosy pink candle. I picked out tapers for each member of our family, trying to choose an appropriate color to suit personalities. Sara gently cradled the Birth Family Candle in her hands as we went to the check-out lane.

We did the ceremony that evening when the kids were eight, five, two, and one year old. We got out all the candle holders we could find and gathered them in the middle of the table, placing one taper in each (one for each member of our family). The candle holders don't match; they are different colors, heights, and styles (quite by accident, but fitting since each member of our family is also unique). Our Family Candle goes at one end of the tapers, and the Birth Family Candle goes at the other end. My husband and I sit at either end of the table and the kids on the sides.

My husband or I light the Birth Family Candle to start. Then my husband and I both pick up our taper candles and touch them to the Birth Family Candle to light them. We tell how we were both born into our birth families as tiny babies. We then tell the story of how we grew up, were two separate people who met, fell in love, married, and decided to form a family. We then use both our tapers to light our Family Candle. Our tapers then go back into their holders in the middle.

The story of our family continues to be told, and then we get to the oldest child. She picks up her taper and lights it first from the Birth Family Candle, while we talk about her family in Korea. Then she touches her taper to our Family Candle at the appropriate point in the story. When the story is over, her candle then goes back to the middle. Each child's story is told in the same way, lighting first from the Birth Family Candle, then moving the flame to touch our Family Candle, then standing as individuals in a group in the center. Even though it is only one child's arrival day, all have their stories told.

To close, Mom and Dad talk about how wonderful it is to have the honored person in our family, and about how lucky we are as parents. We then go around the table and give a compliment or say something nice about the person whose day it is. Afterwards, we go watch the airport video of the arrival of the honored person and eat popcorn. We usually eat dinner before the ceremony at a Korean restaurant.

We do not give gifts, as we want this to be distinctly different from a birthday. It is a family celebration/ritual. The gift is the children themselves—from their birth families to our family.

The first time we did this I thought my husband and I would do all the talking. We were promptly informed by the eight- and five-year-olds that they could tell their own stories, thank you (they had heard them a zillion times, after all), and not only that, but they could also tell the stories of the younger kids. Now that they are 11, 7, 4, and 3, they each tell their own stories and have ownership of that portion of the ceremony. They *love* doing "the candle thing," as it has come to be known, and ask often when the next Arrival Day is.

This is a wonderful, yet easy, no-fuss ceremony. It takes all of 10 to 15 minutes to do. We keep all the candles in a special drawer and reuse them each time. We have done it about ten times now, and each time it is different, as the kids grow and understand adoption differently. It is a wonderful touchstone for us. Four times a year we set aside an evening to celebrate who we are as individuals with unique origins, and who we are as this family. Four times a year we openly reaffirm, in a concrete and symbolic way, our commitment to *being this family* for the long haul.

We were not so sure about it the first time we did it, thinking perhaps the kids would find it too corny or silly. That has not been the case. Based on the kids' reactions, I think it touches something deep inside them every time we do it. I know it does in me.

I must tell you, though, that one time the Korean restaurant idea was vetoed, and we had to have McDonald's Happy Meals for everyone, including Mom and Dad (extra toys, you know). Another time the three-year-old had been behaving so badly all day that when we did his ceremony and got to the compliment part, we were speechless—none of us could think of a nice thing to say about him right then! We ended up falling out of our chairs laughing instead and were able to recognize the levity he brings to our home with his wild antics! There is, of course, the usual bickering about who gets to put their candle in which holder, etc. This reminds us that they are indeed siblings.

This ceremony, which started out as a trial balloon, has turned out to be a deeply moving ritual for us. Thanks to Holly Van Gulden for the basic idea, and thanks to my kids for giving us so many wonderful reasons to celebrate the privilege of being their parents.

John and Jenny Bailer are the parents of four children, all born in Korea and all adopted as infants. Jenny first wrote this article as part of a talk on "Rituals for Adoption" presented at the Adoption Awareness Alliance Conference in November 1997. The Bailers live in Oxford, Ohio.

Enjoying the Journey

Jim Omans
FCC–Capital Area

"Excuse me, if you don't mind my asking, but, is your daughter adopted from Korea?" asked the guy standing over me at Boston Market.

I looked up from my meatloaf and said, "No, she's from China." Well, that's what I tried to say, but when you have a mouth full of mashed potatoes it comes out unintelligible. Fortunately, my wife Monica, ever the lady, was ready to speak for us all.

"No," she said, "we adopted her from Guangdong province in southern China. A lot of Koreans, though, think she is Korean. It seems everyone from an Asian country thinks she comes from their country. I think it's because she's so pretty. Then again, I'm a little prejudiced."

"How old is she?" he asked.

By now I'd managed to swallow my spuds. "Almost two," I answered, ever the proud father.

"It's amazing," the guy said. "She reminds me so much of my daughter at her age. We also adopted a little girl, but from Korea. You know, it was the best thing we ever did."

"How old is your daughter?" I asked.

"Well, she'll finish graduate school this spring."

For a brief moment the guy flashed back 25 years or so, reliving the adoption of his daughter. He lingered over that memory, savoring it as the precious gem that it was, and then let it go. I flashed forward 25 years or so and thought, "Graduate school! Kira hasn't even started preschool! How am I going to afford that!" Then we looked at each other and knew what the other was thinking.

He smiled and said, "Enjoy the journey. I have."

Jim Omans lives in Alexandria, Virginia.

On Tiananmen Square, 1992

Karen Braucher
FCC–Oregon and SW Washington

Swarms roam the square, which can hold a million.
A huge color portrait of the late Chairman
hangs from the Gate of Heavenly Peace
in front of the Forbidden City where emperors
lived with hundreds of concubines. Nearby,
the Great Hall of the People stands, where,
according to our guidebook, the "dictatorship
of the proletariat" is conducted. But here
in front of the Museum of the People's Revolution,
there's a gigantic green inflatable beer bottle,
so out of place we laugh at the hint that markets
are opening. So much gray concrete, scrubbed
clean of blood. Who cares now about Mao's
permanent revolution? Who cares now
for the wisdom of Confucius or Lao Tzu?

Perhaps there is some new way for this country
to rise up. I wish I could speak to these mothers
with their only daughters, dressed in layers of frills.
I approach them sitting on the sunny square. They
rise politely smiling, willing to pose for a foreigner.
They speak no English and I, no Beijing dialect.
I want to say my daughter is Chinese; these photos
are for her. Pictures she may study years from now
when she considers why her birth mother
might have let her go, why that mother might
still dream of her from a compound
near the rice paddies, imagine her, happy.

Acknowledgments

A book like this simply could not exist without the support, cooperation, and roll-up-the-sleeves participation of a good many people. I would like to thank the newsletter editors and their associates who made the initial selections, put up with my nagging about deadlines without complaining, and gave their enthusiastic support to this project:

Lillian Bando, FCC–Los Angeles

Deborah Borchers, FCC–Greater Cincinnati

John Bowen, Families with Children Adopted from China (British Columbia)

Kristin Castiglione, FCC-Arizona

Susan Caughman, FCC–New York

Carrie Daniel and Sherry Agard, FCC-Colorado

Mike Feazel, FCC–Capital Area

Julia Fleming, *Mosaic* (UK)

David Horstmann, Upper Midwest FCC (Minnesota, Wisconsin, Iowa, North Dakota, South Dakota)

Steve Huettel, FCC–Tampa Bay (Florida)

Valerie Kaye and Wyndham Parry, Children Adopted from China (UK)

Chris Kukka, Maine Families with Children from Asia

Robyn Leo, FCC–Connecticut, Rhode Island, and Central Massachusetts

Mary Jo Leugers and Cary C. Hintz, Families of the China Moon (Virginia)

Jean MacLeod, Metro Detroit FCC

Julie Michaels, FCC/New England

Pat Kluzik Stauch, Carol Nelson, and Kathy McMahon, FCC-Chicago

Karen Braucher Tobin, FCC–Oregon and SW Washington

Linda Uram, New Mexico FCC

Julie Watson, FCC-Baltimore

Sarah Young and Jan Frederick, FCC-Northwest

Michael Zessner, FCC-Toronto (Central Ontario FCC)

San Francisco Bay Area FCC did without an Autumn 1998 newsletter as I neglected my duties to work on this book. Thanks to all our subscribers for their patience.

I owe special thanks for special assistance to Chuck Bouldin (FCC Webmaster), Susan Caughman (New York), Shanti Fry (New England), Martha Groves (Los Angeles), Rita Guastella (New England), and Aileen Koger (New York). Thom Henninger (Chicago) graciously volunteered his proofreading skills and saved me from going to print with embarrassing errors. The elegant Chinese calligraphy is the work of Pearl Weng Liang Huang, who also saved me from an embarrassing error. I benefited from the moral support of Pam Carlisle (Indiana), Caroline Diepeveen (Scotland), and Cindi Woolery (Kansas City). Time constraints meant I had to do without the assistance of Ruth Laseski (Texas) and Peter Silverman (Delaware Valley), and I apologize; I missed some good ones.

I'd like to thank the accomplished poet and FCC mom Karen Braucher for permission to reprint selections from *Heaven's Net,* Braucher's award-winning 20-poem chapbook concerning her journey to China to adopt a baby girl. Copies of the complete work may be ordered through any fine bookstore or directly from the publisher by sending a mere US$5.00 to The Bacchae Press, c/o The Brown Financial Group, No. 10 Sixth Street, Astoria, OR 97103, USA.

I'm grateful to all the authors who gave their permission to reprint articles in this volume. I wish we could have included them all, there were so many good ones. The final decisions were very difficult, requiring a balance of geography as well as more usual considerations like range of content and points of view. I regret disappointing anyone but take full responsibility for the final cut. Others would have chosen differently, I'm sure. I also regret any errors that may have been introduced in transmitting or editing these articles.

Many thanks to all who submitted photos to this volume; again, I wish we could have included them all. On the front is the Chang-James family: Linda, Walton, Kam, and Deanna (photo by David Sanger); on the back are Martha and Nora Groves (photo by Jim B. Clarke); the Quan-Yee family (Betty, James, and Jane; photo by Betty Quan); Erin Helena Cherry, Jackie Noel Hing-Pacheco, and Joe Pacheco (photo by Jeanne Cherry); LiLi and Jesse Johnson (photo by Kay Johnson); Breana and Hannah Park (photo by Linda Park); our Changsha families: the Izumizaki-Kistler family (Joanne, Larry, and Mei Mei), the Rosenberg-Fried family (Judith, Alan, and Emma), the McCarthys (Carol, Dennis, and Jenny), the Chans (Laurie and Jana), and the Klatzkin-Fry family (Terry, Amy, and Ying Ying). Inside are Mei Li Isaacson (p. 1, photo by Virginia Stearns), those Changsha girls again (p. 75; photo by Terry Fry); Anne Goodman, Allie Lang, and Hana X. (p. 113, photo by Diana Allison); Sarah Zhen Miller (p. 163, photo by Linda M. Miller); Jana and Laurie Chan (p. 197, photo by Lincoln Chan); Julia Mei Irwin (p. 215, photo by Judith Gamble); Yang West and Myah Revilock (p. 235, photo by Anna Schmitz); Megan and Anna Stocking (p. 263, photo by John E. Hall); Mei Mei Kistler and her grandma, Amy Izumizaki (p. 303, photo by Joanne Izumizaki). The photos on pp. 25 and 285 are, shamelessly, of my own family.

I am deeply indebted to the designer Mark Ong—philosopher, writer, artist, friend—for donating his time and talent to making this a beautiful book to look at and to read. He gave far more than he ever set out to, and the book is all the better for it. May his cup overflow with *dahongbao* tea!

To Brian Boyd of Yeong & Yeong Book Co., my profound appreciation for your vision, your professionalism, your good humor, and your generosity. *Kamsahamnida.*

Above all, I thank my family for allowing me the time to do this work. Terry, your love and support never faltered, and the dinners were great. When Terry flew off to work in Egypt, my mom, Libby Klatzkin, flew in and saved the day (the month, really) by keeping the household afloat while I learned to typeset. And then there's Ying Ying, my little Mulan: "The greatest gift and honor is having you for a daughter."

To the writers of the articles I couldn't include, to the editors of the newsletters I couldn't find, and to anyone whose help I inadvertently failed to acknowledge, I offer my apologies. If there's a next time, I'll try to do better.

A.K.